Fear Not

Living a Life of No Regrets

D1367661

Fear Not

Living a Life of No Regrets

(A Weekly Devotional)

* * *

Fear not, for I have redeemed you;
I have summoned you by name; you are mine.
When you pass through the waters,
I will be with you;
and when you pass through the rivers,
they will not sweep over you.
When you walk through the fire,
you will not be burned;
the flames will not set you ablaze.

(Isaiah 43:1b-2)

James Cha

ISBN: 9798567645314

DEDICATION

To Faith (Sun-mi),
My lovely bride and BFF in yellow dress.
You are God's precious gift to me (Proverbs 18:22).
Thank you for going through life's adventures with me.

To our children, Joniel, Josiah, and Karis.
May our ceiling become your floor…as you seek first
God's Kingdom and His righteousness (Matthew 6:33).

To my parents, Rev. Moon-Jae and Yong-Ha,
Who faithfully served the Lord for many decades,
And are now in heaven with Him (2 Timothy 4:7).

ACKNOWLEDGMENTS

It has been ten years since my family and I returned to the U.S. from our missionary adventures in Central Asia. Over these ten years, the Lord has graciously opened the door for me to preach and teach at numerous church services, retreats, conferences and seminars, including over a hundred eighty Perspectives missions classes across the East Coast. My wife was able to accompany me and teach and minister with me on many of those occasions. Invariably, several people at those events would encourage me to write a book about our missionary journey. Of course, my wife and my children also encouraged, prayed, and supported me to write this book. Thank you for your words of encouragement and prayers.

The Lord has blessed our family with numerous churches that have partnered with us financially and with prayers over the years. They include Korean Orthodox Presbyterian Church (now Open Door, Virginia), Renewal Presbyterian Church (Pennsylvania), Nam-Seoul Pyongcheon Church (Korea), Hanmaum Church (North Carolina), Grace Christian Fellowship (Virginia), Grace Covenant Church (Pennsylvania), Korean Central Presbyterian Church (Virginia), Korean United Church of Philadelphia (Pennsylvania), Yuong-Sang Presbyterian Church (Pennsylvania), Emmanuel Church in Philadelphia (Pennsylvania), GraceLife Bible Church (Maryland), Ekkelsia-USA (Virginia), Community Church of Great Neck (New York), New Covenant Fellowship Church (Virginia and Maryland), Rock Church (Maryland), Worship Center (Virginia), Leesburg Community Church (Virginia), Evergreen Church (Virginia), Centreville Presbyterian Church (Virginia), Christ Central Presbyterian Church (Virginia), and Cornerstone Chapel (Virginia). Aside from these churches, there were (and still are) hundreds and even thousands of individuals who have faithfully prayed for us and blessed us with their time, talents and treasures to make this ministry possible. Thank you for your faithful partnership!

I am also grateful to two ministry agencies, Pioneers and Crescent Project, through which my family and I have been able to fulfill our calling more effectively.

My wife and I are grateful to our parents, who have raised us to love God and to share His love with others. All four of them were born in what is now North Korea; they had to flee to the south during the Korean War. We are also grateful to every Korean War veteran who fought to keep our entire country from being swallowed up by communism. By far, the U.S. has provided the most number of soldiers during that conflict. Without their service and sacrifice, my wife and I would not be here. God bless America!

I also want to thank Tom Siebert for providing excellent proofreading and copyediting help for this book, and Corinne Browdowski for using her God-given creative talent to help with the book cover. Special thanks also to Pastor James Lee for his advice on steps towards publishing this book.

My utmost gratitude is to Jesus Christ, Son of the living God, my Lord, and my Savior. You have not only taken my place on the cross and died for my sins, but you have also given me a purpose to live...for Your Kingdom and glory. May this book, and my life, lift You higher than anything or anyone else under heaven. May Your government and peace increase to no end (Isaiah 9:7).

Table of Contents

PREFACE

From my observation, there are two great obstacles for any Christian to fulfill the Great Commission (Matthew 28:18-20) to the ends of the earth. The first is choosing a life trajectory that does not put priority on the command of our Lord to make disciples of all nations. If we do not seek first God's kingdom and His righteousness, then we will end up building our own kingdom here on earth, making ethical compromises along the way. Or, as is common in Asian cultures, we struggle to uphold our parent's kingdom, and accept their mandate to never leave them for the mission field. Those who are on this life trajectory are like the seed that fell among the thorns, bearing little or no fruit because of the worries of life and the deceitfulness of wealth (Matthew 13:22).

The second obstacle is fear—fear of man, fear of persecution, and ultimately, fear of death. Fear keeps Christians living in countries like Somalia from sharing the gospel with the lost people around them, including their own family members. Fear also keeps missionaries from being bold witnesses in a hostile environment (Acts 1:8; Ephesians 6:19-20). They are like the seed that fell among the rocky soil, bearing little or no fruit because of fear (Matthew 13:20-21).

The Lord's desire is that all of His followers would be like the seed that fell on good soil, bearing abundant crop (Matthew 13:23) *of souls* to fulfill what was declared in Revelation 7:9. Those Christians who spend their lives building their own kingdom or wallowing in a state of fear will come to regret the outcome of their life's endeavors when they finally stand before the Lord.

This book is intended for those followers of Christ who are either already on the mission field or sensing God's call to go. Nonetheless, the book may also be a source of encouragement and challenge to Christians of any setting. The book is designed to be a weekly devotional; hence, the fifty-two chapters. Each chapter begins with a few verses from God's Word, followed by one or two snippets of testimonies, and closes with biblical principles, promises or warnings.

If you are not yet a follower of Jesus Christ, then I invite you to join me as I reflect upon His impact on my life and those around me through this book. There is no one else like Him. You can encounter Jesus at a deeper level by reading through the Gospel of John in the Holy Bible. My prayer is that you, too, will choose to make Jesus Christ your Lord and Savior, and invite Him to dwell in your heart.

In closing, my wife and I have asked the Lord to use our testimonies and teaching (including this book) to launch over a thousand fulltime laborers into His harvest field all over the world. Our sincere prayer is that, through this book, our ceiling would become the floor of the next generation of laborers—those who would bring hundreds and thousands of souls into God's kingdom. If you have any questions about global missions or cross-cultural ministry, feel free to contact me at book.fearnot@gmail.com.

1 – Called by the Living God

Judges 6:11-16 - Now the angel of the LORD came and sat under the terebinth at Ophrah, which belonged to Joash the Abiezrite, while his son Gideon was beating out wheat in the winepress to hide it from the Midianites. And the angel of the LORD appeared to him and said to him, "The LORD is with you, O mighty man of valor." And Gideon said to him, "Please, my lord, if the LORD is with us, why then has all this happened to us? And where are all his wonderful deeds that our fathers recounted to us, saying, 'Did not the LORD bring us up from Egypt?' But now the LORD has forsaken us and given us into the hand of Midian." And the LORD turned to him and said, "Go in this might of yours and save Israel from the hand of Midian; do not I send you?" And he said to him, "Please, Lord, how can I save Israel? Behold, my clan is the weakest in Manasseh, and I am the least in my father's house." And the LORD said to him, "But I will be with you, and you shall strike the Midianites as one man."

I was born as the third of six children into a Presbyterian pastor's home in the summer of 1963. Both my parents, Rev. Moon Jae and Mrs. Yong Ha Cha, were born in the northern part of Korea (now North Korea) in the late 1920s during the Japanese occupation. (My wife's parents were also born in North Korea.) They both escaped from North Korea when the Korean War erupted in the summer of 1950. My mother came to faith in Jesus as a refugee in Seoul, but my father was already a Christian as he was growing up in Pyongyang. He was in fact an assistant pastor (jundosanim) at a local church in that city between the few years of peace from 1945 to 1950. He had been arrested by the communist authorities around 1950, and was put to work in a concentration camp. By God's hand of mercy he was set free with the outbreak of the Korean War. Many U.S. soldiers fought and died on our soil to secure

5

freedom for our people. My wife's parents also fled from the communist regime during the war. My wife and I are forever indebted to the Korean War veterans. Eventually, the Lord brought my parents together as a couple in South Korea in the spring of 1958, and my father continued to serve as a pastor wherever the Lord led him. We immigrated to the U.S. (Los Angeles) in the spring of 1972.

Even though I grew up in the church, my heart was not fully committed to Jesus until after my freshman year in college. Of course I believed that Jesus was the Son of God and that He had died for my sins, but trusting in Him as my personal Lord and Savior had not happened during the first eighteen years of my life. It was at Cornell University that I met a small group of students in the Korean Bible Study; they had a genuine relationship with Jesus. When they prayed, they earnestly prayed as if they were talking to God. And when they studied the Bible, they read and discussed it as if the text were actually the Word of God. I knew the stories of the Bible well, for it was customary in my home to have family devotion twice a day, morning and evening. We would usually sing a hymn, read a chapter from the Bible, and pray...all in Korean. However, my approach to family devotion or Sunday worship was more mechanical (even legalistic) and lacked intimacy and genuine faith. The living faith of the Korean Christian students at Cornell sparked two things in me: a desire to know God as they knew Him, and a serious question as to whether I was an authentic Christian or not. [As a freshman at college I attended church on Sunday, and Bible study on Saturday night, but on the other days I was trying out the "fun" things of campus life. I would occasionally drink beer with my roommates and even hang out at fraternity parties with my classmates.]

A few weeks after I came back home for the summer in 1982, my older sister Sharon started taking me to revival gatherings for young adults called "Saturday Night Alive" at Church of the Apostles (Fairfax, VA). It was at the first

6

meeting that the Holy Spirit broke through my hardened heart. Everything the speaker was saying seemed to apply to me, especially concerning my desire to run my own life. He said that if Jesus wasn't the Lord over my life, then I was heading in the wrong direction...towards hell. It was not enough to know Jesus as Savior; I needed to trust in Him as the Lord over my life. When the invitation was made to surrender one's life to Jesus, I stood up and went forward; it was as if the Holy Spirit would not let me sit still in my chair.

That fall when I returned to Cornell as a sophomore, I joined a campus Christian group called the Navigators. [The Korean Bible Study group lacked a full-time trained staff, and I felt that I needed the oversight of a mature believer in my life.] The Lord would cause me to grow in my faith through the Navigators over the next four years (including one year as a graduate student). I am indebted to the ministry of my Bible study leaders—Ron Bostic, Pete Cassetta, and Jim Neathery—and the campus staff, Gary Bradley and Jeff Kraines.

Then in 1983, at a Navigator retreat at Watson Homestead (NY), the Lord began to guide my steps towards long-term missions. I attended a workshop conducted by a Wycliffe Bible translator in one of the cabins. At the end of his talk, the missionary showed a film clip of a tribal group in the Amazons celebrating with joy as they were receiving the first set of New Testaments in their own language. The men of that tribe were shouting and enthusiastically performing the "victory war dance." Everyone in the cabin shouted "amen" or "praise the Lord" and clapped with joy at the close of the film. Strangely, however, tears began to flow down my cheeks. At first they were a couple of drops, but within seconds there were two steady streams of tears falling towards the floor. I began to feel very embarrassed because I could not stop the tears. I asked God why I was crying when others were clapping and shouting with joy?

In the midst of those tears, I heard a quiet inner voice: "Would you give your life for something like this?" I knew that this was the voice of my Lord, and I responded: "Lord Jesus, if you want me to serve you overseas amongst a people like this, then I am yours." The tears stopped, and I was able to wipe my face dry before the lights came back on.

A few months later there was a special seminar on Muslim outreach by Zwemer Institute at Bethel Grove Bible Church. The instructor was Don McCurry; he was a veteran missionary to Pakistan and other parts of the Muslim world. He taught about the Muslim beliefs and practices, and their overwhelming need for Jesus Christ. At the end of the three-day seminar, Mr. McCurry gave the following invitation: "Right now we have one missionary for one million Muslims; at this rate, they will never hear the gospel. We need more missionaries to the Muslim world. Who will go to the Muslims for the Lord?"

It was at this moment that the Lord reminded me of my commitment at the Navigators retreat a few months prior, and the Spirit seemed to say that this invitation was for me. He had chosen me to be His ambassador to the Muslims (John 15:16 and 2 Corinthians 5:20), and how would I respond? I raised my right hand and stood up before God and Dr. McCurry. That was the start of my long journey of preparation for the mission field. The Lord would guide and prepare me in a manner similar to what He did with Gideon.

The Lord came to Gideon, a fearful farmer, and called him to be a mighty warrior that He would use to deliver the people of Israel from the hands of the Midianites. God gave him a new identity...a mighty man of valor. God gave him a new purpose...to deliver Israel from Midian. And God gave him a divine promise...the Lord's presence would go with Gideon, and He would give Gideon victory.

The Lord came to me over a period of several years to reassure my doubting heart towards my calling as ambassador of Jesus Christ to the Muslim world. He needed to strip away any worldly or fleshly identity that I was latching onto, so that the identity He spoke into my heart would not be compromised in any way.

Every person who has put faith in Jesus Christ as his/her Lord and Savior has a new identity in Christ. We are God's children (John 1:12)...no longer citizens of the kingdom of darkness (Colossians 1:13) but the kingdom of light. We are Christ's disciples and His ambassadors (2 Corinthians 5:20).

We have a new purpose in life. As Christ's ambassadors to the world that is lost, we no longer live for ourselves, but for Him who died for us (2 Corinthians 5:15). We must give up the "American Dream" or any such worldly dreams, and embrace God's will and purpose for our lives. We must uphold the Great Commission (Matthew 28:19-20), taking the gospel to the ends of the earth.

We have this promise from God, that He will be with us wherever we go, to the very end of the age. His presence will go with us all throughout our days here on earth. And He has given us His Spirit, who lives in us (Acts 1:8), to empower us to be Christ's faithful witnesses (martyrs).

If you are contemplating about going overseas as a missionary, then I hope that you have had an unforgettable and distinct call from the Lord. I firmly believe that you need a subjective experience that confirms the call of God...an encounter with the Lord similar to what Gideon or Moses (Exodus 3) or Paul (Acts 9) experienced. The simple reason is because of periods of doubt and fear that will come during times of persecution, serious illness, seemingly fruitless periods in ministry, relational conflicts, or even betrayal. A secure and unquestionable call of God will sustain you through those periods. Even if your sending church or mission agency questions the validity of your approach, or even location of ministry, you will not waver but believe that the Lord who has called you to the people and place of ministry will bless you with Christ-honoring fruit in and through you.

John 15:16 – You did not choose me, but I chose you and appointed you that you should go and bear fruit and that your fruit should abide, so that whatever you ask the Father in my name, he may give it to you.

If the Lord has given you an unforgettable calling to overseas missions, thank Him for it and continue to seek the Lord for guidance in how to prepare for the field. If you lack such an encounter with the Lord, ask Him. You want to be assured that God has sent you to the field so that you don't make decisions based on human reasoning or fear. The same God who led the people of Israel with the pillar of fire and pillar of cloud is able to lead and guide you similarly throughout your lifelong journey. All you have to do is ask (Jeremiah 33:3).

I want to share about God's calling in the rest of my siblings' lives. As we were growing up together in a pastor's family, we remembered our parents' words of advice not to step into fulltime ministry; they warned us that serving the Lord fulltime in whatever capacity would not be easy. Hence, we were encouraged to pursue careers in medicine, engineering, or teaching in public schools. All six of us, however, were called by God during our young adult years into fulltime ministry: Peter (the oldest) is an ordained minister and professor at Trinity Evangelical Divinity School in Chicago; Sharon (second oldest) served as a Cru (Campus Crusade for Christ) staff member for many years, and is currently leading youth ministry in northern Virginia; I (third) am an ordained minister and a missionary to the Muslims; Rose (fourth) served several years as Cru and Youth With A Mission (YWAM) staffs, and is currently leading a missionary training program in northern Virginia; Lily (fifth) is serving as a youth pastor at an immigrant church in northern Virginia; John (sixth) is an ordained minister and lead pastor of the English congregation at Open Door Presbyterian Church in

10

northern Virginia. We are all grateful to the Lord for allowing the six of us the privilege of carrying on the heritage of serving Him, just as our parents had done.

Recommended readings:
Practicing the Presence of God by Brother Lawrence
My Utmost for His Highest by Oswald Chambers

2 – Confirmation from the Lord

Judges 6:17-24 - And he said to him, "If now I have found favor in your eyes, then show me a sign that it is you who speak with me. Please do not depart from here until I come to you and bring out my present and set it before you." And he said, "I will stay till you return."

So Gideon went into his house and prepared a young goat and unleavened cakes from an ephah of flour. The meat he put in a basket, and the broth he put in a pot, and brought them to him under the terebinth and presented them. And the angel of God said to him, "Take the meat and the unleavened cakes, and put them on this rock, and pour the broth over them." And he did so. Then the angel of the LORD reached out the tip of the staff that was in his hand and touched the meat and the unleavened cakes. And fire sprang up from the rock and consumed the meat and the unleavened cakes. And the angel of the LORD vanished from his sight. Then Gideon perceived that he was the angel of the LORD. And Gideon said, "Alas, O Lord GOD! For now I have seen the angel of the LORD face to face." But the LORD said to him, "Peace be to you. Do not fear; you shall not die." Then Gideon built an altar there to the LORD and called it, The LORD Is Peace. To this day it still stands at Ophrah, which belongs to the Abiezrites.

Even though I believed that God had called me to be a long-term missionary to the Muslims, there were periods when I wrestled with doubt. When I looked at myself in the mirror, I saw an introverted engineer with only a layman's training in ministry. I was not a gifted evangelist; I had led only two students to Christ during my five years at Cornell. What made me think that I could start a church in a Muslim country? The more I looked at myself in the mirror, the more I felt like Gideon in Judges 6:15. And like Gideon (v.17), I needed a sign from the Lord to confirm His calling in my life.

In the spring of 1991, a few months before I would be married to Faith, I decided to take a short-term mission trip to Cairo, Egypt. As I prepared for the trip, I began to pray and ask God to show me that indeed He was calling me to the Muslim world. Confirmation came in two ways.

About two months before the trip, I woke up suddenly from my sleep, gasping for breath. It was around 3 a.m., and the fluorescent streetlight shone through my bedroom window to give adequate definition to all the furniture and wall hangings. But there was something new, something very evil in the room. It was a spherical, glowing red fireball about the size of a grapefruit. It was floating about a meter above me, and was causing me to suffocate. Each time I exhaled, this evil spirit (a demon) took my breath and I could not take in any air. I panicked and tried to get up, but soon realized that I was completely immobilized. I could not even move my head. *I am going to die*, I thought to myself.

And then I remembered that there was power in the name of Jesus, so I shouted in my mind, *In the name of Jesus, I ask you to leave!* [It's quite amusing to me now how I could have confronted the demon with such polite words…but then it was my first direct encounter with an evil spirit.] At the mention of the name of Jesus, the red fireball flew right through the window without breaking it, and then disappeared beyond the trees.

Finally, I was able to breathe, and sucked in as much air as I could. Never did oxygen taste so sweet to my lungs. And then I got up and ran out the front door to see if the demon was still hanging around the house. It was nowhere to be seen. I went back into the house and sat quietly in my room. I was thankful to be alive, saved by the power of the Lord when I called upon His name. But now I was curious why the Lord allowed this demonic attack to happen.

Two possible answers popped into my head. First, the demon was acting as a vanguard to the host of evil spirits that dwell in Egypt, and they were threatening to kill me if

I made the trip there. Second, Satan did not want me to go to Egypt, and sent one of his servants to attack me and put fear into me so that I would cancel my trip. Knowing that Jesus had just set me free from the demon, I decided that the latter was the correct answer. And so I decided to take my two-week trip to Egypt in June of 1991, and visit a missionary team that was encouraging me (and my future wife) to join them after our wedding.

During the flight to Cairo, I prayed to God that He would allow me the privilege of sharing the gospel with at least one Muslim man, and to even see that person come to Christ. The Lord graciously fulfilled part of that request. I was staying with a single missionary in his apartment, and the neighborhood mosque was only a block away. On one of the nights, I decided to take a prayer walk around the neighborhood. As I approached the mosque, I saw droves of men walking out after having made the last prayer of the day. Just as I neared the entrance of the mosque, I met a young Egyptian lad who was about eighteen years old. We greeted each other first in Arabic, and then to my joy and surprise, I discovered that he was quite fluent in English. As we began to introduce ourselves, he took great interest in me, and my engineering career, and so I invited him to the apartment where I was staying. My roommate was out for the evening, so we had nearly three hours of uninterrupted conversation. We shared about our families and our countries, and then eventually I began to share about Jesus using my English Bible. He was very attentive and curious. I could see that he had a load of questions concerning Jesus and Christianity, and the best thing I could do for him was to give him a Bible in Arabic. I did not have a copy with me at the moment, but I told him to come back to the same apartment within the next few days, and there should be a Bible for him. He thanked me and left. I was in Cairo only a couple more days, and did not get a chance to see him again. My missionary host wrote me later that the young man didn't come back to his apartment again. However, the Muslim lad did hear the good news through our meeting…enough to understand that Jesus is more than a prophet, that He is God.

As I flew back from Cairo, I sensed that the Lord was saying to me to take both the encounter with the demon in my room and the encounter with the Egyptian Muslim youth as His confirmation upon my calling.

A few months later Faith and I had our wedding and settled down in Arlington, VA. After a few years of both of us working in our careers (Faith as a pharmacist and I as an electrical engineer) and paying off student loans and other debts, we decided to move to Columbia (SC) to study at Columbia Biblical Seminary. During our third year at the seminary, we decided to take a break from the school and take a mission trip as a family. Faith had never gone on an overseas, short-term mission trip, and she eagerly wanted to take one as a family. By this time we had two sons (Joniel was age five; Josiah was four) and a daughter (Karis was one).

As we were looking for an agency or ministry that would accept a family for a short-term mission trip, the Lord connected us with the Korean American Center for World Mission in Pasadena, CA. By God's sovereign will, this organization was looking for a family to join an ethnographic research team (similar to the Caleb Project) to an Asian country. We believed that the Lord was opening this door for us, and agreed to join them. We looked at the map of Asia, and excitedly ran our fingers over countries like Indonesia, Vietnam, and Thailand. Faith confessed to me and to the Lord, "I will go anywhere but India!" [She had just read the biography of Amy Carmichael, a single missionary to India, and was horrified by the accounts of forced temple prostitution of little girls in that land.]

About two weeks after we signed our name, the organization wrote us and said that they would be sending the team to INDIA, to an ancient city called Varanasi. Although Faith was initially apprehensive about taking our

15

three kids to that city, the Lord spoke to her through a fellow seminary student family. By God's sovereign will, this family was on furlough from their ministry in Varanasi! So Faith decided to take our kids and visit the missionary wife and her two little girls one day. Faith asked rather apprehensively, "Do you like living in Varanasi?" The missionary answered, "I love Varanasi. It's my home!" As the missionary continued to share about what God was doing in that city, Faith's doubts and fears began to melt away.

In the fall of 1997, our family of five joined a team to Varanasi, India, for three months of ethnographic research amongst the Ansari Muslim people group.

About halfway into our trip, our daughter Karis became very ill. For about ten days she had a temperature of 103+ degrees. She also had huge bumps or welts on her scalp, and her head smelled like it was rotting. During this time of illness she wasn't sleeping well at night, and Faith and I took turns rocking her to sleep. The best antibiotic medicine that we had brought with us from the U.S. was not making any impact on our daughter. We consulted our doctor friends in the States, but no one could offer any explanation or treatment strategy. Was it meningitis or encephalitis? No one knew. During one of those nights I went outside the house to pray to God. I asked Him why the attack was on my daughter and not on me. I was the one who decided to take my family on this mission trip. If anyone was to be attacked by the enemy or any illness, it should have been me. And then, triggered by the thought of foul smell from Karis' scalp, I asked God that if there were to be any permanent damage to her brain, I would rather that He take her to be with Him than to have her live the rest of her life with a severe mental disability. My wife and I would fast two meals a day, sometimes the whole day, to pray for God's healing touch upon our daughter.

Then about the eighth day, we met a local Indian doctor at the hotel lobby where we were making international calls to doctors back in the U.S. A middle-aged Indian man came over after overhearing our phone conversation, and told us that he would like to help. He took out his stethoscope, listened to Karis' lungs, and informed us that she had an infection in her lungs. He explained that this particular illness is common amongst infants in the area, and that he had the right medicine to cure the disease. He took out his syringe and administered a shot of local antibiotic, and gave me two more vials to administer over the next two days. By the tenth day, the fever was completely gone and Karis was back to her old self. We never saw the doctor again...but he was a definite answer to our prayers.

It was through this ordeal that Jesus reaffirmed His declaration in *Matthew 28:18 - And Jesus came and said to them, "All authority in heaven and on earth has been given to me."*

Because Jesus has all authority, He could send us to Varanasi and take care of our family, including the youngest one. God wanted us to completely trust in the fact that Jesus has all authority in heaven and on earth. Our trip to Varanasi was the final confirmation that we needed from the Lord. Upon our return from India, we finished up our studies at Columbia Biblical Seminary, joined a mission agency (Pioneers), and raised prayer and financial partners to head overseas.

Do you have a confirmation from the Lord to reassure you of your calling to the mission field? It is not sin to ask the Lord for a sign (Gideon in the above passage; Moses in Exodus 4), especially if we are yet weak in our faith. He knows that we are frail and easily discouraged, and He will even send signs without our asking to bolster our faith (King Hezekiah in Isaiah 38). Confirmations are necessary so that we do not struggle with serious doubts about the Kingdom task before us when we face overwhelming challenges on the mission field.

3 – Consecration (Part 1): Repent!

Judges 6: 25-32 - That night the LORD said to him, "Take your father's bull, and the second bull seven years old, and pull down the altar of Baal that your father has, and cut down the Asherah that is beside it and build an altar to the LORD your God on the top of the stronghold here, with stones laid in due order. Then take the second bull and offer it as a burnt offering with the wood of the Asherah that you shall cut down." So Gideon took ten men of his servants and did as the LORD had told him. But because he was too afraid of his family and the men of the town to do it by day, he did it by night. When the men of the town rose early in the morning, behold, the altar of Baal was broken down, and the Asherah beside it was cut down, and the second bull was offered on the altar that had been built. And they said to one another, "Who has done this thing?" And after they had searched and inquired, they said, "Gideon the son of Joash has done this thing." Then the men of the town said to Joash, "Bring out your son, that he may die, for he has broken down the altar of Baal and cut down the Asherah beside it." But Joash said to all who stood against him, "Will you contend for Baal? Or will you save him? Whoever contends for him shall be put to death by morning. If he is a god, let him contend for himself, because his altar has been broken down." Therefore on that day Gideon was called Jerubbaal, that is to say, "Let Baal contend against him," because he broke down his altar.

The Lord was willing to authenticate His call in Gideon's life by demonstrating His power through the burning up of the sacrifice. But now it was the Lord's turn to bring up a matter before Gideon. God asks the young Israelite to destroy the idols in his father's house. God wants Gideon to physically destroy both the altar to Baal and the Asherah pole next to it. God could have done this task Himself (1 Samuel 5), but He commands Gideon to do it. These were idols that Gideon grew up with. He saw his father and other family members offer worship to the idols that the Sovereign Lord detests. Perhaps Gideon also held a measure of faith *in* and devotion *to* Baal and Asherah. If the altar and idols were not destroyed, then during the upcoming battle against the Midianites, there may have been a crisis moment where Gideon may have turned his heart towards these gods. The Lord did not want that to happen; He wanted Gideon to trust solely on Him, and not in anyone else (Psalm 20:7). Also, He did not want to share His glory with anything or anyone else (Isaiah 42:8). He would give an incredible victory to Gideon's 300, and God alone deserved praise and glory for this miracle. If the altar to Baal were still standing in Gideon's home throughout the battle, then the townspeople would say that the victory belonged to both Yahweh and Baal.

As I was finishing up my engineering studies at Cornell University, the Lord began the lifelong work of purifying my heart. Whereas Isaiah confessed that he was a sinner when he saw the glory of God (Isaiah 6), Gideon and I needed the prompting of God towards repentance and consecration after the calling.

I was enrolled in Cornell's one-year Masters in Engineering program, and this gave me the opportunity to be around Christian brothers who would impact my life. Pete Cassetta was my Bible study leader, and since his apartment was a few hundred yards from mine, we spent much time outside of weekly Bible study to talk about our spiritual walk. He had many godly attributes, and I wanted to be like him. And as I made such pursuit towards godliness, the Lord began to bring out idols and sins in my life…one by one.

One buried sin that the Lord uncovered was something that I did when I was in elementary school in Los Angeles. I would walk to school, and sometimes my friends and I would stop by at the local 7-Eleven. They always seemed to have change, and they would buy candy and share with me. My stern and conservative parents did not give any allowance to their children, and I was envious of the American families in which weekly allowance was a way of life. Then one day I decided to go into my parents' bedroom and steal pocket change (literally from my dad's suit pocket) when no one was around. I stole from my own parents to satisfy my thirst for sweets, and also to be able to proudly show my friends that I too had money to spend. This went on for about a year, and then I stopped.

I never told my parents about this, nor prayed to God for forgiveness, until my last year at Cornell. As I continued to study and memorize God's Word, I began to be more concerned about my sexual purity, especially in the area of lust and pornography. I started fasting and praying for the Lord to give me the strength to overcome lust and also grow closer in my walk with Him. I wanted to be more like the older, more mature brothers in my campus ministry. Then the Lord brought up to my mind the childhood sin of stealing from my own father. I asked God to forgive me for the repeated sin of theft, thinking that confessing privately to Him was enough. But the Lord kept bringing the matter to my mind. It seemed as though the Lord wanted me to confess my sin to my father in person and ask him for forgiveness.

And hence, during winter break, I went back home with a heart to obey; but I was also nervous about possible consequences after my confession. Korean culture is embedded in the shame and honor worldview, and it would be countercultural for me to confess my childhood sin to my father. After a few days of wrestling in my heart, I finally decided to knock on my father's bedroom door. He told me to come in, but he was seated at his desk with his back turned towards me. He was preparing his Sunday sermon. In Korean, he asked me, "What is it?" Then, in my terse Korean, I explained to him how I used to steal from him when we were living in L.A., and said that I was sorry. I asked him to forgive me. He simply said, "Okay."

He didn't say anything more than that or turn around and give me a hug. Such are the customs of Asian fathers. Anyway, I left his room and closed the door. And although my earthly father did not give me a hug, I felt a huge embrace from my Heavenly Father warm up my heart.

Another buried sin that the Holy Spirit brought to my mind during this period was an incident in the summer of 1984. I was working as an assistant manager at a motel near Kings Dominion in Virginia. The owner was an elder at our church, and I was grateful for the fulltime job. Although it was very demanding work (sixty to seventy hours per week), I was able to save up $3,000 during the summer to help pay for college tuition. The motel owned a huge, brown utility van that was used to haul equipment and supplies. While doing one job on the motel premise, I accidentally put a huge gash on the side panel from driving too close to a tree branch. I got out of the van to examine the damage, and saw that there were other similar scratches on both sides of the van. Apparently, I was not the only careless driver. I decided not to tell the owner; I reasoned that the van already had scratches, and more importantly, I needed the money for school. God knew that.

So when the Holy Spirit brought up the utility van incident, I first tried to suppress it. I thought that it was my restless mind bringing up trivial mishaps when I wanted to wrestle with more serious sins like lust. But when the Holy Spirit brings up a matter, even if it's very trivial, He does not relent. So now I had a choice…do I confess the "crime" to the church elder, or do I dismiss it? After a few days of struggle in my heart, I decided to pen a letter to the elder. I explained in the letter what had happened at the motel, asked him to forgive me, and included a $200 check to help pay for the necessary paint job. I also offered to send more funds in the future if my check was not sufficient.

21

A week later I received a letter from the elder. He wrote that he had forgiven me and that the matter is resolved; the van had already been sold, and he did not need the money. He sent back the voided check.

Out of thousands of sins that I committed since childhood, the Holy Spirit brought up these two sins for me to confess and resolve if I wanted a closer walk with Jesus. After the confession of the two sins, the Lord brought revival to my heart. I began to have greater thirst for His Word…it came alive as I read it from cover to cover. And when I began to pray, I felt like I was sitting before the throne of God. Although I still had a long way to go, the Lord was opening up my heart more and more to realize that He desires simple obedience from me as He took me through the process of consecration.

Upon closer inspection, we can see that the two sins were rooted in having money as my God. I stole from my father because I wanted money (even if they were only few coins) to buy what I wanted. I did not tell the owner of the van about my accident because I did not want to spend the money to pay for the repair. The Lord knew what was at the root of my heart, and so He would wisely and sovereignly use a spiritual mentor to show me how I should treat money and possessions as a disciple of Jesus Christ.

What are the idols in your life? Is it career, success (including ministry success), money, security, children, comfortable retirement, or youthfulness? Ask the Lord to guide you in your steps of repentance that honor Him and also reconcile any broken relationships. It is the Lord's desire to use consecrated vessels in a mighty way to advance His kingdom.

Joshua 3:5 – Then Joshua said to the people, "Consecrate yourselves, for tomorrow the LORD will do wonders among you."

Recommended reading:
The Pursuit of Holiness by Jerry Bridges

4 – Nightmare from Horror Movies

Galatians 6:7-8 - Do not be deceived: God is not mocked, for whatever one sows, that will he also reap. For the one who sows to his own flesh will from the flesh reap corruption, but the one who sows to the Spirit will from the Spirit reap eternal life.

Growing up as a PK (pastor's kid) was not easy, especially since my father was a well-known and respected conservative Presbyterian pastor. The fact that he was elected numerous times to lead the regional and national presbytery in Korea and later in the U.S. attest to his stature and respect by his fellow clergymen. At home, he was very strict and the six of us feared our father's discipline, even if they were a few stern words of chastisement. He did not abuse us in any way; whatever spanking we received at early childhood years was well deserved.

As I grew older, however, I decided to rebel against my father's conservative and restrictive boundaries and explore the "fun" side of the world. I began to listen to heavy rock 'n' roll and watch horror movies surreptitiously. It was the latter indulgence that took me deeper and deeper into a world that glorifies the activities of Satan. During my high school years I would join my youth group friends at the movie theatre to watch the latest release of *Halloween* or *Friday the 13th*. It is rather ironic that we would study Bible one evening, and then watch a gruesome and demonic movie a few days later.

I did not realize that the horror films were opening a door for the enemy to come in and tear at my heart and my mind with his claws. The more I watched horror movies, the more I was drawn to films that depicted maiming and killing with ever-increasing gore. It was like being addicted to drugs. This fascination to horror movies continued even after I became a born-again Christian in college. I had daily quiet time with the Lord and even memorized Bible verses, but about two or three times a year, I would watch a horror movie alone or with my friends. And then the Lord decided to intervene one night; actually, He allowed a demon to step into my dream.

I was already working in Boston for about a year, and I had gone to the theater to watch a newly released occult, horror movie with my high school friend while visiting my family in Virginia. A few days after the movie, I had a chilling nightmare. In my dream, I saw my younger teenage brother sleeping in his bedroom. Then I saw someone enter the dark room with an ax and brutally murder my brother by landing multiple blows to his head. There were spatters of blood, flesh and bone pieces all over the wall. And then the ghoulish murderer turned around and I was able to see his face...it was ME! To my shock, I saw my own face, drenched with the blood of my own younger brother, someone I loved dearly. What was even more disturbing was that I was smiling in the dream, as if I had enjoyed the mayhem. It was at that very moment I woke up from the nightmare with a scream; I was relieved that it had only been a horrendous dream. But immediately I sensed that there was someone else in the room. It wasn't a person, but the chilling presence of an evil spirit. I decided not to look around the room, for fear of actually seeing a demon. Rather, I turned over on my bed, got on my knees and hunched over to pray. I asked God to forgive me for indulging in horror movies and made a commitment not to watch them again.

I thank God that He allowed me to see through that demonic encounter that I was only reaping what I had sown.

Psalms 1:1-2 give us the following spiritual principle.

Blessed is the man who walks not in the counsel of the wicked, nor stands in the way of sinners, nor sits in the seat of scoffers; but his delight is in the law of the Lord, and on his law he meditates day and night.

Although I may not have been making personal visits to serial killers and witches for their counsel, as I watched horror movies, the actions and words of the ghastly characters portrayed on the screen would gradually but surely influence my thoughts, my speech, and my actions. [In 2013 a teenager living in Texas killed his mother and sister after watching *Halloween* three times in one week. He claimed that he heard a voice telling him to kill his family. He came to his senses after the gruesome murder. He is currently serving a prison sentence.] Horror movies glorify Satan and his works. Even the movies that seem to have priests or pastors overcome the demonic spirits (e.g., *The Exorcist*) draw unnecessary attention *to* and celebrate the works *of* Satan and his demons.

The Lord wanted me to conform no longer to the pattern of this world (Romans 12:1) but be transformed by the renewing of my mind that comes from meditating on His Word. The world of entertainment will continue to offer hybridized horror movies that are sprinkled with tantalizing amounts of romance (*Twilight* series), science fiction (*Alien* series), or apocalyptic themes (zombie series). Even children's movies that foster curiosity towards witchcraft, like *Harry Potter*, can have negative impact on the viewers of all ages.

Let us guard our eyes, ears, and minds against the destructive patterns in this world. Movies and books that try to entertain the audience through witchcraft (*Harry Potter*) or apocalyptic warfare (zombie series) are not from the King of kings but from Satan.

What are you sowing into your mind and your heart? Is the Holy Spirit challenging you to uproot ungodly music, video games, or social media from your life?

Philippians 4:8 - Finally, brothers, whatever is true, whatever is honorable, whatever is just, whatever is pure, whatever is lovely, whatever is commendable, if there is any excellence, if there is anything worthy of praise, think about these things.

5 – From Rejection to Invitation

Isaiah 37:14-20 - Hezekiah received the letter from the hand of the messengers, and read it; and Hezekiah went up to the house of the LORD, and spread it before the LORD. And Hezekiah prayed to the LORD: "O LORD of hosts, God of Israel, enthroned above the cherubim, you are the God, you alone, of all the kingdoms of the earth; you have made heaven and earth. Incline your ear, O LORD, and hear; open your eyes, O LORD, and see; and hear all the words of Sennacherib, which he has sent to mock the living God. Truly, O LORD, the kings of Assyria have laid waste all the nations and their lands, and have cast their gods into the fire. For they were no gods, but the work of men's hands, wood and stone. Therefore they were destroyed. So now, O LORD our God, save us from his hand, that all the kingdoms of the earth may know that you alone are the LORD."

The wintry days of January 1986 brought promises of hope as I took time away from my graduate studies at Cornell to have an interview with Raytheon Corporation in Wayland, MA. The previous year, when I was finishing up my bachelor's degree in electrical engineering, I sent resumes to over fifty companies…there was no response, not even an interview. I had no choice but to enroll in the one-year masters program at Cornell to improve my chances of being employed the following year.

The interview with Raytheon went well (so I thought), and I shared with my parents about the possibility of working in Boston; they were eager to share in my hopeful excitement. A week after the interview, however, I received a letter of rejection from Raytheon. I had hoped to make my immigrant parents proud by announcing that I had a great job lined up after graduation, but that wasn't going to happen. I was too disappointed and ashamed to inform them over the phone, so I wrote a very brief letter.

A week later, I received a letter from my mother. As usual her letter was more than a page long. [My father's letters were typically less than half a page, and in terse, bulleted sermon format. He would repeatedly remind me to 1) stay away from women, 2) stay away from alcohol and 3) focus on my studies. And he would include a $5 or $10 bill...whatever he could spare at the moment.] My mom's letter on this occasion was three pages long.

She wrote that when she read about my rejection from Raytheon, she decided to take my letter to the church that Saturday night. She and my father would usually keep a prayer vigil at the church for ministry needs. They would arrive at the church around 10 p.m., and then leave the next morning (Sunday) around 6 a.m. Since the Sunday service didn't start until 1 p.m., they could take a quick nap before coming back to the church around noon.

On this particular Saturday night, my mother took my letter and spread it out before the Lord at the front of the church, just as King Hezekiah had done with the letter of threat from Sennacherib. She had been fasting that day, and she interceded on behalf of her son so that he could find employment. She instructed me to read Isaiah 37 to understand what God did for Israel when its king cried out to God in His holy Temple.

A week after I received her letter, I received a second letter from Raytheon. This time it was a letter of employment! Apparently, another department from within the company reviewed my résumé and application papers, and decided to offer me a position. I was so ecstatic and grateful...this time that I ran to the student union with a handful of quarters and used the pay phone to share the good news. My parents rejoiced with me.

In between the two letters from Raytheon, one of rejection and the other of acceptance, was my mother's fervent prayer vigil before God's throne of grace. She taught me a great lesson about the power of prayer. Nothing is impossible with God. Jesus reminds us in

Matthew 7:7 – Ask, and it will be given to you; seek, and you will find; knock, and it will be opened to you. For everyone who asks receives, and the one who seeks finds, and to the one who knocks it will be opened.

[A year and a half after I began my career with Raytheon, I had to give up that job voluntarily to come back home to northern Virginia to be with my family; my father was struggling with stage-four colon cancer. I will share more about this later.]

Several years later, my wife and I were preparing to move down to Columbia, SC, to pursue seminary training. We had been married four years and had two boys already. We were on an aggressive plan to pay off our debts (student and auto loans) and didn't have a huge financial margin for unexpected expenses.

Then one day our four-year-old Mazda 626 broke down; it had a crack in the engine. We had faithfully kept up with maintenance, but the engine failed any way. The car had been driven only 3,000 miles beyond the factory-backed warranty. I approached the local Mazda dealer for some leniency and help with the repair, but he would not budge. He insisted that the warranty had expired, and proceeded to give me a print out of the estimated cost. It would cost $3,000 to replace the engine. We only had a few hundred dollars in our savings account. [Besides paying off our loans and debts, we were also supporting both our widowed mothers each month.]

One coworker jokingly suggested that I report the cracked engine as the result of an accident and try to have the insurance company pay for it. This was tempting, but it would not be right before God.

And so my wife and I decided to take this need to the Lord. We decided to fast and pray for three days. On Friday night, after we put our boys to sleep, Faith and I spread out the dealer's repair estimate on the floor of our living room. We cried out to God for help. We didn't have any reserve funds to repair the car.

We continued to fast and pray through Saturday and Sunday. On Monday, when I came back from work, a letter was waiting for me in the mailbox. It was from my best man at the wedding, Horace. I had not heard from him for several years, and it was a great surprise to get a personal letter from him. As I read his letter, my heart burst with joy. He wrote that his rich aunt had just passed away to be with the Lord, and that she had left a huge inheritance to her nephews and nieces. And as Horace was thinking and praying about people with whom to share this unexpected blessing, our names came to his mind. And hence the letter with a check attached. And how much was the check for? Exactly $3,000. We were able to fix the car and continue to use it for the next six years.

The Lord made sure that Horace's letter didn't come to us before that weekend; otherwise, Faith and I would not have fasted and prayed. But also it did not come too many days later...we may have become very discouraged. God sent it just at the right time. He wanted to remind us that we needed to be utterly dependent on Him, and beseech Him, as both King Hezekiah and my mother had done. The Lord knew that serving as missionaries amongst Muslims would not be easy, and He wanted to train us to know how to fast and pray for strength, wisdom, and even general provision.

Hebrews 4:15,16 - For we do not have a high priest who is unable to sympathize with our weaknesses, but one who in every respect has been tempted as we are, yet without sin. Let us then with confidence draw near to the throne of grace, that we may receive mercy and find grace to help in time of need.

Are you facing some impossible challenges right now? Perhaps it's an opportunity for you to fast and pray, and approach God's throne of grace with confidence solely in the faithful High Priest, Jesus Christ our Lord.

6 – Working as unto the Lord

Colossians 3:23-24 - Whatever you do, work heartily, as for the Lord and not for men, knowing that from the Lord you will receive the inheritance as your reward. You are serving the Lord Christ.

My work at APTI (Advance Power Technologies, Inc.— now part of BAE Systems) in Washington, DC, was such a blessing to me in so many ways. I was earning a higher salary than my previous job with Raytheon, engaged in more interesting projects, and enjoyed an incredible work environment. My coworkers were experienced, skilled, and gifted engineers and scientists, including several Christian men who were about ten years older than me. One of them named Bob would become a lifelong friend, mentor, and ministry partner. Several times Bob displayed wisdom from heaven that brought peace and unity to our marketplace setting (James 3:17-18). Another man was Mark, who was the program manager over various projects that I was involved in. Mark was gifted in bringing laughter to any tense situation; he lived out his faith as a peacemaker (Matthew 5:9).

My project involved developing a workable rectenna system at 35 GHz. [Briefly, a rectenna, or rectifying antenna, is a device that can receive power transmitted at high frequency and convert it to usable DC energy.] My immediate supervisor, Pete, was about forty years older than me; he was an experienced and gifted engineer who guided me in this project. [He not only memorized Maxwell's Equations, but also knew how to apply them readily to describe any electromagnetic phenomena.] He grasped the theoretical aspect of the system, and would coach me on how to bring it to reality. And so the two of us were on a journey to "invent" an efficient 35 GHz rectenna. The challenge was that at such a high frequency, the circuit dimensions are so small (micrometers to millimeters) that I would have to use a powerful microscope to build or modify the circuits.

Thomas Edison once said that invention is 95 percent effort and 5 percent genius. How true. It would take me about an hour to prepare the circuit, set it up in the laboratory for testing, which only took a few seconds, and then record the data. My task was to try out different circuit designs to determine the optimum configuration for best performance. Easier said than done. There were months when I would be spending each day testing five to eight different circuit configurations. Pete was eager to see good results, and on some days there were no satisfactory data to report. After a while, I was losing interest in the project. I found myself working at a slower pace, and even playing solitaire on my computer between each testing.

To help me work better, I had written and posted Colossians 3:23-24 right next to my computer. These verses reminded me to work with excellence regardless of who my employer is and what type of project I am given. Whether I am a school teacher, a janitor, or an engineer, I need to persevere in working with all my heart and to the best of my ability...for I am working for Jesus, not just for men.

One autumn Friday in 1988, I was particularly struggling with working diligently. The tests were not going well, and I found myself dozing off after lunch. Some people call it "food coma." I definitely was feeling the effects of a big lunch in my stomach. I meditated on apostle Paul's exhortation from Colossians 3, and then got down on my knees and prayed to God to help me to work better. The Lord gave me the strength to finish all the circuit tests that I had on my schedule for the day, and I was thankful to leave the lab at 5 p.m. On the drive home I rolled down the windows and turned on "Handel's Messiah" to help me take my mind off work and to start thinking about Christmas, which was still two months away.

Somewhere along Route 50 West in Arlington, I came to a huge intersection. The light just turned red so I put my gear in neutral. Suddenly, I felt intensifying heat in the car. I felt as if the whole car was on fire and my body was engulfed in flames as well. But I could see with my eyes that there was no physical fire nor any damage to the car. And then I began to feel the intense presence, pleasure, and love of the Lord Jesus. Tears began to flow down my cheeks as my mouth began to say, "I love You" to the Lord. I did not understand what was happening, so I asked Him to explain. Immediately, the Lord brought the following verse (which I had memorized in college years) to mind:

John 14:21 - Whoever has my commandments and keeps them, he it is who loves me. And he who loves me will be loved by my Father, and I will love him and manifest myself to him. [The original Greek word for "manifest" points back to the moment when Moses asked God to show Himself – Exodus 34:18.]

And then the Holy Spirit began to explain to my heart that because had I obeyed the Lord's command to work wholeheartedly for Him in my lab that day, I had shown authentic love to Him. And now He was delighted to love me and manifest Himself to me. Right there in my small, blue Plymouth Colt hatchback.

The Lord wisely and graciously chose that moment, not too long after I drove out of DC, and when I came to an intersection where the stoplight is rather long. And just a few seconds before the light turned green, the epiphany came to a close, and the car cooled down again. The crisp autumn air gushed in once more to remind me that what just happened was not my imagination. The rest of the drive home I kept meditating on John 14:21. The Lord wants me to love Him by obeying Him. Yes, lifting hands and shouting praises during worship gatherings are important, but without a concomitant heart of humble obedience, there is no true worship. A disciple who truly loves Jesus will fully obey His commands, even at his mundane workplace.

Whether taking an online class for a graduate degree or working as an IT consultant at Google, are you fulfilling your commitments as if unto the Lord? All legitimate (noncriminal) work is sacred if done unto the Lord. You can take the rich, powerful presence of the living God that you experience on Sunday mornings at church with you into your work place, if you steadfastly live out the truth that you are working for the Lord Jesus.

The powerful encounter with Jesus and His intense presence happened again a few months later; this time, it was in my engineering office. As I was writing up a few lines of code in C (programming language) to better simulate rectenna circuitry, I felt an intense pleasure of God in what I was doing. And again the tears flowed down my cheeks as I felt His love. I sensed that God was pleased that I was working faithfully for Him as an engineer. Eric Liddell, a Scottish missionary to China, said something very relevant to what I experienced. Eric was a gifted sprinter who would win a gold medal in the 400-meter dash at the 1924 Olympics in Paris. He once made a confession that when he ran, he felt the pleasure of God. [For those of you who are not familiar with the life testimony of Eric Liddell, I encourage you to watch Chariots of Fire, released 1981.] God had gifted Eric with fast legs; He had given me engineering skills...both to bring Him glory and pleasure. That was over thirty years ago. To this day, I have not had such a singularly powerful, intense and burning presence of God during any worship service or conference, even if the speakers were God's mighty preachers like John Piper, David Platt, Francis Chan, etc. Neither did it happen during early morning prayers, days of fasting, nor prayer vigils. It happened at my workplace or as I was driving home from work.

I believe that Jesus wants to come to your office and make it a place of worship unto Him. He wants you to walk with Him during the other six days, not just on Sundays. Your office or workplace is where He is often absent or even not welcomed. That's where the lost sheep and those living in darkness are thirsty for His truth and grace. Won't you invite Him to your workplace? But in order for Him to come and feel at home, you will first need to work as if working for Him. And the Holy Spirit will show you what steps to take...addressing issues like integrity, honesty, mercy, refusing to gossip, etc.

[NOTE: I want to share the rest of the story about the rectenna project at APTI. But first, we have to rewind a few years to when I was a junior year at Robinson High School in Fairfax. I was invited to apply for Virginia Governor's School for the Gifted, specifically in the science program. One section of the application required a brief essay on a particular engineering or science project that I would like to be engaged in. I had recently read a *National Geographic* article about the bountiful electromagnetic energy that is trapped between Jupiter and one of its moons, and decided to write about a project that would transfer the Jovian "free" energy back to earth. I also included a portion about converting the transmitted energy into usable form employing a device called rectenna. I had read about the works of power beaming and rectenna systems by Dr. Brown at Raytheon in a science magazine at the local library. By God's grace, I was selected to attend the Governor's School that summer. Amazingly, my first employment would be at the very company (Raytheon) where rectenna systems were developed. But it was my second place of employment at a small engineering company in Washington, D.C., where I would actually work on a project I had written about while in high school.

The Lord blessed our 35 GHz rectenna system project. My supervisor and I received two patents for the system, and subsequently were invited to present our accomplishments throughout the country and even overseas. One such place was Paris, France, in the late

August of 1991...just about the time Faith and I had our wedding.]

Recommended readings:
Living in the Light of Eternity by Paula and Stacy Rinehart
Your Work Matters to God by Doug Sherman

7 – Consecration (Part 2): Man of Unclean Lips

Isaiah 6:5-7 - And I said: "Woe is me! For I am lost; for I am a man of unclean lips, and I dwell in the midst of a people of unclean lips; for my eyes have seen the King, the LORD of hosts!" Then one of the seraphim flew to me, having in his hand a burning coal that he had taken with tongs from the altar. And he touched my mouth and said: "Behold, this has touched your lips; your guilt is taken away, and your sin atoned for."

After my father went to be with the Lord (he passed away with colon cancer at the age of 63, in early 1988), the Lord provided a wonderful engineering job in Washington, DC. I also began to serve as a youth group teacher at my home church, Korean Orthodox Presbyterian Church. After about two years, I began to be restless, especially concerning my calling to be a missionary to the Muslims. I had been sure that God had called me when I was at Cornell, but now that I was living at home and taking care of my widowed mother, doubts began to creep in. Did God really call me? If He did, why did He take my father away so early in his life? When will the doors open for me to go overseas? My doubts and restlessness gave rise to subtle complaints and grumblings towards the Lord.

At the end of 1989, I called my older brother Peter, who was living in Chicago with his family and serving as InterVarsity staff on a local college campus. I told him that the next year was a new decade, and that I wanted to join a mission agency and go overseas to a Muslim nation. Hence, he should think about a way to take care of our widowed mother.

After our phone conversation, he called my older sister Sharon, and gave her the assignment of finding me a wife. They both knew that I did not have the gift of celibacy, and that I needed a wife if I were to survive on the mission field. A few weeks later Sharon, a gifted evangelist, was speaking at the youth group service of Immanuel Presbyterian Church in Philadelphia. During her visit at the church, my sister noticed a young Korean-American lady who was serving as one of the teachers.

After inviting herself over to Faith's home for a meal, Sharon set up a "blind date" for the two of us to meet. I was reluctant at first to start a long distance relationship (Washington, DC and Philadelphia are about three hours apart by car.) But eventually I gave in to my sister's persuasion and decided to drive up to Cherry Hill, NJ, on a cold January day of 1990.

As I approached Faith's home, I saw that it was a fairly large home in a middle-class neighborhood. I slowly drove past the house, turned the car around at the end of the street, and headed back to Virginia; anyone who lived in such a nice home would probably not want to go overseas and live humbly in a poor Muslim country. After about fifteen minutes, however, the Holy Spirit prompted me to reconsider and give the relationship a chance. After all, He had used my older sister to screen out the young lady. So I turned the car around and arrived thirty minutes later than promised.

When I rang the doorbell, I was taken aback a second time…by her professional attire and her beauty. As I mentioned before, I grew under the discipleship ministry of Navigators at Cornell. We jokingly called ourselves "Navigator never-daters." I did not date while I was in college, and drove up to my first date with a casual attitude, wearing a flannel shirt and jeans. Faith, however, opened the door wearing a stunning professional dress (she was already working as a pharmacist) and a beautiful, bright smile. I had not expected such a first encounter, and after a brief handshake and exchange of names, I asked if we could sit down and pray. So during my prayer I nervously blurted out to God that He would have to lead and guide us in our new relationship. All the while I was thinking out loud in my head, "God, You are making a big mistake...first the big house, and now a woman of stunning beauty who is elegantly dressed. We're not connecting at the same level."

During our lunch at a nearby Chinese restaurant, however, the Lord opened up our conversation and we shared about our childhood years, testimonies of our faith journey, and our ministry commitments.

After my first date with Faith, I needed to take some time to pray. I was taken by her beauty and aura, and didn't want to be drawn only by her personality and external features. So after work the next day, I decided to stop by at my church to pray. At the time, our church (Korean Orthodox Presbyterian Church) was renting space from Calvary Gospel Church in Arlington, VA. Since the church was on the way home from work, I would often stop by to pray and prepare for youth group Bible study, especially if the rush hour traffic was particularly heavy. On this evening, I went in to specifically pray for my new relationship with Faith.

I had just been hearing Keith Green's "Make My Life a Prayer to You" in the car, and decided to take the cassette tape with me into the church. It would serve as the background song of worship as I prayed. I went to the front of the sanctuary, and knelt down at the steps leading to the pulpit to pray. Suddenly, I felt a gentle but firm hand push me towards the floor. With my face to the ground I began to hear the Lord speaking to my heart: "It's not about your time, but Mine. You don't decide when you want to go to the mission field; it is I who make that decision."

I began to wail and weep like never before. It was as if the gates of my heart were torn apart, and the waves of repentance of my soul gushed forth. I'm not exactly sure how long I was in that place of weeping and repenting; perhaps it was for a couple of hours, although it seemed like moments. The Lord wanted to rid my heart of wanting things done my way in my time; if Jesus were to truly be my Master, then I needed to surrender everything unto Him…my past, present, and future.

After the tears dried up, the Lord began to show video clips of my life. It was His version of Facebook or YouTube…memories from my past that were brought up right before my "eyes" to communicate several important messages to me.

One of the first memories was playing on the balcony of our home in Gunsan, Korea. I was playing with my siblings, and decided to surprise my mother who was just below, hanging up laundry. As I leaned over to shout her name, the concrete block I was leaning against gave way (it had not been properly cemented), and I fell headlong with it. My four-year-old head would have been dashed against the concrete ground below had it not been for the clothesline. Somehow, my right foot got caught in the clothesline, and I swung completely around the line one revolution. It was the Lord's hand that guided my foot to be caught on the line. My swing around the clothesline gave my mother enough time to rush over and catch me with her arms. Lynn Swann (famous receiver for Pittsburgh Steelers) could not have done any better.

And then the Lord took me to the next memory. This time it was in Seoul, Korea. I was playing with my neighborhood kids on the second floor of one of their homes. We decided to jump from one balcony ledge to another, the gap between the two being about half a meter. (Little boys can indulge in the dumbest games.) Somehow, I tripped as I made the jump, and fell between the two ledges towards an artisan well below. This time, my body fell on the concrete wall of the well, and the Lord's hand guided my body to fall towards the ground. Had I fallen into the mouth of the well, I would certainly have drowned.

There was yet one more memory of falling from a cliff while playing Tarzan with old ropes tied to a tree. As I swung out from one side of the cliff to another, the rope snapped. Again, the Lord's hand guided me from a fatal accident. (Boys will never learn!) I was unconscious for a few minutes, then got up and walked home crying with bloody head and body. With each memory, the Lord showed me that He was there to preserve my life. And then the Lord showed me of the time when He healed me of polio. I recalled the time (perhaps in first grade?) when I could not go to sleep at nights because my body was racked with pain; I felt like my leg bones were on fire. My mother would hold me and rock me to sleep. She had attended nursing college before she met and married my father, so she had medical awareness of my illness. She knew that there was no cure for my illness at the time. A few days later she and I took a taxi to Pusan (about a six-hour ride at a cost of $100 equivalent), where an old Korean woman with the gift of healing would pray for the sick. When we arrived at the ministry house, there were already dozens of people waiting outside the walled gate, lining up to enter in. Somehow, because of the distance that we had traveled to come for prayer, the crowd allowed me and my mother to go towards the front of the line. My mother half carried me through those who were seated near the elderly woman. I could see and smell death: rotting flesh of lepers and people coughing up blood (tuberculosis). They came to find healing from their sickness and life for their souls in Jesus. After about an hour of waiting, I was laid before the elderly Korean woman. People called her "Byun Kwonsanim." As soon as she put her hands on my chest and prayed over me, I felt the pain in my bones leave. All the weakness and pain left immediately. And I rose up and began to walk around without pain for the first time in weeks. I ran out the front door and began to run around the courtyard. Through this memory, the Lord was now showing me that He had saved me numerous times in my life for a special purpose. Perhaps the enemy wanted to take my life, starting from my early childhood years, but the Lord delivered me each time. Even from a debilitating illness so that I could walk, run, and travel to places near and far. He had not forgotten about me. He did not abandon me, as I had accused Him of doing when my father passed away.

And then He spoke to my heart: "Did you know that you had buried your pain of rejection in your heart?" The Lord was referring to a girl that I had started to date in Boston about two years prior. She and I were Sunday school teachers in the same Korean church, and I had grown in affection for her. However, when my father became terminally ill and I had to move back home, she was the one who initiated the breakup in our relationship. At the time I said to myself that it was for the better, and didn't let it bother me. But the Lord knew that I my pride (male ego) had been hurt, and He wanted to heal me. As the Lord asked that probing question, it was as if His hand reached into my heart and brought out the pain…and I could sense the deep pain of rejection. And then He said gently, "But I am healing you." And with that, the pain was suddenly and completely gone. I no longer felt the heart pain.

And then the Lord showed me the image of a beautiful young lady, wearing a bright yellow dress, opening the door for me at Korean Cambridge Church in Boston. In a previous chapter I had wondered if I had met Faith before in Boston…and the Lord was giving me a clear answer through this image: "Yes you did. You met her two years ago, in Boston, at her church. She was the one who opened the door for you when you knocked." Once the image came up in my memory, I realized that I had met Faith before.

And then the Lord spoke these words to my heart: "I am your pillar of fire and pillar of cloud. Trust me." And the time of intimate fellowship and the powerful presence of God ended in the church sanctuary. And I knew that the Lord has been, and will continue to be, the One who would faithfully lead and guide me throughout my life. Numerous times He preserved my life from serious injury, terrible illness, or even death. He even introduced me to the woman who would be my life partner while I was working in

Boston. But perhaps at that time neither of us were ready for a lifelong commitment to one another, so He set aside our second meeting until about two years later. He is truly wise beyond our comprehension.

Are you grumbling at God for the closed doors to your dreams? Regardless of your present circumstances, do you see God's handprint all over your life since birth? Would you take some time to meditate on the verses below, and embrace the Lord as your pillar of cloud and pillar of fire?

Exodus 13:21-22 - And the LORD went before them by day in a pillar of cloud to lead them along the way, and by night in a pillar of fire to give them light, that they might travel by day and by night. The pillar of cloud by day and the pillar of fire by night did not depart from before the people.

A genuine encounter with the Lord will often result in a deep confession of our sins, much as Isaiah did in Chapter 6. When he saw the glory of God, he realized how sinful he was. His confession would lead to consecration, which would then open his heart to hear the Lord's call to a specific mission. Perhaps you cannot hear the voice of the Lord because of your unclean lips. Seek His face, even as Moses sought the face of the living God. Dare to ask the Father that you want to speak with Him as Abraham, Moses, Elijah, and Isaiah did. This privilege has been made possible for you through His Son (Hebrews 4:15-16). And when He does speak to you, and you are unclear about His words, ask Him to clarify using Scripture. And He will. The Lord has confirmed His words (spoken to my heart) with verses from Scripture when I asked Him for clarification or confirmation. He is our loving Father.

8 – Heaven's Gift with a Lifetime Warranty

Proverbs 18:22 - He who finds a wife finds a good thing and obtains favor from the LORD.

After the time of prayer at Calvary gospel Church and being affirmed by the Lord in a vision that there was something very special about Faith, I decided to write her a card. I picked out a simple card showing a bouquet of bright yellow flowers and a matching yellow envelope. In the card I wrote her that I greatly enjoyed our time of fellowship, and that subsequent to our first date that I remembered meeting her previously in Boston. I wrote that when I visited her church and knocked on the side door about two years prior, she was the one who opened the door for me wearing a bright yellow dress!

[Later she confessed that when she received the card and the note, she was a bit shocked that I even remembered the color of her dress. She did remember opening the door on a rainy fall evening for a total stranger who came to an intercollegiate fellowship meeting at her church. But neither of us had exchanged our names, and never saw each other again. Who was this stranger who even remembers what she wore two years prior? Was he a creepy stalker? But somehow the Lord gave her a sense of peace over our relationship, and she decided to respond positively to my card.]

About a month later, I drove up again to Philadelphia for our second date. As I was driving up, I was readying my heart and mind for a very critical question that I had to pose before Faith: "God has called me to be a missionary to the Muslims. Are you open to going to the Muslim world as a missionary? Do you have a sense of calling to overseas mission?" Her reply would determine whether our relationship would continue or not.

Faith then shared about her family's commitment to praying for and supporting a long-term missionary to

China. And then she reiterated the commitment she made as a sixteen-year-old student to give her life to fulltime ministry, either as a pastor's wife or a missionary's wife. She had written this down on a 3 x 5 index card in response to the question from the conference speaker: What will you be doing for the Lord ten years from now? I sensed that Faith was the right one for me, and I was determined to propose to her.

Two weeks later, I woke up on a Saturday morning with a very bizarre experience: for some reason, I could not recall Faith from memory, and my heart held no affection for her. During the past six weeks, my mind and heart were passionately taking in everything about Faith…my affection for her was growing day by day. Just the night before, I was reminiscing fondly about the first two dates. Every card or note she wrote was tucked away in my daily journal.

But that strange Saturday morning, I had no memory of Faith. I knew her name, but the image of her face could not be drawn up in my mind. It was as if she was erased from my heart and my mind. I called her at home, and her mother said that she had already left for work. I called the pharmacy where she usually works, and the clerk told me that she had been reassigned to another store, but did not know exactly which location. I took care of some chores around the house and then left for youth group meeting that evening. All day I was disturbed by this unique phenomenon. As the meeting was coming to a close, we began to sing "Thou, O Lord, Are a Shield About Me." All day I tried to relive a faint memory of Faith, and I failed miserably. I knew that somehow the Lord could remedy this sudden absence of the woman whom He had brought into my life. As we sang the song two more times, I began to pray to God to bring Faith back into my life. Suddenly, all the memory and affections for Faith began to surge back into my mind and heart. And the Lord reminded me gently but firmly: He is to be the first in my life, and that not even

44

my wife (nor any other thing or person on earth) is to replace Him. He wanted me to guard my heart (Proverbs 4:23). I quietly prayed that commitment to Him as I left the church. I knew that the Lord who had brought Faith into my life could easily take her away.

A week later, I called Faith to fast and pray for the Lord to direct our relationship, and to read the entire Book of Hebrews to prepare for our third date. I told her that both of us were getting older (I was 26 and she was 25), and that we should not be dating for the sake of dating. I also wanted to share with her the recent blessings I had received through the readings in Hebrews. A week after giving her these two "assignments" I drove up to Immanuel Presbyterian Church in Philadelphia. I met her in one of the smaller chapels, and after a time of praise and brief devotional, I said to her: "There is no one else on the face of the earth with whom I would rather spend the rest of my life with than you." She was quiet for a few minutes, with her cheeks becoming more and more flushed. She then asked, "Is this a proposal?" I guess she was confused; she had not expected me to propose to her so soon. It was only our third date!

When I confirmed that it was a proposal, she then said, "Yes." Praise the Lord! The woman whom God had brought into my life (first in Boston, and then two years later in Philadelphia) agreed to marry me, and journey with me through adventures that God would have for us. Driving up to Philadelphia that early March Sunday, I knew in my heart that Faith would say "YES" to my proposal. This conviction was the result of the strange experience that I had a week prior...when the Lord had taken away and restored my affections for Faith, I knew that she was the one for me.

A formal engagement ceremony was held about a year later, and the wedding ceremony was held on August 24th, 1991. [The main reason for the delay in the engagement and wedding was to wait for Faith's two older sisters who were yet unmarried. Korean traditions encourage marriages in sequential age order, and we were requested to wait for a year.]

The wedding date, August 24th, was chosen because my supervisor (senior engineer) and I had been invited to present a paper on our research work at a science symposium in Paris, France, during that last week of August. I decided to surprise Faith by proposing that we have our honeymoon in Paris and south France (near Toulon). She was ecstatic about the prospect, and readily agreed even though the wedding day itself would most likely be very hot and humid.

As we wed, the Lord reminded me that my wife was a gift to me from Him (Proverbs 18:22). And the Lord only gives good gifts. His gift comes with a lifetime warranty; we are to be married until He takes us home to be with Him. Furthermore, heaven is not like Walmart; there is no customer service desk in heaven to offer refunds or allow exchanges. Once we are married, we are married for life…there is no divorce.

In the spring of 1999, about seven years after our wedding, we were finishing up our time at Columbia Biblical Seminary and preparing to move back to northern Virginia. As Faith was sorting through our books and collection of folders and papers, she came across a thin folder labeled "Students for Christ 1981." It was the folder from the retreat she attended at Rosemont College (Philadelphia) when she was sixteen years old. It was at that retreat that she had made a commitment to become the wife of a fulltime pastor or missionary within ten years from the time of the retreat. By God's leading, she was now the wife of a pastor and a missionary. And the retreat was held during the third week of August, almost exactly ten years before our wedding date! When Faith saw the folder, she understood right away that God had allowed her to fulfill her commitment to the Lord.

46

A careful reading of Genesis 2 will reveal that the Lord did not create man and woman at the same time. He created Adam first and gave him work to do in the Garden. And as Adam was working, including giving names to God's creation, the Lord expressed that there was not a suitable partner for the man. And so God created Eve (out of Adam) to be the man's helper for all their lives together. She was to help him fulfill his mission here on earth.

I believe that God wants each young man to seek the Creator to understand what his purpose on earth is. And as he engages in that work (a school teacher, lawyer, pastor…laboring to advance God's kingdom), he is to ask God to provide a suitable helper to help him fulfill that work. Too often, young men, being influenced by the world, think that the only criterion for becoming a groom is financial stability…to be able to provide for his wife and future family. As soon as he finds a well-paying position, he then focuses on marrying a pretty gal who will say, "Yes." The Lord has created every man and woman with a purpose, and for those who come to faith in Jesus, there is good work that He has prepared for us in advance to accomplish (Ephesians 2:10). If the Lord has called a man to ministry overseas, whether as laity (business as mission) or clergy (fulltime missionary), he needs to ask the Lord for a wife who will share in his journey. Quite often we meet couples in ministry where one of the spouses does not share in the calling of the one serving fulltime in ministry. We have seen several couples struggling in their marriage and even going through divorce because of such differences.

If you are considering long-term missions, I encourage you to ask God for a spouse who shares a similar calling. Brothers, if you are young and single, and not sure what God wants you do with your life, fast and pray until you hear from Him. And then ask for a godly woman who will journey with you. And sisters, if you are single and dating a fellow who is a Christian but has no idea what he wants to do with his life, I recommend that you take a break for a few weeks and encourage him to go and fast and pray until he hears from the Lord. If you are going to trust him with your life, don't you want a man of God who walks with Him and hears from Him (like Enoch, Abraham, David, Philip, Paul, etc.)? Furthermore, from now until Jesus's return, life on earth will become only more difficult. The coronavirus pandemic of 2020 is just the beginning. Jesus warned of all the challenges that believers will face as the end time draws near (Matthew 24). Ask the Lord for a man of God who knows how to face and overcome challenges through fasting and prayer.

9 – Not Loving the World

1 John 2:15-17 – Do not love the world or the things in the world. If anyone loves the world, the love of the Father is not in him. For all that is in the world—the desires of the flesh and the desires of the eyes and pride of life—is not from the Father but is from the world. And the world is passing away along with its desires, but whoever does the will of God abides forever.

The Lord knew that soon after finishing up my graduate studies at Cornell, I would be working as an electrical (RF/microwave) engineer with generous salary. Without His guidance and intervention, I would be pursuing the "American Dream" like the rest of the young adults (including many Christians) in the country.

And so the Lord placed several Navigators Bible study leaders in my path. The first, Ron B., was a Christian who pursued excellence. He showed me what it means to excel in my studies for the glory of Jesus. He was also a great athlete, well respected on the soccer field and the basketball court...and yet he remained humble about his athletic prowess. But the attribute I admired most about Ron was his love relationship with Jesus. It came through in his daily actions, relationship with other students, and especially in prayer. When he prayed, I sensed his deep love for the One who died for him, and gradually the presence of God would fill the room. But he didn't just pray that he loved Jesus, he lived it. His life genuinely reflected his prayers. This was an aspect of Christian faith I was not familiar with, and the Lord encouraged me to grow in this area of intimacy with Him.

The second Bible study leader was Jim Neathery. He was also a one-of-a-kind Christian. He was handsome (could be Tom Cruise's double), smart and a gifted athlete. Although he came to Cornell with an ice-hockey scholarship and played as a star goalie during his freshman year, he followed the Lord's leading to give that up and become a "fisher of men." His distant cousin, Lance Nethery, had also come through Cornell on a hockey scholarship and went on to play professionally for the New York Islanders. Jim could have followed a similar path to fame and riches, but his heart was for making disciples for Christ. Jim had a way with teaching and preaching God's Word; his insights were often radical and challenging. Through Jim Neathery, God continued to grow my faith to embrace a path of "reckless abandon" unto Him. From time to time, he and the other Bible study leaders pulled money together to pay for me to attend Navigators retreats and conferences. (It was at one of these retreats that God called me to fulltime missions.)

I know that Jim Neathery regularly led Bible study lessons during my junior year at Cornell, but it's not for those lessons for which I remember him best. It was rather a simple breakfast meal at his basement apartment one cold Saturday morning. Jim stayed in Ithaca one extra year after graduation to help with Navigators ministry, which included leading Bible study for a group of underclassmen, meeting up with them one-on-one during the week, and sharing the gospel with non-believing students. There were four of us in his Bible study group, and none of us were accomplished athletes like Jim; rather, we were all "nerds"—two engineers, one pre-med, and one business/commerce major. After few weeks of study together, Jim invited us to a small room that he was renting from a fraternity house. As we went through the basement hallway, we could see and smell the aftermath of the previous night's raucous revelry. The four of us sat ourselves on his bed and a couple of mismatched chairs. And then Jim served us toast, scrambled eggs, and orange juice for breakfast. As we sat there enjoying the simple meal and a thought-provoking devotional from God's Word, I came to the incredible realization that Jim Neathery had given up the possibility of a professional hockey career to feed breakfast to four "nobodies" in the basement of a messy frat house. He had made such series of decisions because of His love for Jesus, and in obedience to the Lord. Tears began to well up, and I tried hard not to cry at the moment and embarrass myself and the group.

Two thousand years earlier and thousands of miles away from Ithaca, NY, there was a similar breakfast scene on the shores of Galilee. On that occasion, the King of kings served breakfast of grilled fish and bread to a group of men who needed words of encouragement and challenge (John 21). He was particularly interested in restoring and firmly reestablishing the faith of a fisherman who would be used mightily of God to advance His Kingdom in the days and years to come.

Jim Neathery probably does not remember the occasion; it was one of many acts of service he did unto Jesus for our Bible study group. But I shall never forget that breakfast. And when the time came for me to resign from a well-paying engineering position to head overseas, my heart had very little resistance. I was indebted not only to my Lord Jesus, but also to those like Jim Neathery who loved not the world. They were aliens here on earth, and their lives exemplified Galatians 2:20 and 2 Corinthians 5:15 faithfully.

Galatians 2:20 - I have been crucified with Christ. It is no longer I who live, but Christ who lives in me. And the life I now live in the flesh I live by faith in the Son of God, who loved me and gave himself for me.

2 Corinthians 5:15 - and he died for all, that those who live might no longer live for themselves but for him who for their sake died and was raised.

My third Bible study group leader was a strong Christian of Italian descent named Pete Cassetta. He came to Cornell to study chemistry (on a pre-med track) and play polo for the school. Along the way the Lord reeled him into the Navigators ministry, and he also became a fisher of men. He stayed at Cornell two years beyond his graduation.

He had a brilliant mind, and from what his friends told me, he had a near 4.0 GPA and could have applied to any medical school of his choice. But it was during his senior year at Cornell that the Lord redirected his steps towards Bible translation and church planting work amongst the unreached people groups. Pete was also a skilled programmer, and the Lord gave him favor to find a well-paying position with the university computing services.

One peculiar but admirable attribute of Pete Cassetta was that he was very frugal. For someone who was earning a decent salary at Cornell, Pete was content with clothes from thrift shops and yard sales. He chose not to buy a car and instead purchased a used bike to commute to work. He often had a group of other brothers over to his home for meals, and like a true Italian, he made spaghetti sauce from scratch. One of the key ingredients to his special recipe required bell pepper. And when he would go shopping at the local grocery store for the peppers, he would break off the stem first and then bag only the peppers so that he could save a few ounces and thus, a few pennies. (And I thought Koreans were frugal...Pete Cassetta takes the cake!) I had never met someone so "cheap." And yet, at the end of that school year, Pete spent the money saved up to purchase an Apple McIntosh (computer plus printer) for the Navigators staff couple serving at Cornell. Apple had just introduced their version of a personal computer around that time, and the price for the system was very high (over $2,000). When I heard about this generous gift a few weeks later—of course through the staff couple and not from Pete himself—I was both shocked and challenged. Here's a Christian who is very frugal with himself, but knew how to lavish the love of God upon others. It was Pete's sacrificial giving that launched me to meditate further on Biblical passages concerning giving, and to examine my own convictions and practices. My parents had always taught me to tithe, and even give a few dollars to the Lord even if I didn't have a job. And even though my father received a pastor's salary that barely covered our house mortgage and family expenses, both he and my mother practiced giving twenty percent of their salary to the Lord.

And now as I was about to graduate, the Lord challenged me to be generous towards Him and others who are in need. By God's grace I was able to work part-time for a RF engineering company in Syracuse, NY. I happened to be reading through the Book of Proverbs, and the words from Proverbs 3:9-10 spoke to me.

Proverbs 3:9-10 - Honor the LORD with your wealth and with the firstfruits of all your produce; then your barns will be filled with plenty, and your vats will be bursting with wine.

I decided to give my entire first paycheck to the Lord...giving some of it to the local church I was attending, and the rest to the Navigators ministry. And just as He promises in Proverbs 3:9-10, the Lord has faithfully provided for me and my family's every need to this day.

During the last few months at Cornell, the Lord spoke to me through a book called Living in Light of Eternity by Stacy Reinhart. (This book is out of print, and is not to be confused with the one with a similar title by Yohanan.) He was challenging me to think critically about how I would like to spend the rest of my life, including the way I would spend my wealth. And as I was researching for my first automobile, the Lord kept afresh in my mind the sacrificial giving of Pete Cassetta. Instead of looking at the popular Honda Accords and BMW sedans that my colleagues at Raytheon were driving, I decided to purchase a Plymouth Colt...a small but reliable hatchback with manual transmission, no radio, and no air conditioning. Because of its low price tag, I was able to save considerable amounts of money, and the Lord gave me the opportunity to send significant sums of money to two campus ministry staff couples who were in need of new vehicles. If the Lord had not brought Pete Cassetta into my life during my final two years at Cornell, I probably would be driving a brand new Porsche convertible by now.

A few days after I bought my new car, the Lord challenged me with the verses from Luke 14:26-27 - *If anyone comes to me and does not hate his own father and mother and wife and children and brothers and sisters, yes, and even his own life, he cannot be my disciple. Whoever does not bear his own cross and come after me cannot be my disciple.*

How do I "hate the world?" What about the possessions I am beginning to acquire, including my brand new car? Already I was thinking about ways to add a cassette deck and speakers to help with the long Boston commute. Guys making improvements to their vehicles can be endless and costly. I needed to do something radical and drastic before my heart went astray. So one afternoon, I drove the car to an old but spacious cemetery in Lexington, MA. I parked the car in a quiet place where no one was around. I stood in front of the car and preached to it: "You are not going to get in the way between me and my Jesus." And I laid my hands on the hood of the engine and prayed to God to let nothing that I ever own keep me from loving Him and pursuing His calling in my life.

This was the "Gideon-destroying-Baal" moment in my life. Perhaps you have idols in your life that the Holy Spirit has been pointing out. It can be your technology gadget (smartphone, tablet, computer), video games, social media, ungodly relationships, career, family, home, or car. The Lord usually does not destroy our idols with a lightning strike; rather, He wants us to deal with them ourselves. Is the Lord asking you to put to death such idol(s) even today?

10 – Why Don't You Get a Job?

Deuteronomy 8:17-18 - Beware lest you say in your heart, 'My power and the might of my hand have gotten me this wealth.' You shall remember the LORD your God, for it is he who gives you power to get wealth, that he may confirm his covenant that he swore to your fathers, as it is this day.

It was a hot and muggy Monday morning. There was another long delay on the Orange Metro line, and I was briskly walking past the slower-moving people to get to work before 8 a.m. Just as I turned north on 23rd St., I noticed a homeless man sitting at the edge of the sidewalk panhandling with an oversized Styrofoam cup. He was a familiar face, and on other days I had given him extra fruit or sandwich from my own lunch bag. But today I had nothing with me, and I had resolved previously not to give money to the panhandlers no matter how hungry or impoverished they may seem; the money may go towards drugs or alcohol.

As I got closer to the homeless man, I purposely veered away from where he was sitting. I wanted to quickly pass by him, giving him neither a glance nor a greeting. At the last second the man thrust his cup even further into my path. Obviously, he didn't want to be ignored. I almost tripped over his arm; my immediate response was one of irritation and condemnation. He looked to be a man in his early 30s, of about my height and quite healthy…he was not emaciated nor disabled. I had seen him several times pushing his shopping cart, loaded up with personal belongings, up and down Pennsylvania Avenue. In my heart I said to him: "Why don't you get a job and stop begging for money from people?"

Even though the homeless man did not hear my caustic words, the Holy Spirit did. Immediately, the Spirit of God said these words to me (not audible words, but the inner voice of God): "There is no reason why you should not be in his place, and he in yours." The Holy Spirit was faithfully and cleanly probing through my mind and heart to reveal the darkness within (Hebrews 4:12). He guided my thoughts further along the path initiated by His penetrating statement. If I had been born somewhere in southeast Washington, DC, and had to grow up in its harsh environment, I may not have survived my teenage years. Either I would already be dead or incarcerated. But because of God's grace I was born into a Korean family that took education seriously, and I was able to study electrical engineering at an Ivy League school. Furthermore, it was my Christian parents who instilled Biblical values and helped me maintain godly boundaries that kept me away from sinful and harmful lifestyle. These thoughts filled my mind as I stepped away from the homeless man.

Even as I was walking, I asked God to forgive me of my pride, my prejudice towards the homeless, and my neglect or ignorance of His grace in my life. The verses from Deuteronomy above state well the sentiment I had. I was just like the Israelites, who thought and believed that it was their superior intelligence, amazing business acumen, incredible physical strength, and/or charismatic and winsome social skills that brought them the abundance of wealth. God was warning them even before they entered the Promise Land that they would soon forget about the One who made their blessings possible.

Although I did work hard through high school, college, and graduate years to obtain a masters degree in engineering, it was ultimately God who provided the ability to accomplish it. Furthermore, He provided generous scholarships and grants along the way to reduce the financial burdens. But I was quickly forgetting about such important details and assuming that it was all my hard work and effort. Consequently, I began to embrace the secular (nonbiblical) worldview that because I had made academic and career achievements, I was entitled to spend my wealth (the fruit of my success) according to my will and pleasure. My pride and ego were growing, and the Lord was not pleased with that.

And so it was on a hot Monday morning that the Lord placed a homeless man as a "prophet" in my path near Foggy Bottom metro station to confront me of my pride. After saying a prayer of repentance, I continued to walk towards my workplace. I did not turn back to give the homeless man money, but I did resolve to do something about the welfare of the homeless community in the DC area.

As I was praying and seeking the Lord's guidance, He eventually led me to several ministry opportunities. One was volunteering as part of the kitchen crew that served breakfast to hundreds of homeless people at an old church (perhaps it was Lutheran or Methodist) near Washington Circle. So once a week, I would get up at 4 a.m. to drive into DC and help make and serve breakfast. It was during one of these serving sessions that I believe I met an angel. He was an African American man in about his late 30s. He was in line to get breakfast for the morning, but when he saw me, he walked over and volunteered to help me set up tables. As I gave him the instructions, I connected with him momentarily. As I gazed into his eyes, I thought that I was gazing into eternity. There was something about his eyes that suggested that he knew eternity and that he knew me. I did not have time to dialogue with him because the breakfast lines would soon open. After the last table was cleared, I looked for the "man of eternity" but he was no longer on the church grounds. Even to this day, I believe that he was the fulfillment of Hebrews 13:2…I had the privilege of serving breakfast to one of God's angels.

After a few months of serving breakfast to the homeless, the Lord opened a more "reasonable" ministry opportunity…one that did not require getting up at 4 a.m. (Plus, I got a parking ticket once for not moving my car before the rush hour. And yes, I did grumble at God: "God, this is unfair! How can You give me a parking ticket when I'm trying to serve Your people?") This new ministry was aptly called the "Sandwich Patrol." It was established by the businesses in Georgetown that wanted to care for the homeless community but also did not want them to frequent their shops for fear of driving away the clientele. A local church near Wisconsin Avenue and M Street organized the volunteers to be part of the Sandwich Patrol. So once a week, I would stay after work and make about twenty brown-bag meals: ham and cheese sandwich, fruit and chips/cookies, and a small box of juice. And then I would walk around a pre-determined route in Georgetown where the homeless people live or linger during the day, and hand out the brown bags. Most of them were expecting someone to come around evening time, and appreciated the meal. I had opportunities to talk to some of them and even pray for them.

The Lord opened the way for others to join me in the Sandwich Patrol ministry. The youth group students (about 20+) from a nearby Korean-American church came out one evening to make and pass out the meals. For some students it was their first exposure to life-on-life ministry outside the church walls.

It was also during this time that the Lord encouraged me to attend worship services at African American churches in DC. The first church I attended was Shiloh Baptist Church in the NW section of the city. I was greatly blessed by their worship service, and decided to attend their services whenever I had time. (Since the service at my own church, Korean Orthodox Presbyterian Church, began at 1 p.m. on Sundays, I had the opportunity to visit other churches in the morning.) Over the next few months, a partnering relationship grew between KOPC and SBC, and several outreach events were held in DC by the two churches.

It's incredible to think that such a series of ministry opportunities grew out of a timely but sharp rebuke from the Holy Spirit on the streets of DC. In the Old Testament times, confession of sin and repentance were publicly declared through animal sacrifices (Leviticus 4). These sin and guilt offerings were acts of "worship" unto the Lord, acts of obedience to the Lord, who is worthy of our reverent submission. I believe that God honors genuine prayer/act of repentance as an aspect of worship unto Him. Perhaps the Holy Spirit also wants to reveal to you sinful attitudes of pride, prejudice, entitlement, etc. Would you take some time to pray and ask the Holy Spirit to search your heart, and reveal ways that are offensive to Him? And ask also for the Holy Spirit to guide you to ministry opportunities in keeping with genuine repentance.

Psalm 139:23-24 - Search me, O God, and know my heart! Try me and know my thoughts! And see if there be any grievous way in me, and lead me in the way everlasting!

11 – Competing with Horses

Jeremiah 12:5 - If you have raced with men on foot, and they have wearied you, how will you compete with horses? And if in a safe land you are so trusting, what will you do in the thicket of the Jordan?

A few weeks before our move from northern Virginia to Columbia, South Carolina, for seminary training, we met for lunch with a Baptist pastor who had been a member of my father's Presbyterian church. Over the course of the meal, the pastor encouraged me to consider going to Southeastern Baptist Seminary in North Carolina. He shared briefly that he studied at Southeastern because the denomination had offered him a generous scholarship. Furthermore, for those who are considering fulltime missions (like us), the denomination's International Mission Board is the largest in the U.S. and will fully fund qualified candidates. The Korean Baptist pastor finished his talk with this simple question: "Why would you want to struggle with paying for seminary tuition, and afterwards face the challenge of raising financial support for years before you go to the mission field? Don't you want to take the generous offer that God has for you through the Southern Baptist?"

As we left the lunch meeting, my mother, who was the one who had connected the old church member with us, reminded us that we don't have to change denomination or mission agency because of fear of not having enough funds: God will faithfully provide. My wife and I had both seen God's faithful provision for each of our families as we were growing up. I resolved that I would not switch denomination or mission agency simply because of money. If I had to leave the Presbyterian denomination, it would have to be for doctrinal reasons.

A few weeks later, we moved into a three-bedroom apartment that was about twenty minutes from Columbia

Biblical Seminary. Although the rent was very low, the apartment had several issues (heavy tobacco smell, fire ants, roaches, etc.), and we decided to move into a three-bedroom trailer home (14 feet by 80 feet) that was located on campus grounds. The owner, who had served many years in Southeast Asia, had to suddenly move to his agency's headquarters in Philadelphia. We agreed to purchase the home for $12,000 and gave him a $1,000 down payment with the agreement that we would send him the balance within thirty days.

I assumed that my wife and I would have no problem taking out a loan from a local bank. After all, we both had excellent credit history, and Faith was working as a part time pharmacist at a well-known drug store chain. However, the first bank I walked into rejected our application. It was the same with the second bank. Both times, the loan officers explained that, historically, loans for trailer homes were a terrible risk for the banks, and that unless my wife worked full time, the bank could not approve our application. I submitted application at one more bank, and then we wrote a prayer letter to our family and friends back in northern Virginia. We asked them to pray that the Lord would allow the bank to approve our loan. The deadline for the required $11,000 payment to the owner was less than two weeks. Did God bring us all the way to seminary just to make us homeless? We could not understand why God was not opening the door for a bank loan.

So we decided to fast and pray for three days. My wife and I spread out the trailer home contract on the living room floor (similar to what King Hezekiah did with Sennacherib's letter and my mother did with Raytheon's rejection letter) and cried out to the Lord. On the third day, as we came back from a day of worship and serving in the children's ministry at the local church, we received a phone call from Bob, a colleague at previous workplace and a close friend. He started his conversation with these words,

"James and Faith, I don't think God wants you to be in debt when you are in the seminary. We will send you the money to purchase the trailer home."

We could hardly believe his words. We were fasting and praying for God to grant us the bank loan, and the Lord had a different plan. Bob and his friend, someone we had never met in person, decided to bless us with this generous offer. He explained that the $11,000 gift would be a "loan"...when we were finished with the seminary and eventually sold our trailer home to the next family, we could return the funds to him. [Because trailer homes depreciate, we eventually sold the home for $8,500 and sent the funds to charitable ministries designated by Bob and his friend. Bob would explain that the sum of money was already given to the Lord, and he wanted the proceeds from the sale to bless other ministries.] This trailer home became a sanctuary for our family for the next four years. All three of our children have wonderful memories of growing up in a small house that shook every time storms pass by.

Through this experience during our first few weeks at Columbia, God was intent on training our heart, mind, and knees for the battle to come. He was concerned that if we did not grow in our faith, we would not be ready to meet the barrage of attacks from the enemy on the mission field. There could be unexpected illnesses, persecution from the local authorities, arrests, team conflicts and even demonic attacks...but if we were not ready, we would respond with fear rather than faith. We were complaining to God for rejected bank loans...we were already tired from running with the footmen, and God was warning us that we would be competing against horses in the years to come. If we did not learn to fast and pray, and seek the Lord earnestly in prayer, we would not be able to survive on the mission field. [Read again 1 Samuel 17. While King Saul and the rest of Israel soldiers cowered before Goliath, David stood firmly against the mortal giant with unswerving faith in the immortal God.]

Are you preparing to go to the ends of the earth for the Lord? Then ask Him to get you battle ready. You may be going through financial crisis, and about to be evicted from your home in a few days; then rise to the challenge. Worship the Lord, fast and pray, and see Him provide a breakthrough. You are created to race against horses, and win! Do not give up, but take every challenge, every detour, every setback as an opportunity to be better prepared for the mission field.

I am amazed at the incredibly rigorous training men have to go through to qualify as SEAL soldiers. They have to endure days and days of tormenting stress put on their mind and body in order to be America's elite soldiers, ready to complete their mission regardless of insurmountable odds set against them. However, their superiors (generals and even the president of the United States) are only mortal and unable to guarantee neither safety nor success of their tactical mission. Furthermore, their warfare is only against flesh and blood.

You are being equipped with spiritual weapons to overcome demonic forces, set the prisoners free from the dungeons of darkness, heal the sick, and even raise the dead. And even if you are struck by a sniper's bullet, the Lord can raise you back to life. Your Superior is immortal, and knows exactly where and how to send you, and always accomplishes His purposes. The government of the United States will come to an end one day. But the government of our Lord Jesus Christ will endure forever. You have nothing to fear. Take time to recommit your life to the King of kings…to do as He bids.

Isaiah 9:7 - Of the increase of his government and of peace there will be no end, on the throne of David and over his kingdom, to establish it and to uphold it with justice and with righteousness from this time forth and forevermore. The zeal of the Lord of hosts will do this.

63

12 – God's Plumb Line

Amos 7:7 - This is what he showed me: behold, the Lord was standing beside a wall built with a plumb line, with a plumb line in his hand.

James 5:16 – Therefore, confess your sins to one another and pray for one another, that you may be healed. The prayer of a righteous person has great power as it is working.

In the spring of 2000, our home church (now Open Door Presbyterian Church) commissioned our family to the target Central Asian country as ambassadors of Jesus Christ to the lost. Our kids were quite young—ages 3, 6, and 7. Just prior to going to the mission field, the Lord led us through a time of spiritual cleansing. He wanted us to be as free as possible from our sinful past.

2 Timothy 2:19-21 – "Let everyone who names the name of the Lord depart from iniquity." Now in a great house there are not only vessels of gold and silver but also of wood and clay, some for honorable use, some for dishonorable. Therefore, if anyone cleanses himself from what is dishonorable, he will be a vessel for honorable use, set apart as holy, useful to the master of the house, ready for every good work.

Paul wrote this last letter in prison after more than three decades of faithful and fruitful ministry. He wanted his disciple Timothy (and all of us who are followers of Jesus Christ) to know several principles pertinent to ministry. In Chapter 2, Paul gives two exhortations: to commit to correct teaching (vv.14-18) and to practice correct living (vv.19-22). Or to put it another way, be committed to orthodoxy and orthopraxy. We can serve God as a preacher, public school teacher, IT consultant, or hospital custodian. The Lord is not concerned with the title of our job or office, but the status of our heart and mind. Are we upholding the truths of God's Word without compromise, lifting up Jesus to the highest place in every context? Are our hearts free of lust, idols, fears, pride or prejudice? The Lord who saved and called us into the ministry of reconciliation (2 Corinthians 5:20) is holy, and wants us to be holy. This does not mean that we have to be perfect or sinless, simply blameless (Psalms 19:13; 1 Timothy 3:10). And when we do sin, we are to quickly and humbly confess our sins and ask for cleansing (1 John 1:9).

Imagine yourself to be a cup in God's hands. It is not the color nor the composition of the cup that God is concerned about...the color of your skin, your academic degrees, linguistic abilities...but the status of your heart. Is it pure and clean, or is it filled with immorality, greed or bitterness? If our hearts are not emptied of our idols or habitual sins, what comes out on the mission field is not only the gospel but also our idols, prejudices, lust, and other sins.

On the mission field we have seen missionaries engaged in extramarital affairs, struggle with pornography, pursue after material gain, and treat our local population (believers and nonbelievers) with condescension and prejudice. The Lord knew that if He did not cleanse our hearts, we would be taking our idols, habitual sins, and prejudices to the field. Some of the consecration He did gradually over time as we were preparing to go overseas.

During our first year at Columbia Biblical Seminary, we met a missionary family from South Korea. They had served for seven years in the Philippines, and were granted their request of having Sabbath rest and graduate study in the U.S. during their eighth year. As they shared about their mission journey, they humbly confessed of their experience of discipline from the Lord. Knowing that they would be allowed to spend a year in the U.S., the missionary couple began to save up some of the funds that were sent from the supporting churches in Korea. These were funds that were to be used both for their living expenses and ministry needs on the field. Over time they had saved up about $8,000;

with that money they had planned on buying a used automobile and traveling throughout the U.S. and visiting famous landmarks or popular tourist sites. As they made a layover in Hawaii, the bag of money was stolen at the airport. The missionary said it himself: "It was God who took the money away. He was not pleased that we could not trust Him to provide for us when we came to the U.S. We should have used the funds on the mission field." Both he and his wife teared up as they confessed their sin of distrust in God, and we and other seminary families present prayed for them and for ourselves. Within a few weeks, a local church in Columbia donated a used vehicle for the missionary family, with which they were able to travel to tourist sites all over the country. I am so thankful that the missionary couple was humble enough to share their faith experience; we have been encouraged to trust God to faithfully provide as we labor for His kingdom.

On the mission field, we have seen some families purchase promising local homes, renovating and restoring them with Western features and amenities, and putting them on the market for up to ten times the original purchase price. Some missionaries owned several properties. Such "fix and flip" endeavors, however, do require significant investments of time, and missionaries can easily be distracted from the original purpose of their calling. Perhaps the missionaries struggle with their future financial security, and are seeking for ways to build up funds for children's college education or purchasing a home upon return to their home country. However, Jesus did not send us to the mission field to "fix and flip" homes. He sends us to build His kingdom, to seek His kingdom first, not ours. And He promises to provide what we need, including housing upon our return to our sending country.

On other issues, the Lord took drastic measures. One such blessing happened at Kona, Hawaii. We were there as a family from July to September 2000, to attend Crossroads Discipleship Training School at the Youth With A Mission base. There were twelve weeks of teaching by anointed and powerful speakers on topics like "Spiritual Warfare," "Father Heart of God," and "Plumb Line." The latter teaching came about halfway through the training program, and the emphasis was on using God's Word as a plumb line against the framework of our lives. God brought us to face sins and hidden hurts in our lives, which we had not dealt with before. We had been married for nine years by then, but our marriage relationship had several trouble spots. We took one day off to fast and pray, and then as the Spirit led us, each of us shared with one another about things in our past (unconfessed sins, hurts from childhood, etc.). The context of James 5:16 is about a physically sick person asking for prayers from the church elders. In our situation, our marriage relationship was very unhealthy, and it needed a "healing touch" from the Lord. We forgave one another and prayed for each other. We also had the whole Crossroads group (about seventy) pray over us and bless our marriage. Our marriage was restored and revived and relaunched with a new beginning, centered on honoring Christ, and it grew stronger on the mission field. Our ten years of marriage on the mission field were incredibly better than the first ten years in the States. (Typically, marriage relationships suffer on the mission field due to stress and anxiety.)

God also took our children through a time of purification. During our time in Hawaii, our two sons kept having nightmares. At the same time, their drawings/sketches made during playtime showed increasingly horrifying demonic figures. One night, Josiah, our second son, told us that he did not want to go to sleep...because Satan had told him in a dream the previous night that he would kill him on the next night. As we prayed with one of the YWAM staff, we came to the conclusion that there was demonic influence from Pokemon toys and stuffed animals. Our sons repented of their attachment to Pokemon toys, and then we burned up all their Pokemon cards and toys. The nightmares stopped that very night. The Lord knew that we would be stepping into a country that was steeped in shamanism, where demonic spirits thrive. He wanted to prepare even our children for the spiritual warfare to come. Ask the Lord to consecrate your children as well.

We encourage every person, especially married couples, considering missions overseas (or even full time ministry in your home country) to attend YWAM Crossroads. I believe it's a great setting for the Lord to address issues of your heart, including marriage relationships. Seminaries typically provide theological training of the mind; ministries like YWAM Crossroads/DTS provide training of the heart. Both are necessary to be Christ's ambassadors to the nations. Will you allow God's Word to minister as the plumb line in your life?

Proverbs 28:13 – Whoever conceals his transgressions will not prosper, but he who confesses and forsakes them will obtain mercy.

13 – A Prophecy from the Lord

1 Corinthians 14:3 - On the other hand, the one who prophesies speaks to people for their upbuilding and encouragement and consolation.

Besides the cleansing work in our lives, the Lord also spoke to us through one of the teachers at YWAM Crossroads in the summer of 2000. The middle-aged man had the gift of prophecy, and during one of his lectures, he paused and pointed at me. He asked me to stand up and then identified me as a missionary and a church planter. (Prior to that day, we had never met.) And then he prayed over us...that we would, through the lives of a handful of national leaders, plant many churches on the mission field. His prophetic prayer was a great source of encouragement to us, and served to confirm God's calling in our lives.

Even though I grew up in a conservative Presbyterian pastor's family, I believe that all of the gifts of the Holy Spirit are functioning today, including the charismatic gifts like prophecy and tongues. I believe that the Holy Spirit still guides the Church (and missionaries) to make those decisions that not only bring glory to Jesus, but also bear abundant fruit. It was the Holy Spirit who spoke to the Church at Antioch to set apart Barnabas and Saul (Paul) for the special ministry of evangelism and church planting (Acts 13:1-3). It was the same Spirit who guided Paul away from Bithynia and westward towards Macedonia, where the apostle would see abundant fruit. Eventually, the Seven Churches (Revelations 3) would be established in what is today's Turkey.

Acts 13:1-3 – Now there were in the church at Antioch prophets and teachers, Barnabas, Simeon who was called Niger, Lucius of Cyrene, Manaen a lifelong friend of Herod the tetrarch, and Saul. While they were worshiping the Lord and fasting, the Holy Spirit said, "Set apart for me Barnabas and Saul for the work to which I have called them." Then after fasting and praying they laid their hands on them and sent them off.

The church at Antioch was led by godly, Spirit-filled men. I believe any one of the men listed in the first verse one can easily take the place of CEO of any global ministry (Cru, Compassion, IMB) or the lead pastor role of any megachurch today. And yet these leaders fasted and prayed to hear from the Lord concerning how to proceed with their ministry of advancing God's kingdom. In response, the Holy Spirit spoke to them clearly. Sadly, we are neglecting this incredible privilege in our private and public life today. The church leaders should expect to hear from the Holy Spirit concerning whom to send out as cross-cultural missionaries. Loren Cunningham, the founder of Youth With A Mission, wrote a challenging and inspirational book titled *Is That Really You, God?* In that book, Loren encourages every believer to draw closer to God and to learn to hear God's voice.

Ever since I was called into missions (1983), I have met hundreds, if not thousands, of missionaries. Of course it would be impossible to have deep, meaningful conversations with every one of them, but there are occasions where I can at least have a five-to-ten-minute exchange. I sometimes meet missionaries who chose their mission field simply because of statistical facts. One young seminarian at CIU said that he is choosing to go to Saudi Arabia because it was the most difficult place for missionaries to access. I'm not sure what happened subsequently, but his remark made me ponder about our choice of mission field. Shouldn't the Holy Spirit have something to say about where we should go and serve the Lord? If apostle Paul, the greatest missionary in the history of the Church, and a man filled with the Holy Spirit, had to be guided away from Bithynia towards Macedonia, should we not seek similar guidance from the Lord? It seems rather prideful for a man to choose a mission field simply because it is the place of greatest challenge.

As Jesus looked at the Jews and Gentiles around Him in 1st Century Palestine, He declared that the field was ripe for harvest (John 4:35; Matthew 9:37-38). He asked that we pray to the Lord of the harvest for more laborers to be sent to the field. I believe that what Jesus said 2000 years ago is also true today. There are places in the world today where the harvest is plentiful. And we are to pray and ask the Lord for more laborers to those places; for missionaries, this means to ask God to send us to those places where the field is ripe for harvest. The Spirit guided Paul to such places, and He can do the same today.

So why can't we hear God's voice? I believe that the main reason is because of our sin.

Matthew 5:8 - Blessed are the pure in heart, for they shall see God.

Psalm 24:3-4 – Who shall ascend the hill of the LORD? And who shall stand in his holy place? He who has clean hands and a pure heart, who does not lift up his soul to what is false and does not swear deceitfully.

Would you ask God to cleanse you so that you can hear clearly from Him? Regardless of your church/denomination background, confess to Him that you believe He speaks to those who earnestly seek Him with all their heart. And then quiet your heart and listen for His Spirit to speak to you. The Father delights to speak to His children, including those areas where we are not behaving like His children. But remember that He points out our weaknesses and sins not to condemn us, but to set us free and allow us to live in the abundance of His grace. And ask the Lord to take you to those places where the harvest is ready, so that you can experience not only the privilege of sowing seeds of truth in people's heart, but also the joy of bringing the lost into His Kingdom, raising them up as disciples of Christ.

I want to close this chapter with one more testimony of God's affirming vision at Kona, Hawaii, before we left for Central Asia. There were two visions, separated by a few minutes; both visions came during one of the powerful praise and worship sessions in the chapel. As we were singing "These Are the Days of Elijah," the Lord showed me a vision of the heavens, with thousands and thousands of soldiers mounted on horses. Each soldier was fully armored and equipped with swords and spears. I could sense that all eyes were fixed on Jesus, who was brilliantly white, also mounted on a horse. I noticed that I was in the midst, but dressed only in a white tunic...no armor, no weapons. I began to wonder why I was not in full armor. And then a few minutes later, there was another vision. This time there was a smaller group of soldiers, perhaps dozens. I was part of this group, this time in full armor. Jesus was at the very front, galloping towards a town that was engulfed in huge flames. I believe that the Lord gave me this vision to reassure us that He was sending us to a possibly dangerous place where His mission needed to be accomplished, just as He did with Gideon just before the battle against the Midianites (Judges 7:9-15).

I believe that the Lord was using our time at YWAM's Crossroads in Kona to prepare our heart and mind for the kingdom warfare to come. Through the times of repentance and confession, of learning about evangelism, spiritual gifts and spiritual warfare, of prayers of healing and anointing over us, we were putting on the full armor of God. Once we were ready, the Lord would send us to the very town where the enemy must surrender the lives of the lost sheep who would respond to the voice of the Good Shepherd.

Recommended reading:
Surprised by the Power of the Spirit by Jack Deere.

14 – Trusting in the Lord of the Harvest

Proverbs 3:5-6 - Trust in the Lord with all your heart, and do not lean on your own understanding. In all your ways acknowledge him, and he will make straight your paths.

Acts 16:6-10 - And they went through the region of Phrygia and Galatia, having been forbidden by the Holy Spirit to speak the word in Asia. And when they had come up to Mysia, they attempted to go into Bithynia, but the Spirit of Jesus did not allow them. So, passing by Mysia, they went down to Troas. And a vision appeared to Paul in the night: a man of Macedonia was standing there, urging him and saying, "Come over to Macedonia and help us." And when Paul had seen the vision, immediately we sought to go on into Macedonia, concluding that God had called us to preach the gospel to them.

As our family returned to the States from our three-month mission trip to Varanasi, India, my wife and I were settled on going back to the Ansari Muslim people group after finishing seminary. The Lord had endeared our hearts towards these silk carpet and tapestry weavers, and we wanted more than anything for them to know the true Master who would like to see the scarlet thread of the gospel woven into their lives.

During our final year at CIU (Columbia International University), we decided to actively look for mission agencies to join. We decided to join Pioneers more for gastronomical than spiritual reasons. Donnie, the recruiter for Pioneers, came over to our trailer home twice with pizza, and quickly became our kids favored "uncle." He understood how seminary families struggle financially, and kindly met our physical needs before sharing with us the ethos of Pioneers. Of course Donnie also had a contagious heart of worship and passion for the lost. After his second visit with a box of Domino's Pizza, we decided to apply with Pioneers as long-term church-planting missionaries.

During this time we also began to engage with our church mission committee about the possibility of returning to Varanasi, India. Our missions elder met with us over lunch and explained the current missions vision of the church. While we were in seminary, the church had begun to connect with Korean missionaries in Central Asia. The church had been sending summer mission teams to work with missionaries in one of the capital cities, and they were seeing much spiritual fruit. Elder Lee, a godly man who is now with the Lord, explained that the church was focusing on sending long-term missionaries to the selected Central Asian country, and strongly encouraged us to consider that Muslim country as an option. If, however, we were still determined to go to India, we would need to spend the next two years at our home church to bring the leadership and congregation alongside our Ansari vision. We would probably have to lead one or two short-term mission teams to northern India to acquaint the church members with the needs of the unreached, unengaged Ansari people group.

Faith and I were in a dilemma…we wanted to go to the mission field as soon as possible, especially because our kids were getting older. Seasoned missionaries had told us that the younger the children were when they arrived on the mission field, the more readily and easily they adjusted to the new culture and language. We knew very little about Central Asia, and the fact that it had been a Soviet republic made us think of it as a cold, sterile land. Then in the summer of 1998, I had the opportunity to join a short-term mission team to the target Central Asian country for exploratory and ethnographic research project, and found the local people group to be warm and hospitable. It was during this trip that I asked the Lord for a sign of confirmation. One Friday I approached the largest mosque in the city, where three to four thousand men gather to pray. I asked the Lord to allow me to meet one person who would be interested in the gospel. And then I walked through the gate. Within a minute a young Muslim man walked up to me and asked me if I spoke English. I told him, "Yes," and then he proceeded to give me a tour of the mosque. He allowed me to stay close to him as he washed and prepared himself for the salat (prayer). He even found a place in the shade where I could observe the men praying. After about thirty minutes, the ritual was finished, and he and I went to a nearby café to talk about prayer and Jesus Christ over tea. He was eager to receive a copy of the Gideon pocket Bible (New Testament only). We met one more time to talk about the teachings in the Bible, and then I had to return to the States. God had answered my prayer.

And yet back at home Faith and I still felt drawn to the Ansari people group. We decided to take a couple of days away at a retreat center about two hours south of DC. Faith and I would fast a day and our three kids (ages seven, six and three) would fast one meal (lunch). We told them that we needed to pray and ask the Lord of the harvest where He would like to send us: India or Central Asia? I'm not sure if the kids understood the purpose of their fasting a meal, but later that evening as we roasted hot dogs on a campfire, they quickly forgot about the purpose of skipping lunch and enjoyed a simple meal of hot dogs, potato chips, punch, and marshmallows. At the end of the day, Faith and I decided to submit to the leadership of the church and head towards Central Asia; we prayed that if the Lord wanted us to go to India instead of Central Asia, He would have to close the doors to the latter. We also reasoned that both India and Central Asia were relatively new places of ministry for us; we had not invested significant amount of time learning the language and culture of Ansari people group.

What we did not know was that the Lord had been preparing His harvest field for our arrival to Central Asia in 2000. About sixty years before our arrival, Joseph Stalin had forcibly taken nearly 200,000 Koreans from Manchuria and transported them by rail to Central Asia...to Kazakhstan, Kyrgyzstan, Turkmenistan, Tajikistan, and Uzbekistan. According to the grandchildren of these migrants, nearly a third of them died during the brutal first winter. Those who survived, however, were determined to thrive in their new environment, and eventually became prosperous and successful as farmers, merchants, physicians, professors and even KGB agents. The other people groups in the region held deep respect for the Koreans for their tenacity for life and strong work ethic. Furthermore, when the Soviet Union fell apart in the early 1990s, many South Korean companies rushed in with their electronic merchandise and even automobiles. The Central Asians began to appreciate both the culture and manufactured goods of Korea.

Hence, when we arrived in Central Asia and identified ourselves as Koreans from the U.S., the community recognized us as being hardworking and intelligent. Right away we were given a measure of trust and respect that opened doors for the gospel. The Lord of the harvest knew His laborers (us) and His harvest field (people groups of Central Asia), and prepared the hearts of the latter so that they would be eager to build relationship with "Korean-Americans."

In our own journey, we had initially wanted to join a church-planting missionary team in Cairo, Egypt, in the early 1990s. The Lord closed that door when the team imploded and was forced to leave the country. I also had sensed that the Arabs in the '90s held prejudice against Asians and treated Koreans with condescension. Ten years later the Lord took us into a country that respected Koreans and were willing to hear the reasons why the small peninsula country had been blessed by God with progress and prosperity.

Perhaps the Lord is leading you to a place or on a path that you had not expected. If you are seeking to fulfill His will in your life (remember the Lord's prayer..."Thy will

76

be done"), trust that He who knows you, and the harvest field, will take you to a place that is an optimal environment for abundant fruit. Continue to approach God with an open heart to hear from Him. He is not mute; ask Him speak to your heart...just as He did with Philip.

Acts 8:26 – Now an angel of the Lord said to Philip, "Rise and go toward the south to the road that goes down from Jerusalem to Gaza." This is a desert place.

15 – Fear Not!

Isaiah 43:1-2 - But now thus says the LORD, he who created you, O Jacob, he who formed you, O Israel: "Fear not, for I have redeemed you; I have called you by name, you are mine. When you pass through the waters, I will be with you; and through the rivers, they shall not overwhelm you; when you walk through fire you shall not be burned, and the flame shall not consume you.

Isaiah 41:10 - fear not, for I am with you; be not dismayed, for I am your God; I will strengthen you, I will help you, I will uphold you with my righteous right hand.

There were two significant exhortations from the Lord as we began our ministry in Central Asia. The first exhortation came in the early summer of 2001 while we were attending a retreat for the missionaries serving in our country. The guest speaker was Len Bartlotti, a veteran missionary to Pakistan. He had served more than a dozen years in that country, and was blessed to see many Muslims come to Christ through his team. Just recently, the Pakistani government had decided to rescind his visa, and thus he and his family were forced to leave.

As he shared about his missionary journey, he challenged all of us to think about what we came to teach the local believers. He shared about the survey he took amongst several hundred believers from Muslim background (BMBs) just before he had to leave Pakistan. He had asked them what they had learned from the foreign missionaries. Of course there were varied answers, ranging from how to have personal devotions to preaching at church meetings. However, the most common answer on the survey was "how to fear." The BMBs explained that the expatriate missionaries had taught them how to fear man. Of course the missionaries would not explicitly teach this; on the contrary, they would ardently teach and preach about how great and sovereign the Lord is. And yet, the missionaries would often act as if God had little or no power when it came to persecution against the Christians. The missionaries had inadvertently shown an overwhelming attitude of fear as they tried to protect their own lives, or the lives of the national believers from the local authorities or fanatic Muslims in the community. Some missionaries perhaps did not even engage in any religious activities so that they could preserve their visa. Such statements from the BMB community shocked and greatly disappointed Len, and he asked all of us at the retreat: "What are you going to teach your disciples? I'm afraid that we mainly taught our disciples how to fear man."

When we heard this challenging message, we were just eight months into the country. The Lord spoke words of hope and courage into our hearts. He reminded us that He will be with us (Isaiah 41:10) and that He will preserve us through trials of fire (Isaiah 43:1-2). The Lord knew what we would face in the months and years to come, and so He gave us an apt warning through one of His servants at a missionary retreat.

Later that evening, my wife and I committed ourselves to be fearless in our ministry. We resolved that we would not teach fear to our disciples. The gospel of Jesus Christ is nothing to be ashamed of, and we decided that we would not keep quiet in order to secure our visa. We asked God to make us bold like the apostle Paul (Romans 1:16).

The Lord also used Transformations, a video documentary by George Otis, Jr., to confirm His message of "Fear Not!" We were introduced to this video while attending Crossroads DTS with YWAM at Kona, Hawaii. The video took us through four cities around the world where the Holy Spirit brought about amazing transformation to the community as the body of Christ came together to fast, worship, and pray. The first featured city was Cali, Colombia, where a Bolivian evangelist named Julio and his wife labored to bring unity to the body of Christ and revival to their city. The Lord does bring a mighty transformative revival to Cali, but at the cost of Julio's life; he was gunned down by a criminal neighbor. The Lord used his death to bring about reconciliation and restoration of unity between the pastors and ministry leaders in the city. A great revival is ushered in after his death. A few weeks before his death, Julio said the following in response to threats against his life: "I am immortal until I have done everything that God has for me to do." What an awesome expression of faith! [I highly recommend both Transformations and its sequel, Transformations II, for every Christian, especially missionaries.]

The Lord challenged us through Julio's testimony to come up with our own convictions concerning our missionary endeavors on the field. First, our visa in the country is in God's hands, and not in the hands of the local authorities. If the Lord wants us to stay in the country, even the president of the country cannot kick us out! However, if the time has come for us to leave the country, then no matter how many international lawyers or U.S. government leaders we enlist, we will not be able to stay.

Second, we are truly immortal (or invincible, bulletproof, untouchable, etc.) until we have done everything that God wants us to do. Our Lord Jesus was sent by the Father with the purpose of redeeming mankind through His death on the cross at the appointed time. Hence, no one could mortally wound Him prior to that; for instance, He was able to walk through a crowd that wanted to throw Him off the cliff (Luke 4:28-30). Storms could not drown Him (Mark 4:35-41). But when the time came for Jesus to be arrested, beaten and crucified, even the angels of heaven could not (and would not) save Him (Matthew 26:53-54). So it will be for us.

The Lord knew that we would need His exhortation to be bold and courageous as we began our ministry in Central Asia. About three months after the missionary retreat, nineteen Muslim terrorists attacked America on September 11th. We were alerted to the tragic event by our ex-KGB landlord. He took us to his family quarters, and we saw the repeated images of the twin towers being blown apart by the two passenger planes. Although the broadcast was in Russian, we could understand what was happening. Our landlord, a Muslim himself, felt terrible for the tragic deaths of nearly three thousand innocent civilians. Once the identity of the perpetrators were revealed, our landlord expressed his disgust against the brutal attack by Al-Qaeda. He also expressed his support for the U.S. military's campaign against this terrorist group hiding in Afghanistan.

A few days after the war in Afghanistan began we received an email from the U.S. embassy in the capital city. They advised that we leave the country since the war against Al-Qaeda could have easily spilled over into the former Soviet country. There may have been Osama bin Laden sympathizers who could have attacked U.S. citizens in the region. My wife and I prayed, and after consulting with our team leader and other missionaries in our city, we decided to stay and not leave the field. The Lord also moved the heart of our landlord to assure us that he would do everything he could to protect us from any terrorist attacks. We were very grateful for his gesture of help and protection.

The U.S. embassy sent out similar alerts to American missionaries serving in other Central Asian countries. In one particular country, several missionary agency leaders decided to heed the warning and organized a mass evacuation of the missionary teams; they would return when the country was "safer." After a few months, the U.S. missionaries returned to the mission field, and several local church leaders expressed that they had lost respect for the missionaries. (Some of the local church leaders had advised the missionaries not to leave the country.) They felt that the evacuation was prompted more by fear of man than by the guidance of the Holy Spirit.

We are ambassadors of Jesus Christ, the risen Lord who has been given all authority in heaven and on earth. We must entrust Him with our visas and our very lives. He knows exactly where He is sending His ambassadors, and is more than able to protect them and provide all their needs to accomplish His mission. Nearly ten years after the 9/11 attack, the U.S. government launched a surprise attack against Osama bin Laden, who was then living in Pakistan. There is a historic photo of the White House Situation Room where President Obama and his staff sat in solemn silence, anxiously waiting for the news from Pakistan. There were two clear unknowns: 1) Were the intelligence reports accurate about bin Laden's whereabouts and 2) Would the elite SEAL soldiers succeed in their mission? Even the leading earthly government could not guarantee a successful outcome of the mission.

The power and authority of Jesus Christ is not like that. He knows exactly where the lost sheep are, and can send one or several missionaries to bring that person to Himself. And He is able to protect the lives of His missionaries from every evil attack, whether by flesh and blood or by evil spirits (2 Timothy 4:18).

Will you take time now to recommit your life and your mission to the King of kings? He not only knows exactly what storm or persecution you are facing (or will be facing in the near future), but also has the power and the authority to resolve it according to His will. Declare to the heavens and the earth Who it is that has sent you.

16 – Worship of the Living God

Psalm 22:3 - Yet you are holy, enthroned on the praises of Israel.

Psalm 46:10 - "Be still, and know that I am God. I will be exalted among the nations, I will be exalted in the earth!"

Acts 16:25-26 - About midnight Paul and Silas were praying and singing hymns to God, and the prisoners were listening to them, and suddenly there was a great earthquake, so that the foundations of the prison were shaken. And immediately all the doors were opened, and everyone's bonds were unfastened.

The first message from the Lord had been "Fear Not!" The second message from the Lord was "WORSHIP." We had just completed three wonderful months of YWAM training at Kona, Hawaii, and had been blessed by incredible times of worship. We had also seen the *Transformations* videos (I and II), and we were praying that God would transform our city with the gospel as the believers from different denominations and ministries began to worship, fast, and pray together.

About nine months into the country, we began to meet with a German missionary family. We decided to meet twice a month, on Friday evenings. We would begin with a meal, and then proceed to praise and prayer. They had three children close to our own children's ages, and we encouraged all the children to join us for the time of praise. After about 30 to 45 minutes of lifting up praises unto the Lord, we would pray over our children and then release them to go and play together. The four of us would spend the next one to one and a half hour praying specifically (by name) for the Muslim neighbors, friends, and acquaintances in our lives.

We would often pray through portions of Scripture, asking the Lord to repeat His miracles in our day. We asked the Lord to fill us with the Holy Spirit, as He did with the believers of the early church in the Book of Acts.

Two weeks after we started our time of praise and prayer, the Lord blessed us with our first fruit of conversion. A young Central Asian Muslim widow and her two sons came to faith in Christ.

As we continued to meet with our missionary friends, the Lord of the harvest opened up more opportunities to share the gospel with our Muslim friends. Of course we did not know who would come to faith in Christ, and hence we shared the gospel with as many people as possible. We watched JESUS movie (produced by Cru ministry around 1979) in Central Asian languages with our Muslim friends. On the average we showed this incredibly powerful movie two to three times a week. Because the movie is based on the Gospel of Luke, there is great opportunity after the movie to explore passages in Luke and launch into heart-stirring discussions. We prayed and asked the Lord to speak to our Muslim friends through the movie.

Over the next five years, we continued to meet with other missionaries to worship the Lord and pray that He would open doors for the gospel. Children were always included in our gathering. As we continued our biweekly prayer meetings, the Lord added sixty new believers to our house church. Other missionaries experienced fruit in their ministry as well.

In the Old Testament the Kohathites had the responsibility and privilege of carrying the ark of the covenant where the LORD would come and manifest His glory. Often, the Kohathites also carried the ark of the covenant into the battle field, leading Israel's army against their enemies. The people of Israel were reminded over and over again that their God would fight on their behalf.

2 Chronicles 20:13-15, 21-23 - Meanwhile all Judah stood before the Lord, with their little ones, their wives, and their children. And the Spirit of the Lord came upon Jahaziel the son of Zechariah, son of Benaiah, son of Jeiel, son of Mattaniah, a Levite of the sons of Asaph, in the midst of the assembly. And he said, "Listen, all Judah and inhabitants of Jerusalem and King Jehoshaphat: Thus says the Lord to you, 'Do not be afraid and do not be dismayed at this great horde, for the battle is not yours but God's.

And when he had taken counsel with the people, he appointed those who were to sing to the Lord and praise him in holy attire, as they went before the army, and say, "Give thanks to the Lord, for his steadfast love endures forever." And when they began to sing and praise, the Lord set an ambush against the men of Ammon, Moab, and Mount Seir, who had come against Judah, so that they were routed. For the men of Ammon and Moab rose against the inhabitants of Mount Seir, devoting them to destruction, and when they had made an end of the inhabitants of Seir, they all helped to destroy one another.

The Lord comes to the aid of His people when they put their trust completely in Him, and are ready to offer genuine worship for what He is able to do regardless of the outcome (Daniel 3:16-18). We knew that even if we had the best church planting strategy and the most capable team members, if the Lord's presence was not with us, there would be no fruit.

In his book, Let the Nations Be Glad, John Piper reminds us that "missions exists because worship doesn't." We know from Revelations 7:9 that people from all languages and ethnic backgrounds will be worshiping our Lord in heaven. Missions exist to implement that future reality here on earth until the return of Christ.

Although we are not directly involved in "house of prayer" movements across the globe by ministries associated with International House of Prayer, Bethel, or even YWAM, we do agree with their general approach that offering up pure and passionate worship of Jesus Christ the Son of the living God will bring His glory and power into the harvest field. He will send dreams and visions, empower His servants to heal the sick and cast out demons, and boldly proclaim God's Word without any compromise. Will you set aside time in the busyness of culture and language learning, remodeling your home so that it becomes somewhat inhabitable, meeting with both local and expatriate people...to worship the living God who has called you to the place where you are now serving? Perhaps you can reach out to another missionary family(ies) that shares your heart and vision for worship, and exalt the name of Jesus through songs and prayer of proclamation that He is the King of kings and Lord of lords, the Son of the living God. And then lift up the names of the lost people around you, that the Lord may open their hearts to respond to the gospel with complete repentance and surrendered lives.

Recommended reading:
Let the Nations Be Glad by John Piper

17 – Spiritual Warfare

1 Peter 5:8 - Be sober-minded; be watchful. Your adversary the devil prowls around like a roaring lion, seeking someone to devour.
Ephesians 6:12 - For we do not wrestle against flesh and blood, but against the rulers, against the authorities, against the cosmic powers over this present darkness, against the spiritual forces of evil in the heavenly places.

In the fall of 2000, our family moved in to live with a group of local Muslims. There were four extended families living at this compound...an elderly couple and three of their four sons with their spouses and children. Our landlord was the eldest of the sons, and was a retired officer with the secret police (KGB during the Soviet era). We were introduced to this man through our team leader.

My wife and I had to pause and pray for a while about our living situation: Isn't it foolish and risky for a missionary family to live with an ex-KGB agent? What if this Muslim man becomes suspicious of our intentions of being in his country? Can we even have family devotions in our living quarters?

But as we and our team leaders prayed, we sensed peace from the Lord for us to move in. What necessitated this particular living situation was the fact that his second son was the only one in our village who spoke English. And we would initially need as much translation help as possible with our settling down. The landlord's first son was the village imam (Muslim priest). Our landlord's family belonged to a tribe similar to the Levites in the Old Testament...Muslim priests would come out of this line. For some reason we weren't as concerned about moving in to an imam's home.

The landlord's parents owned about an acre of land, and on this land the fours sons had built their own living quarters. Our landlord rented out his own living quarters to us to make extra income. We had two bedrooms, a large meeting room, kitchen, and our own bathroom. The landlord had taken extra effort to make the kitchen and bathroom as modern and Western as possible, and we were grateful for a modern flush toilet (and not a hole in the ground).

I became like the fifth son to the landlord's aging parents, and my wife became the fifth daughter-in-law. We moved in to learn the language and the culture of the local people, and at the onset we had planned to live with them for about three months. However, as our relationship deepened with the landlord's extended family, we decided to stay another twelve months.

By God's grace and His sovereign protection, we were able to have Bible studies, prayer meetings, and even Sunday worship services with other missionaries in our own home. As I mentioned earlier, our initial fears or anxiety about moving in with this Muslim family hinged on the fact that the landlord was an ex-KGB agent. We had been worried that our landlord would turn us over to the local police once he found out that we were having worship services at our home. But that never happened. We did, however, experience another type of attack on our family.

The very first night that we slept in our new home, I had an intense nightmare. In it I saw an old woman with wrinkled face, a dark scarf (hijab) covering her hair. She neither looked Korean nor American (Caucasian), so in my dream I assumed that she was of local ethnicity. She had fierce black eyes, and she approached me suddenly and thrust both her hands into my stomach. I felt a horribly sharp pain as her hands went deep into my stomach and come out of my back. I woke up from the nightmare with an immense scream, and Faith woke up with me. What was shocking was that I still felt the old woman's hands in my stomach as I sat up. Faith and I both felt the presence of an evil spirit in the room.

It was as if Satan was saying to us: "What are you doing in my territory? This is my domain, my kingdom. Don't touch any of my people. You are not welcome here. You are no longer with your Christian friends in America. Get out!" Satan did not want to release anyone who was a citizen of his kingdom. So he came to us like a roaring lion (1 Peter 5:8), wanting to inject fear into us so that we would either leave that place or be so immobilized with fear so that we became ineffective. Faith and I got down on our knees and prayed for about an hour to the Lord for protection and deliverance from the enemy.

The next morning, we decided to fast and pray the entire day. We also took our guitar and sang worship songs unto Jesus Christ, the Lord of lords and King of kings, throughout our living quarters. We cried out to the Risen Savior to come and chase out the evil spirits and fill the rooms with His presence. We did not know what kind of Muslim rituals (both orthodox and folk Islamic) were performed in our rooms, but we were now asking the Holy Spirit to sanctify the rooms for the worship of the true God. We asked the Lord to break down and annul any curses that were directed towards us. (Weeks later we would learn more about folk Islamic/animistic rituals that our landlord's family members regularly practiced.)

Whereas we had been concerned about the physical threat and possible persecution from the landlord and the secret police, the Lord wanted us to be more focused on the spiritual warfare that we were now engaged in. We were living amongst a group of people who worship idolatrous spirit called Allah (of the Quran), bow down towards a created object called the Ka'ba, and practice witchcraft for protection from demonic spirits.

By allowing the demonic spirit to come into my dream and attack me on the first night, the Lord opened our eyes to the reality of spiritual warfare around us. And when we called upon the name of Jesus, and sang praises unto Him the next morning, we were (unknowingly) inviting Him to come and fulfill the necessity of Matthew 12:28-29 before salvation could come to the Muslim home.

Matthew 12:28-29 - But if it is by the Spirit of God that I cast out demons, then the kingdom of God has come upon you. Or how can someone enter a strong man's house and plunder his goods, unless he first binds the strong man? Then indeed he may plunder his house.

Over the next fifteen months the Lord began to open doors of opportunities to share the gospel with the elderly parents and each of the son's families living in our compound. The landlord's father was a devout Muslim and respected me for not drinking alcohol. His sons, however, would occasionally drink, especially at wedding banquets. He knew that I was a Christian, but would acknowledge me as a man "who feared God." Gradually, we would invite our "Central Asian parents" to our home for tea and/or meals. They enjoyed kimchi and other Korean dishes that my wife made. During those visits we would play the local dialect version of the Life of Jesus DVD (produced by Cru) and watch with them. We must have watched it together about half a dozen times. There were some moments where he would exclaim at the wonder of miracles that Jesus performed, and then shed tears when Jesus was being crucified. We gave him a Bible in his dialect as a gift on his birthday. He had a great interest in Jesus, and during our conversations alone, I sensed his deepening faith in the works and teachings of Jesus. Although he never publicly professed faith, nor was he baptized, I believe that he placed his trust in Iso Masih (Jesus the Messiah).

The Lord was also opening up the heart of the fourth daughter-in-law. She had a very difficult marriage, and was often abused by her husband. Faith would invite her to our home and feed her and her three girls whenever she had the opportunity. Eventually, this woman would find the irresistible love of Jesus drawing her towards Him, and she and her three daughters would come to faith in Jesus.

90

As we look back at those first years in Central Asia, and our living situation, we now understand why the Lord took us to the home of an ex-KGB agent; there were lost sheep living there who needed to hear the soothing voice of the Good Shepherd.

Perhaps the Lord may arrange for you to stay in the home of a known jihadist or a drug lord for a few days. Never refuse such an invitation out of fear; pray first to see if the Holy Spirit is leading you there. And if it is the Lord's will for you to be there, He will protect you and deliver you from every evil attack! Who knows if He has sent you there to help Him retrieve a lost sheep?

Recommended readings:
Deliverance from Evil Spirits by Francis MacNutt
Spiritual Warfare by Dean Sherman

18 – The Two Kingdoms

Colossians 1:12-14 - giving thanks to the Father, who has qualified you to share in the inheritance of the saints in light. He has delivered us from the domain of darkness and transferred us to the kingdom of his beloved Son, in whom we have redemption, the forgiveness of sins.

The shocking reality of the above portion of Paul's prayer for the believers at Colossae is that all of us (Christians) were at one point in time citizens of the domain (kingdom) of darkness. To be more specific, every person born into this world, starting with Adam and Eve's first child, is born into the kingdom of darkness. This is the unfortunate consequence of Adam's sin; all posterity was condemned as sinners by his act of disobedience (Romans 5:19). The only exception is Jesus Christ; He was born without sin, conceived by the Holy Spirit in the womb of a virgin.

And because every child, regardless of his (or her) faith heritage, is born into the kingdom of darkness, it is necessary for him to make a personal commitment of faith in Christ in order to become a citizen of God's kingdom. In other words, every person has to be born again (John 3) in order to enter into God's kingdom. This prerequisite is equally true for the offspring of a Baptist preacher, as well as a Muslim cleric, a Hindu priest or a communist chairman. If a personal confession of faith in Christ is not made, then the person would end up spending all eternity in hell, separated from the living God.

A simple corollary is that there are only two kingdoms in this world. There may be many governments, mortal rulers, religious movements, and philosophies in this world, but there are only two kingdoms that will stretch across the entire span of human history: the kingdom of God and the kingdom of darkness. The task of every believer is to invite his/her neighbor to step out of the kingdom of darkness into the kingdom of light through faith in Jesus Christ.

In his letter to the believers at Ephesus, Paul sheds light on another aspect of living in the kingdom of darkness: every citizen of that kingdom follows and serves the prince of the power of air, who is Satan.

Ephesians 2:1-3 - And you were dead in the trespasses and sins in which you once walked, following the course of this world, following the prince of the power of the air, the spirit that is now at work in the sons of disobedience— among whom we all once lived in the passions of our flesh, carrying out the desires of the body and the mind, and were by nature children of wrath, like the rest of mankind.

In a few words, Jesus introduces the rulers of the two kingdoms in John 10:10. *The thief comes only to steal and kill and destroy. I came that they may have life and have it abundantly.*

Whereas Jesus comes to us give life (even everlasting life), Satan comes to us to steal, kill and destroy. Satan destroys peace, hope, people's lives and their relationships, tempts people to kill themselves and others, and steals worship away from God.

Isaiah 14:13-14 - You said in your heart, "I will ascend to heaven; above the stars of God I will set my throne on high; I will sit on the mount of assembly in the far reaches of the north; I will ascend above the heights of the clouds; I will make myself like the Most High."

Satan does not want creation to worship the Creator but himself. He wants to make himself like the Most High so that he can steal God's glory for himself. And he is able to accomplish this through false religions and cults. Except for the Judeo-Christian faith, every act of worship is rendered ultimately unto Satan. Prayers at the local mosque in Dubai, sacrifices to ancestral spirits in Beijing by self-professing atheists, offering of incense to Buddha in Kyoto, and child sacrifice to Molech in ancient Assyria…are all acts of homage to the spirit (Satan) behind respective religions.

1 Corinthians 10:20 - No, I imply that what pagans sacrifice they offer to demons and not to God. I do not want you to be participants with demons.

According to the above verse, sacrifices and any other acts of worship, including prayers, are all offered to the demons, and ultimately to Satan, the overarching authority over those demons. Hence, when the king of Moab offered up his oldest son as a burnt offering to his god, the demons who received such offering responded by unleashing such fury against the army of Israel that the latter had to retreat.

2 Kings 3:26-27 - When the king of Moab saw that the battle was going against him, he took with him 700 swordsmen to break through, opposite the king of Edom, but they could not. Then he took his oldest son who was to reign in his place and offered him for a burnt offering on the wall. And there came great wrath against Israel. And they withdrew from him and returned to their own land.

As Christ's ambassadors (2 Corinthians 5:20), we are all engaged in a war between the two kingdoms, where Jesus is the King over the kingdom of light, and Satan is king over the kingdom of darkness. And this kingdom warfare is waged not over territories but over souls; Satan wants to keep as many souls as possible in his domain. Eventually, he and everyone in his kingdom will spend eternity in hell. Jesus wants to save everyone from eternal damnation and transfer them over to His kingdom (1 Timothy 2:4) so that they may have eternal life.

In our context of ministry to the Muslims, we have learned to take our BMB (believers of Muslim background) disciples through steps of repentance and renunciation of allegiance to anyone but Jesus Christ our Lord.

Exodus 23:32 tells us explicitly not to make any covenant with the gods of the unbelievers. This includes the shahada, the confession of the Muslim faith: "There is no

94

God but Allah, and Muhammad is his messenger." Such a declaration is a covenant with Satan.

Recently, my wife had the privilege of taking a Turkish believer (BMB) through steps of renunciation as outlined in Mark Durie's book, Liberty to the Captives. This particular woman had been a follower of Jesus for over twenty years, and was actively serving as a ministry leader in her church. As the woman renounced her former allegiance to Allah (of the Quran), renounced the shahada and her vow to be a Quranic teacher, she began to feel nausea and convulsed. After a couple hours of repentance prayer, she was finally set free from "covenants" she had made with the enemy under the umbrella of Islam.

Regardless of your context and audience of ministry, you are engaged in kingdom warfare. As one who has been set free from the kingdom of darkness into the kingdom of light, do not forget to declare praises of Him who has made that possible (1 Peter 2:9-10). Acknowledge the fact that there are only two kingdoms in this world, and that even your own precious children, who were born into a believing family, are citizens of Satan's domain until they put their faith in Jesus! Reject the lie that "good" Muslims or Hindus can attain eternal life without Christ. Ask the Lord to lead you this week to someone who needs to hear the Good News of His Kingdom.

Recommended reading:
Liberty to the Captives by Mark Durie

19 – Shame, Guilt and Fear

Genesis 3:7-11 - Then the eyes of both were opened, and they knew that they were naked. And they sewed fig leaves together and made themselves loincloths. And they heard the sound of the Lord God walking in the garden in the cool of the day, and the man and his wife hid themselves from the presence of the Lord God among the trees of the garden. But the Lord God called to the man and said to him, "Where are you?" And he said, "I heard the sound of you in the garden, and I was afraid, because I was naked, and I hid myself." He said, "Who told you that you were naked? Have you eaten of the tree of which I commanded you not to eat?"

When the Lord created man, He did so with the purpose of enjoying a lasting relationship with the one made in His image. The overwhelming characteristic of such a relationship would be unbounded, unconditional (agape) love. However, when man sinned against God in the Garden of Eden, that love relationship would be utterly broken. The Creator would continue to love His creation, but mankind could no longer love God and other people the way He had intended.

Instead of love, the destructive impact of sin was to reframe man's mind where shame, guilt, and fear would become the tri-axial matrix for evaluating experiences and building relationships. Adam and Eve did not recognize that they were naked until they ate the forbidden fruit, and they decided to hide their shame by covering themselves with fig leaves (Genesis 3:8). This was the genesis of man's struggle with shame, and a worldview that propels each person to overcome that shame with acts of honor. Today, in societies indigenous to Middle East or Asia, preserving honor is paramount. If a member of a family brings shame (e.g., a teenage daughter is pregnant out of wedlock), restoring honor often requires taking of a life, either by the sword in the hand of the patriarch or by committing suicide.

It was also in the Garden of Eden that Adam and Eve began to fear God (3:10). Even though they had only experienced love and provision from the Creator, their immediate response to His presence after their sin was one of fear. Perhaps they thought that He would harm or punish them. It was the beginning of a worldview that endeavors to overcome fear (of death or harm) with possession of power. There are societies where people consult men and women of spiritual authority, like witches and shamans, to ward off evil spirits, prevent death or invoke curse upon their enemies.

Thirdly, when God asked Adam and Even if they had broken His command to not eat of the forbidden fruit, their nonverbal response would be: "Yes, Lord, guilty as charged" (3:11). Ensuing generations of Adam and Eve would labor within a worldview that compels mankind to pursue the status of being innocent by abiding by the laws of the land.

Hence, from the time of Adam until the second coming of Jesus Christ, mankind has, and will continue to strive to climb out of a state of shame to a place of honor, from guilt to innocence, and from fear to power.

Jesus Christ came to release us from our bondage to shame, guilt, and fear.

Romans 9:33 - as it is written, "Behold, I am laying in Zion a stone of stumbling, and a rock of offense; and whoever believes in him will not be put to shame."

Isaiah 53:10 - Yet it was the will of the Lord to crush him; he has put him to grief;

when his soul makes an offering for guilt, he shall see his offspring; he shall prolong his days; the will of the Lord shall prosper in his hand.

Hebrews 2:14-15 - Since therefore the children share in flesh and blood, he himself likewise partook of the same things, that through death he might destroy the one who has the power of death, that is, the devil, and deliver all those who through fear of death were subject to lifelong slavery. But Jesus did more than simply take away our shame, guilt, and fear. He did more than elevate us to a place of honor, innocence and power. The Messiah redeemed and transformed our lives so that He could dwell in us. He drew us out of shame to share God's glory living in us. His glory would shine through us. This is beyond any public honor that all the cultures in the world strive to acquire.

2 Corinthians 4:6-7 - For God, who said, "Let light shine out of darkness," has shone in our hearts to give the light of the knowledge of the glory of God in the face of Jesus Christ. But we have this treasure in jars of clay, to show that the surpassing power belongs to God and not to us.

In a subsequent chapter, I will share an anecdote from my own academic journey where Jesus shone His glory through the redemption of my shameful act of plagiarism.

Jesus also removed our guilt on the cross; but He did more than simply make us "innocent" of any wrongdoing in the sight of God and men. He gave us His righteousness.

Romans 1:17 - For in it the righteousness of God is revealed from faith for faith, as it is written, "The righteous shall live by faith."

2 Corinthians 5:21 - For our sake he made him to be sin who knew no sin, so that in him we might become the righteousness of God.

It is the type of righteousness that originates from God Himself, and those in His kingdom live out this aspect of God's righteousness (as taught in the Sermon on the Mount, Matthew 5-7) here on earth. It is such righteousness that allows a man not only to forgive the murderer of his children, but also to pour our God's blessing upon the guilty criminal. Such was the testimony of Rev. Yangwon Son.

Rev. Son lived most of his life during the Japanese occupation of Korea. He was a pastor over a leper colony, but by God's grace neither he nor his family contracted the infectious disease during their many years of ministry amongst them. But because of his staunch opposition to Shinto worship, he was arrested and suffered terribly at the hands of the Japanese officials.

At the end of Word War II, Rev. Son was released from prison, and he continued to pastor the local church in his region. During the postwar years, the presence of communism increased in his city. Then one day, the local communist party incited the local youth to a violent uprising. Rev. Son's two older sons in high school were accosted and beaten by a group of communist youth. The leader of this group subsequently shot and killed the two boys simply because of their Christian faith. The Korean government dispatched soldiers to this city to quell the unrest, and eventually, apprehended the lad who had murdered the two sons. When the soldiers brought the communist youth to Rev. Son and asked him if he would like to press charges, the father gave a surprising response. He told the soldiers that he has not only forgiven the criminal, but has also decided to adopt the young man as his own son. Never had the Korean society witnessed such an unbelievable gesture of forgiveness and mercy. Eventually, the newly adopted son became a Christian and even a pastor. Rev. Son covered the young murderer's guilt with God's mercy and righteousness.

Jesus also became one of us to destroy mankind's bondage to fear of death (Hebrews 2:14-15).

Ever since Adam's sin in the Garden of Eden, death has become an inevitable reality for himself, his wife, and his progeny (Romans 5:12). Mankind has been searching for a way to protect and prolong life here on earth. This endeavor has included such activities as advancement in medicine to overcome all types of illnesses and ailments, development of weapons to protect our loved ones, and even consultation of mediums for protection from evil spirits, curses, and attacks—both physical and spiritual. I believe the goal of each of these (and other similar) activities is to bring us to a place of power where we can manage, control and even overcome our fear. Ultimately, however, every human being will have to taste death...the only exception being those who are miraculously taken up to heaven by God (e.g., Enoch, Elijah, and those who will be raptured when Christ returns).

Amazingly, Jesus did not abolish death upon His first coming. He defeated Satan, the one who has power of death, on the cross. Jesus Himself had to face death (for our sins), but then rose again to life on the third day. Death will finally be destroyed upon Jesus' second coming; it will be thrown into the lake of fire, along with Satan and Hades (Revelations 20:10,14).

An unexpected blessing from Jesus' work on earth was the ensuing ministry of the Holy Spirit in the lives of His disciples. Romans 5:5b tells us that "...God's love has been poured into our hearts through the Holy Spirit who has been given to us."

And it is this perfect love of God, the very essence of God, that has come to dwell in us.

1 John 4:16,18 - So we have come to know and to believe the love that God has for us. God is love, and whoever abides in love abides in God, and God abides in him...there is no fear in love, but perfect love casts out fear. For fear has to do with punishment, and whoever fears has not been perfected in love.

This incredible presence of God's love in our lives keeps us from any fear, including fear of death and even the Judgment Day. It is the everlasting, unconditional love of the Father for His children that keeps us from any harm, persecution, or even death outside of His will. Because we are surrounded by promises of God that He is with us through every storm and trial (Isaiah 41:10; 43:1-2; 2 Timothy 4:18), we can overcome fear of death.

During our time in Central Asia, we learned that the local Muslim mothers will take their newborn child to a special shaman for protection from evil spirits. This shaman would take drippings of blood from a live chicken and then apply the blood on every orifice of the child: eyes, nose, mouth, ears, and even the private parts—all the while reciting Quranic prayers and specialized incantations. This ritual stems from beliefs embedded in the fear and power worldview. The mother believes that there are evil spirits that can harm her child, and thus she is seeking a counter veiling power to protect her child. She believes that an angel (good spirit) will protect her child throughout his/her life. This spiritual transaction, however, would open the door for the child to be oppressed (or even possessed) by demons from that time forward. Hence, when we were ministering in Central Asia, we met many Muslims who were struggling with demonic visits, nightmares, and harassing voices inside their head.

That was the testimony of Dilfuza when we first met her. She was in her late 20s and had been struggling with horrible nightmares (of dark figures attacking her) and sleepless nights. Her parents were devout Muslims and took her to special priests. They even tied Quranic verses around her neck or placed them under her pillow before she went to bed. There was no relief.

And then one day she heard the gospel at my wife's Bible study for women, and she found Jesus. She repented and put her faith in Jesus Christ as her Lord and Savior. That very night she had the most pleasant sleep. In the past she was hesitant to fall asleep because of her fear of impending nightmares. But this night, she had a series of dreams of walking through a beautiful garden, or taking a refreshing swim in a clear pond. Dilfuza slept for fourteen hours, and did not want to wake up the next day! Previously, she had been very eager to come out of sleep, just to end the horrific nightmares.

Subsequently, Dilfuza made a decision to be a worship leader, learning how to play guitar from my wife, and then using her voice and her guitar playing skills to lead our house church to offer up songs of love and devotion to the God who had rescued her. In Christ, Dilfuza had been set free from fear of death to truly love God with all her heart, soul, mind, and strength (Matthew 22:37-38).

As you engage with the local people around you, ask the Holy Spirit to give you understanding and knowledge concerning their worldview, and all the behaviors that stem from such a worldview. Ask the Lord how you can introduce Jesus into their worldview with relevant breakthroughs, ultimately leading them to salvation in Him.

Recommended readings:
Honor and Shame: Unlocking the Door by Roland Muller
The 3D gospel: Ministry in Guilt, Shame and Fear Cultures by Jayson Georges
Ministering in Honor-Shame Cultures: Biblical Foundations and Practical Essentials by Georges and Baker
My Cup Overflows by Tong-hui Son

20 – Jars of Clay

2 Corinthians 4:6-7 - For God, who said, "Let light shine out of darkness," has shone in our hearts to give the light of the knowledge of the glory of God in the face of Jesus Christ. But we have this treasure in jars of clay, to show that the surpassing power belongs to God and not to us.

In the fall of 2001, I began teaching computer classes at the state university. Since the lessons were in English, it was necessary to screen out the students based on their English fluency. Most of my students were majoring in economics, since that seemed to be the only academic path that offered promising career afterwards. Interestingly, a majority of the economics students were also gifted in math and sciences. (Pursuit in engineering or pure sciences would usually result in working for government medical centers or state industries where the pay was extremely low.)

The most difficult class that I taught involved Visual Basic programming. After a few weeks of lessons and simple programming exercises, I decided to give the class of twenty students their first exam. After five minutes, the students began to whisper to one another in Russian. They knew that I was learning the local Muslim language and had very little knowledge of Russian, so they began to ask the brighter students in the room the answers to several difficult questions. Even though I didn't understand what they were saying in Russian, I knew that they were cheating on the test. So I firmly told them that there was to be no talking in the room, but a few students still persisted in whispering.

After the class I talked with one of the brighter students, and also with a fellow missionary who had been teaching in another university for several years. They both suggested that the students were accustomed to not only collaborating on the exams, but also to be provided the answer key to the exam by the professor for a fee. The price tag for a set of answers ranged from $100 to $300, and each student was expected to contribute to the pool. Corruption and bribery in the education system were not surprising since the salary of instructors at most public schools and universities was pitifully lacking.

At the end of the day, I came to the realization that, from the perspective of the students, I was partially responsible for the cheating incident that afternoon in my class; I had failed to "sell" them the answer key to the exam. A few weeks later, I decided to give another exam to the same students. This time, I made the exam considerably easier, and produced two different sets of test papers; the questions were identical except for a change in a few numbers, and also the questions were arranged in different order on the exam papers. I alerted the students to the differences in exam papers so that the students seated adjacently would get the problems wrong if they merely copied one another's answers. To further discourage cheating, I shared my personal testimony of how the Lord dealt with me when I cheated on an exam at Cornell University.

It was my senior year at Cornell and I was struggling in one of the required classes for my major. I couldn't grasp the concepts well from the start of the course, and I was not ready for the first exam. I walked towards the back of the theatre-style classroom and sat down on the last row. The assistant professor handed out the exams and then left the room; the students were expected to adhere to the university honor code. As expected, I was finding the test questions very difficult and tried to answer the easier ones first. Close to the end of the one-hour exam, in my desperation to put down answers to all the questions, I looked over the shoulder of the student seating just below me and copied his answers to two problems that I could not solve. When the assistant professor came back to collect the exam books, I closed the book, signed my name on the front cover, and handed it in. By signing the cover I was acknowledging that I had neither given nor received help during the exam period. So not only did I cheat on the exam, I also lied.

That night, and for the next several nights, I could not sleep well. And each time I tried to pray or read the Bible, the Holy Spirit was bringing up the image of my cheating on the exam. The Lord was not going to let me get by with this one. So about a week later, I knocked on the door of my professor. My heart was pounding thunder and I felt my head turning red with shame as I explained to him what had happened. He looked disappointed and told me that he would discuss the matter with the dean of the engineering college and then let me know of their decision. He told me to come back a week later.

As I left his office that afternoon, I was now burdened with a new set of worries. What if I am expelled from the university because of my plagiarism? And which university would receive me then? And how will my father, pastor of a Korean church, receive the news? I had only one more semester remaining in my bachelor's program, and I was worried that four years of hard work at Cornell would be going down the drain. For the rest of that week, I was again struggling to find adequate sleep. All I could do was to ask the Lord for mercy, and that I may finish my studies at Cornell.

Finally the time came for me to return to the professor's office. He informed me rather mechanically that the university decided to void my test score and I would have to do better on the remaining tests. He also made the comment that this was the first time in his teaching career that a student confessed to plagiarism, and that because I was honest about my offense, the dean of the college decided to show leniency. I let out a big sigh of relief as I thanked him (and the Lord) for showing me mercy. I left the office with a firm commitment not to ever cheat again.

I shared these words with my Central Asian students, and they were very attentive. I concluded my talk with an earnest plea for the students not to cheat on the exams any more. If they regularly relied on the work of others and plagiarized on their exams and papers, then they would only be cheating themselves and failing to gain the knowledge and skills necessary to move their country towards economic and social progress and development. I acknowledged each student as a future leader of their society, and told that their investment in time and effort to excel in the academics would bring future blessing to them and their people.

That afternoon, there was no talking in the classroom as the students took their test. Afterwards, several students came up to me and said that no professor or teacher had ever shared openly and personally on the subject of cheating. They were grateful for my transparency, and even more thankful for my concern for their character development and future success. A few days later, one of my students named Dawud approached me after the class and asked for a copy of the English Bible. I had not overtly shared about Jesus Christ, but my mention of God, the Bible and the Holy Spirit had opened up the heart of a lost sheep. I told him that I would try to find one by the following week. My heart was filled with a mixture of both excitement and anxiety. I was excited to be given the opportunity to share the Word of God with a Muslim student. I was anxious because a fellow missionary professor at the same university was deported a few weeks prior by the local government because of his religious activities. One of his students who pretended to have converted to Christianity was a KGB plant. He had gathered enough information and proof to incriminate the missionary for illegal proselytism with the university students.

I came home and shared about the Bible request with my wife so that we could both pray about this opportunity;

after all, my decision to give the Bible to the young Muslim student would impact the lives of my wife and my children. As we began to pray over this student's request over the next few days, we sensed peace from the Holy Spirit. After the next class session, I met with Dawud and gave him a copy of the English Bible wrapped up in a generic plastic shopping bag. I told him to start reading from the New Testament, since he would be more familiar with the life and teachings of Jesus Christ. I suggested that he read carefully a chapter from the Gospel of Matthew each day, and that we would go through the readings when we met again the following week.

When I met with Dawud after class a week later, I was joyfully surprised to learn that he had already read through Matthew, Mark, and Luke, and was nearly finished with John. What a hunger for God's Word! I sensed in my spirit that this Muslim student was ready to put his faith in Jesus, so I went through the Four Spiritual Laws (by Cru) with him. At the end of the presentation, he prayed with me for repentance of his sins and faith in Jesus Christ as the Son of God, who would now be his Lord and Savior.

Hallelujah! Who would have guessed that an open and personal testimony concerning plagiarism would result in the salvation of a Muslim youth? My purpose in sharing that testimony was to discourage the students from cheating; the Good Shepherd sovereignly used it to speak words of life to a lost sheep. It was through my weakness and failures (cracks in my earthen vessel) that Jesus shone brightly a message of grace and truth.

The Lord of the harvest can easily use our phenomenal victories and crushing defeats, brilliant accolades and resounding failures, and heroic acts of honor and deeds of shame to advance His Kingdom. Would you allow Jesus to shine through your past mistakes and failures as well as your successes? He can redeem your painful divorce to speak tenderly into the heart of a Hindu or Buddhist who is looking for healing from a broken marriage relationship.

Isn't He the one who said, "Come to me, all who labor and are heavy laden, and I will give you rest"? (Matthew 11:28)

21 – Why Did You Come Here?

Matthew 5:14-16 - "You are the light of the world. A city set on a hill cannot be hidden. Nor do people light a lamp and put it under a basket, but on a stand, and it gives light to all in the house. In the same way, let your light shine before others, so that they may see your good works and give glory to your Father who is in heaven."

Colossians 4:5-6 – Walk in wisdom toward outsiders, making the best use of the time. Let your speech always be gracious, seasoned with salt, so that you may know how you ought to answer each person.

As I started teaching computer and engineering classes at the state university, some of my students began to ask about the real reason why I came to their country. They were well aware that I had graduated from an Ivy League school and had been earning a high salary as an electrical engineer in the States. Why would I give up such pay and come to a developing Central Asian country for a professor's salary that was about 1 percent of what I was making in the U.S.? It just did not compute. Hence, some were wondering if I worked for the CIA or a similar organization.

Other students were wondering if we were in their country to convert them to another religion (i.e., Christianity) or even to cult groups like Jehovah's Witness. Prior to our coming, there had already been several missionary teams (long term and short term) who had come and settled down in our city. The local students were well aware of missionary endeavors. A few years before our arrival, there had been a debate at one of the regional colleges on the topic of "Who teaches English better— Peace Corps volunteers or missionaries?" Both sides presented a well-thought-out argument in support of their position.

So when I started teaching at the university, the students were curious about my motives and the source of my income. My initial attempt at offering a plausible explanation was rather unclear and unconvincing. I told the students that I was drawing my salary from a private charitable fund that has, as one of its goals, the socioeconomic development of Central Asian countries. After some thought and prayer, the Lord gave me wisdom on how to answer my students. So at the beginning of each of my set of five classes, I read the following poem:

"The Bridge Builder"
(by Will Allen Dromgoole)
An old man, going a lone highway,
Came, at the evening, cold and gray,
To a chasm, vast, and deep, and wide,
Through which was flowing in a sullen tide.
The old man crossed in the twilight dim;
The sullen stream had no fears for him;
But he turned, when safe on the other side,
And built a bridge to span the tide.
"Old man," said a fellow pilgrim, near,
"You are wasting strength with building here;
Your journey will end with the ending day;
You never again must pass this way;
You have crossed the chasm, deep and wide—
Why build you the bridge at the eventide?"
The builder lifted his old gray head:
"Good friend, in the path I have come," he said,
"There followeth after me today, a youth,
whose feet must pass this way.
This chasm, that has been naught to me,
to that fair-haired youth may a pitfall be.
He, too, must cross in the twilight dim;
Good friend, I am building the bridge for him."

110

And then I explained that I was that old man in the poem; I came to their Central Asian country to build a bridge (engineering education in English) that no one else was building at the state university at the time. I explained that at one time in my life, I was also the youth in the poem. In reality, my forefathers who were living in Korea for many generations were collectively that youth. And "old men" came from Europe and North America to build bridges for our people. They built schools, colleges, and hospitals. Many of them were Christians. They taught my people to work honestly and with excellence. They discouraged plagiarism and bribery, especially in the education system. Many of them died in the process of building the bridge; they became ill with strange diseases in a foreign land. But the impact and fruit of their labor is spectacularly visible today in South Korea; globally successful companies like LG, Samsung and Hyundai are a testimony to the amazing bridges that these foreigners had built.

I told my students that my wife and I are indebted to the bridge builders who came to our native country of Korea. And God had sent me to this Central Asian country to build a bridge for the university students. And my hope and dream was that some of them would be able to study abroad, including in the US, gain professional career experience overseas, and return to their native countries and build necessary bridges for the ensuing generation.

I could see many tear-moistened eyes in those classroom sessions. [Over the five-year period at the local university, I had the privilege of teaching over 500 students. At least five of my students were invited to pursue graduate programs in the U.S. with a full scholarship.] From that day forth, no one ever raised the question of what I was doing in his/her country. They realized that I had come to their country to bless them, making personal and financial sacrifices along the way. It would be terribly wrong in the local culture, which is founded upon the shame and honor worldview, to ask the motives of a person who was doing something that was honorable in their society.

How have you explained your presence to your local community? Is your life and what you are doing in your community deemed as being honorable and a blessing? Ask the Holy Spirit to guide you in providing an answer to those who ask, even to those who are hostile, so that Christ would be exalted in your life and through all your endeavors.

1 Peter 3:13-16 - Now who is there to harm you if you are zealous for what is good? But even if you should suffer for righteousness' sake, you will be blessed. Have no fear of them, nor be troubled, but in your hearts honor Christ the Lord as holy, always being prepared to make a defense to anyone who asks you for a reason for the hope that is in you; yet do it with gentleness and respect, having a good conscience, so that, when you are slandered, those who revile your good behavior in Christ may be put to shame.

22 – Heart Language Above the Gospel?

Revelations 7:9-10 - After this I looked, and behold, a great multitude that no one could number, from every nation, from all tribes and peoples and languages, standing before the throne and before the Lamb, clothed in white robes, with palm branches in their hands, and crying out with a loud voice, "Salvation belongs to our God who sits on the throne, and to the Lamb!"

Acts 2:4-8 - And they were all filled with the Holy Spirit and began to speak in other tongues as the Spirit gave them utterance. Now there were dwelling in Jerusalem Jews, devout men from every nation under heaven. And at this sound the multitude came together, and they were bewildered, because each one was hearing them speak in his own language. And they were amazed and astonished, saying, "Are not all these who are speaking Galileans? And how is it that we hear, each of us in his own native language?

The Creator of all people groups of the world is committed to seeing the fulfillment of Revelations 7:9. The Lord of the harvest wants His ambassadors to cross every cultural, geo-political, and linguistic barrier to present the Good News to the lost in every corner of the world. However, we must remember that the Lord is more concerned about the redemption of lost souls than any specific language and culture. There were Jews living in Roman colonies who no longer spoke Hebrew fluently; their heart language was Greek, the *lingua franca* of the Mediterranean first century, and missionaries like apostle Paul (who wrote the New Testament letters in Greek) chose to communicate in that language.

On the mission field we noticed that some missionaries or mission agencies were quite adamant about using a particular language to establish house churches amongst an ethnic group who lived in a society of two or more languages. Perhaps these missionaries were "purists" or "idealists" who desired to champion a movement amongst people who spoke a particular language. Or perhaps these missionaries wanted to prevent unwanted influences from churches or ministries that stemmed from other language groups. Quite often, these same missionaries were from monolingual backgrounds; perhaps they knew a foreign language, but they grew up in a predominantly monolingual environment.

My wife and I grew up as Korean immigrants in the U.S., in an English-speaking society. We retained our mother tongue (Korean), but in order to progress and prosper in the States, we had to excel in English. Most definitely, our education in public and private institutions was in English, but eventually the language of our religious instruction and practice also transitioned from Korean to English. This transition did not come easily; the first-generation Korean immigrant churches resisted this phenomenon at first, and strongly insisted that all the services and programs at the church be conducted in Korean. They did not want the second and ensuing generations to lose their mother tongue. However, as the children grew up and began to excel in the host society, especially in the English-medium school system, they gradually lost their fluency in Korean. They began to look for churches that were in English. But because of cultural differences, many did not feel welcome in predominantly white congregations. A great majority of these English-speaking Korean-Americans left the Church altogether in the 1980s. Senior pastors of several leading Korean Churches responded to this "Silent Exodus" phenomenon by establishing English ministries within their church. They even hired non-Korean pastors and Sunday school directors to serve the English-speaking members of the church, from children to young married couples. Within a few years, independent English-speaking Korean-American churches would also be established across the United States. In retrospect, the first generation Korean pastors had made the mistake of placing their mother tongue above the gospel. When we arrived in Central Asia, we found some missionaries making similar mistakes; they insisted that a particular minority ethnic group must be encouraged to worship in their mother tongue. They had hoped that a church planting movement amongst this minority people group would be more successful with the added emphasis on using the mother tongue, which was different from the national language. While that may have been more appropriate and feasible during the Soviet era, when the Soviet Union dissolved into fifteen independent countries in 1990s, there were significant changes concerning languages spoken in those new countries. Under the Soviet rule, minority ethnic groups with significant numerical presence in a region were allowed to have a school system in their mother tongue. Of course Russian would serve as the lingua franca, and those who mastered it would have opportunities to study in Moscow, and subsequently, land prominent positions in the government, military, or industry sector. After the collapse of the Soviet Union in 1991, however, the leaders of our Central Asian country decided to phase out minority ethnic group education programs, and established the majority ethnic group tongue as the official language for education, commerce, and governance. This sweeping law forced all children of minority people groups to learn the national language in order to survive and prosper in the country. Their plight was similar to the children of the Korean immigrants growing up in the U.S.: learn the national language or remain being marginalized (just like many of their parents). Master the national language and you have the opportunity to succeed at every sphere of the society.

When we began our house church, which was comprised mostly of a minority people group, we did not implement one-language worship rule. We would read the Bible in the national language, but sing worship songs and pray and

115

preach in the minority language…reminiscent of services in Korean-American churches many years prior.

We encouraged our disciples who were from the ethnic minority group to master the national language while retaining their mother tongue (if possible). This would enable them to share the gospel with the majority population as well as walk through doors of opportunity to every level of leadership in the society.

As missionaries we want our disciples not only to grow in their faith but also excel in their profession so that they can shine the light of Jesus as far as possible. Would we not want them to influence every sphere of their society? If they are to thrive as teachers, musicians, governors, engineers, prosecutors, nurses, soccer players, and even pastors, then they would need to excel in the national language.

Romans 10:14-15 - How then will they call on him in whom they have not believed? And how are they to believe in him of whom they have never heard? And how are they to hear without someone preaching? And how are they to preach unless they are sent? As it is written, "How beautiful are the feet of those who preach the good news!"

You and I have been entrusted with the privilege of sharing the incredibly Good News with the lost people across the world. We need to communicate this with them in the language that they can most easily understand…and sometimes, it can mean two different languages with two different generations within the same ethnic people group. Let us not put anything above the gospel, including the role and significance of the "mother tongue" or any other aspect of the local culture.

23 – Encountering God's Truth

John 3:1-3 – Now there was a man of the Pharisees named Nicodemus, a ruler of the Jews. This man came to Jesus by night and said to him, "Rabbi, we know that you are a teacher come from God, for no one can do these signs that you do unless God is with him." Jesus answered him, "Truly, truly, I say to you, unless one is born again he cannot see the kingdom of God."

Faith and I met Fatima at a friend's birthday party in northern Virginia. Fatima was several years older than us, and was a nominal Muslim from Africa. One of the first things she said to us with great pride in her introduction was that she had been to Mecca eleven times! As soon as I heard her confess this, I said in my heart: Then you did not find what you were looking for. (Muslims are supposed to find the peace of Allah through their pilgrimage to Mecca, and Fatima apparently did not find that peace after the first hajj. Hence, she went ten more times.) And so I asked her to sit next to us and then proceeded to tell her a simple story comparing the teachings of Jesus and Muhammad. This story was developed by a local pastor (Mirzod) in 2005. Mirzod comes from a large clan of devout Muslims, and when he came to faith in Jesus Christ, there was much persecution from his family and relatives. [His parents even threw him and his family out of the house. The father reported him to the secret police, which resulted in the arrest of five men who were attending a Bible study.] As Mirzod started explaining his new faith to his relatives and friends, God gave him the wisdom and insight to come up with this story. The first of the two prophets is Muhammad; the second is Jesus.

Two prophets came to a small town one day, each staying at a different home. By evening that day, the entire town was excited about the two visitors. The hosts had to

117

turn away many people that evening so that the prophets could get some rest after their long journey.

At dawn the next day, the men of the town brought a woman caught in adultery to the first prophet. They asked for his advice. The woman, who was not married, was pregnant with a child. The father's identity was not clear; the woman had given them a name, but the man denied the accusations and said that she was a liar. Besides, it would require the testimony of another woman to validate her claims. They asked the prophet what to do with the woman. The prophet told them that the sin of adultery is a very terrible sin against God and against the society. Such sin must be removed from the land. God is angry about such sins, and if the leaders of the town ddi not show their anger against such sins, others may be tempted to commit the same sin. They should kill her by stoning. The people thanked the prophet for his answer and were preparing to stone the woman. Just then, someone from the group said that since there was another prophet who had just come to their town, they should ask him also. If the second prophet agreed, then they should stone the woman.

The second prophet heard their accusations against the woman, and gave them a simple answer. He told them that anyone amongst them who was without sin should be the first to throw the stone at the woman. Slowly, one by one, starting with the oldest, the men left that place. Only the prophet was left, standing in front of the woman. He told her that neither would he condemn her. He then told her to go and sin no more.

The next day a man came to the first prophet with his marital problems. He had been married ten years, and his wife had not given him any child. Not only that, she often went to visit her friends and came home too late to prepare a hot meal for him. She didn't do the chores at home like the other wives. His shirts were not ironed, the home was not swept, etc. What must he do with her? The prophet told the man that the intelligence of a woman is half of that of a man, and that women such as his wife must be scolded harshly, perhaps even using physical force, to make them better wives. And if God had not given her a child in ten years, then obviously His favor was not with this woman. Evil omens often came with a woman. The man should think about taking a young, healthy woman as a wife so that she may bear him children. And if the first wife is still not behaving properly, he should divorce her. After hearing the prophet's words, the man thanked him and went away.

On his way home, he remembered that there was yet another prophet visiting his town. He went to the second prophet and asked the same question. In his response, this prophet asked the man a question: "How many Eves did God create for Adam?" The man answered, "One." The prophet then told the man that from the very beginning, it was God's will that each man be faithful to the woman that God gave to him as a gift. He must love and cherish her at all times, whether she is healthy or sick, whether they are rich or poor. Even if the wife is rude and unkind, the man must keep her. God does not want divorce at all, even if the wife should not be able to bear him a child. As a matter of fact, God hates divorce. Even the great prophet Abraham was without a child for many years, but he kept his wife. God later blessed him with a child. The prophet prayed for the man and his wife, for God to bless them with a child. He then told the man to also faithfully pray for his wife. Who knows? God may yet give them a miracle child. The man thanked the prophet and went home to his wife.

A few days later, a different man came running to the first prophet. The man was greatly upset about something, and he quickly told the prophet about his problem. He had just moved to a new town few months prior. Some of his neighbors had been very rude and even hostile to him. They would stay up late and drink and make lots of noise. Several times he would go to them to quiet down so that his kids could sleep, but the men would not listen. Instead, *they would make fun of him and even throw stones at him. Over the next few weeks these neighbors became even more hostile and it must have been one of them who destroyed the man's garden in the front and threw trash all over his yard. The children of these neighbors have been throwing rocks at his children, making them cry. The man was running out of patience, and was ready to do something desperate. But what should he do? The prophet answered by telling him to have strong faith. Obviously, the people who drank and party were not believers. Such people were not of God, and must be confronted harshly and even violently. Whatever harm they did to you, you should return to them equally. This world belongs to those who believe in God, and ultimately the pagans must be destroyed and removed from the face of the earth. The man thanked the prophet and went outside.*

On the way to his home, he decided to stop by and see the second prophet. When the man asked the same question, however, he got a different answer. The prophet told the man to love all people, even his enemies. Any man can love those who are kind to him; but those who believe in God must love even those who hate him and are hostile towards him. The reason is because the God of heaven has shown such love to all mankind. The prophet told the man to forgive his enemies and pray for them. Who knows? God may turn their hearts around. The man thanked the prophet for his words and went back to his home.

And now a question for you: Which of the two prophets would you agree with? Whose words would you follow?

When I asked Fatima these questions, she readily chose the second prophet, who is Jesus Christ. Faith was seated next to me, and she shared the gospel with the Muslim woman. In less than an hour, the woman's heart opened up to Jesus, and she prayed to trust in Him as her own Lord and Savior. Praise the Lord!

John 12:32-33 – "And I, when I am lifted up from the earth, will draw all people to myself." He said this to show by what kind of death he was going to die.

Jesus Christ's death on the cross would be the turning point in the history of mankind. Physically, He was lifted up on the cross. I believe that as we place Him high above all other names, titles, celebrity figures, philosophies, and ideologies, the lost people of the world will be drawn to Him.

Philippians 2:9-11 Therefore God has highly exalted him and bestowed on him the name that is above every name, so that at the name of Jesus every knee should bow, in heaven and on earth and under the earth, and every tongue confess that Jesus Christ is Lord, to the glory of God the Father.

As Christ's ambassadors we need to exalt His name and glory above all else…we need to "lift Jesus higher" than any other figure in the history of the world. Muhammad, the founder of Islam, is no mediocre figure; if 1.8 billion people in the world today are following his teachings, emulating his life, and hundreds of thousands (if not millions) are ready to kill and die for him, then he is not to be ignored. However, Muhammad himself is dead and buried, never having conquered sin and death. Our Lord Jesus is alive and reigning in heaven, after conquering sin, Satan, and death through His death and resurrection! He deserves to be lifted to the highest place of honor and glory.

Ask the Holy Spirit to guide you in your conversation with the lost people around you today…so that you may exalt the name of Jesus higher than the idol(s) they are currently trusting in.

Recommended readings:
Connecting with Muslims by Fouad Masri
Jesus and Muhammad by Mark Gabriel

24 – Encountering God's Love

John 13:1, 3-5, 12-15, 34-35 - Now before the Feast of the Passover, when Jesus knew that his hour had come to depart out of this world to the Father, having loved his own who were in the world, he loved them to the end...Jesus, knowing that the Father had given all things into his hands, and that he had come from God and was going back to God, 4 rose from supper. He laid aside his outer garments, and taking a towel, tied it around his waist. 5 Then he poured water into a basin and began to wash the disciples' feet and to wipe them with the towel that was wrapped around him.

12 When he had washed their feet and put on his outer garments and resumed his place, he said to them, "Do you understand what I have done to you? 13 You call me Teacher and Lord, and you are right, for so I am. 14 If I then, your Lord and Teacher, have washed your feet, you also ought to wash one another's feet. 15 For I have given you an example, that you also should do just as I have done to you.

34 A new commandment I give to you, that you love one another: just as I have loved you, you also are to love one another. 35 By this all people will know that you are my disciples, if you have love for one another."

I met Adam two years after we arrived on the field. He grew up as a nominal Muslim, and he was in his early forties. He married his first wife when he was in his twenties. Like most of his Muslim peers of Central Asia, Adam would often get drunk at parties and weddings. Even though alcohol is forbidden for Muslims, the majority of the Muslim men in our country would indulge heavily in vodka at celebrations like weddings. The wealthier the family hosting the wedding, the more the alcohol on the table...which the guests were obligated to finish before the wedding was over. When he was intoxicated, Adam would often fight with his wife and even beat her. She was hospitalized several times with serious cuts and bruises. After one particularly violent episode of beating, resulting in yet another hospitalization, the father-in-law came looking for Adam. There was a skirmish between the two, during which time the father-in-law stabbed Adam with a knife and ran off. Adam's neighbors took him to a nearby hospital, and though the knife wound was not fatal, Adam had to stay there for about ten days. After his discharge, Adam went to his father-in-law's house with an iron pipe. When his father-in-law opened the door, Adam struck his head with such a violent force that the skull cracked and blood began to gush down his face. Adam found a soup bowl in the courtyard and began to collect the stream of blood. He then proceeded to drink his father-in-law's blood as the old man was dying, crumpled on the ground. Adam whispered to his father-in-law, "You took my blood with a knife; now I am taking it back from you." Thus Adam got his revenge.

The horrified neighbors witnessing this gruesome crime called the local police. Eventually, Adam was arrested and sent to a Soviet prison in another country with a twenty-year sentence. It was in that prison, however, that the Lord showed mercy to Adam through several Russian Baptists. The latter were in prison for their faith…Adam was in prison for murder. To the communist Soviet authority, Christians were just as dangerous to the society as murderers. But it was the Lord's will to connect Adam with His ambassadors. Eventually, Adam heard the gospel from the Christian inmates and repented of his sin and put his faith in Jesus Christ the Son of God as his Savior and Lord. While Adam was still in prison, the Soviet Union collapsed, and with the completion of his prison sentence, he was released to go back to his home country.

Understandably, when Adam came back to his house, his first wife had already left him. Adam was able to remarry, by God's grace, to a Christian woman. She was one of our disciples, also a former Muslim, and lived in the same village as Adam. Through their union Adam was blessed with a beautiful daughter.

Adam and his wife attended one of the Russian-speaking registered churches, established by a South Korean missionary. [During the first three years of our ministry in the Central Asian country, we encouraged our disciples to worship at Russian-speaking registered churches. The government did not allow registration for churches that worshiped in the local/ethnic tongue, and violation of attending a nonregistered religious meeting would result in arrest and persecution for both expatriate missionaries and national believers.] After a few months, however, Adam could no longer attend the church. The main reason was that he began to show signs of serious nerve disease that was limiting movement and senses in his limbs. He had difficulty walking and moving his arms. Taxi or bus rides to the bazaar or even to the church was becoming nearly impossible. He was looking for someone to come to his house to disciple him, and the Lord connected us at this time.

[Eventually, Adam's body would succumb to the nerve disease, and he would go home to be with his Savior about a year after we baptized him in the river. At the end of his life he could only move his head; the rest of his body was not functional. I believe that the nerve disease was the result of his drinking the blood of his father-in-law with a bitter and vindictive heart as well as serving twenty years in a Soviet prison. The Lord forgave Adam for his heinous sin of murder, but the physical consequence of his sin was allowed to unfold and be manifest in the form of the nerve disease.]

I carved out time on Wednesday afternoons to visit Adam at his house with my Bible, guitar, and songbook. We would sing worship songs to Jesus in the local dialect for about an hour and then have Bible study and prayer for another one to two hours. Since he was a captive audience, our meetings could be as long as I wanted.

From time to time, whenever I arrived at Adam's house for the Bible study, his wife would hastily leave the house for a couple of hours to do the necessary bazaar shopping for the day. On one particular Wednesday, she left the house with her daughter just as I came in. She said that she had many errands to tend to that afternoon. Adam and I praised Jesus through songs and then continued in our study of Romans. About two hours later, Adam's wife still had not returned from her errands, and Adam needed to use the bathroom. Like most other Central Asian homes, his bathroom was the traditional "outhouse", with a small hole in the ground serving as the toilet. I allowed Adam to rest his weight on my shoulder and we walked together to the outhouse. I helped him squat inside and then closed the door. The outhouse had not been cleaned for a long time, and there were missed droppings towards the back. As expected, there were swarms of flies inside the small space. By God's grace he had enough strength and mobility in his hands to clean himself with toilet paper after relieving himself. Afterwards I helped him wash his hands using a nearby water pitcher, and then we came back to his living room.

An hour later his wife had still not returned, and I had to go back home for another meeting that evening. Adam assured me that he would be all right, and I grabbed my stuff and headed towards my car. After a few steps, however, the Lord prompted my heart back towards the outhouse. It needed cleaning. So I decided to lock up the guitar and my books in the car, grab a bucket of water and broom, and went back to the outhouse. It took several buckets of water to rid the concrete floor of the pile of feces.

The following Wednesday, when I went to Adam's house, a Muslim neighbor named Hasan (in his 60's) was drinking tea with Adam. As we were being introduced to one another, these were Hasan's words to me: "None of our Muslim priests will ever go into someone else's bathroom to clean it because they are afraid of jinns and also because they will be defiled. You are the first teacher of God's Word that has cleaned someone else's bathroom. I want to learn from you." Thus, the Lord allowed our men's Bible study to increase twofold. And one autumn day a few weeks later, Adam and Hasan were both baptized in the river.

A remarkable part of Hasan's journey of faith concerns short-term missionaries. During his first day with our Bible study group, as the three of us were praising Jesus in the local dialect, Hasan said that he knew one of the songs. My wife and I, with the help of some local believers, had translated "Lord, I Lift Your Name on High" (a very simple praise song that is popular worldwide) into the local language. As he sang it with us for the first time in his heart language, he said that he recognized the tune, and that he had heard it before. I was very surprised and asked him where he had heard the song.

He explained that about fifteen years prior, a few years before the collapse of Soviet Union, he met a group of Swedish tourists walking through the city. One of the tourists was fluent in Russian and asked him if he knew a place where they could stay. Like a good Central Asian Muslim (who are very hospitable), Hasan invited the handful of tourists to come and stay at his house. They gratefully accepted the invitation and slept and ate at his home for a few days. What he remembered distinctly was that every time they came to the meal table, they would sing a few songs in Swedish and then pray for the meal. One of the songs that they sang was "Lord, I Life Your Name on High" in Swedish. Although Hasan did not understand the words, somehow the tune stayed in his heart and mind for fifteen years!

Upon hearing his testimony about the Swedes, I told him, "I believe that the Swedish tourists were a short-term

126

missions team that came to pray for your people and your city. And they most likely prayed for God to bless your home with salvation. And fifteen years later the Lord answered their prayer by bringing you to our Bible study group." Hasan came to faith in Jesus that day. Praise the Lord!

So if you are on a short-term mission trip to Kenya or Syria or even North Korea, and you are invited to a home for a meal, always lift up a song of worship unto Jesus (even in your own language). And pray for the Lord of the harvest to bless the home with salvation. Who knows? The Lord may answer your prayer five, ten, or fifteen years later through one of His laborers from another part of the world.

Besides Adam and Hasan, the Lord also brought a little girl to our Bible study. Muhabbat lived down the street from Adam, and was intrigued by the singing and the guitar music. She would often come and join us when we began singing. She learned most of the songs by heart and would sometimes ask me if we could sing a particular worship song again and again. Once we opened the Bibles, however, she would excuse herself and go back home. (I guess she wasn't too impressed with our Bible study.) At her home, Muhabbat would sing the songs about Jesus, and being forgiven as she was doing her chores or homework. Her mother became very intrigued about these songs, especially the one that asked God to create in us a pure heart. Eventually, her interest in the meaning of these songs would lead her to the women's Bible study that my wife was leading.

About six months after Adam and Hasan's baptism, Muhabbat and her mother and older sister were baptized in the river. A year later, Muhabbat's father and then, eventually, her young brother were also baptized as followers of Jesus Christ. The Lord opened up the two families in the village to the gospel simply because one of His ambassadors cleaned the toilet of a disabled, ex-convict. Our Lord Jesus Himself washed the feet of the disciples, and told us to do likewise (John 13:14).

Jesus is not only sending missionaries to places where the gospel has not been preached (like Syria or Afghanistan), but also bringing people from those places to our neighborhoods so that they can hear about Jesus. He does not always use the same method to open the hearts of the people to the gospel. For some lost sheep, a copy of the New Testament in their hands will suffice. For others, like Adam's neighbor, an act of compassion and love may remove the barrier that stands between them and the Good Shepherd...the same One who washed the feet of the disciples caked with mud and even animal droppings. How will you love your lost neighbor?

25 – Can You Teach My Father?

Isaiah 55:10-11 - "For as the rain and the snow come down from heaven and do not return there but water the earth, making it bring forth and sprout, giving seed to the sower and bread to the eater, so shall my word be that goes out from my mouth; it shall not return to me empty, but it shall accomplish that which I purpose, and shall succeed in the thing for which I sent it."

One day at the home of Adam (the ex-convict), I met Kamal. He was a construction worker in his 30s, and presented himself as a devout Muslim who prayed five times a day. [In reality, he only prayed once a week on Friday...but he wanted to impress me with his religious piety.] He joined our Bible study group because he was very interested in finding out more about God, especially in his own tongue. About thirty minutes into our conversation, he began to ask about the prophets in the Bible. He said that according to Muhammad, Allah had sent 124,000 prophets into this world, the last being Muhammad himself. Instead of arguing with him about the validity of such a preposterous statement, I began to explain to him about the lives of the Old Testament patriarchs (who are considered "prophets" in Islam) in chronological order. I began with Adam and finished with Jesus. [I want to commend all the Sunday school teachers who faithfully taught children about the heroes of faith like Noah and Abraham. I am also grateful to my parents, who encouraged me to read through the Bible every year as I was growing up.]

On a clean sheet of paper I sketched out the "family tree" of Jesus Christ, and included the lives of Adam, Cain, Abel and Seth, Enoch, Noah, Shem, Abraham, Isaac and Ishmael, Jacob (and his 12 sons...but could only remember about half, including Judah), Moses, David and Jesus. And then over the next hour, we selectively read from the Bible about the incredible faith and trials of some of them. At the end of the day, as we left Adam's house, Kamal asked me if I could come and visit his home the following week. He gave me detail instruction on which buses to take to his village; with two bus transfers, it would take about two hours to reach his home. Since his house did not have a working phone line, it was imperative that I understood the traveling instructions. And since there was no way to communicate with him again until the following week, I was fully committed to make the visit.

On my free day the following week, when I wasn't scheduled to teach at the university, I made an early morning trek towards his village. I remembered to pick up some fruit, a box of juice, and a couple of naan for the visit. I arrived at his home around midmorning, after asking several of his neighbors about the exact location of his home.

Kamal greeted me with a big smile, handshake, and a hug, and then led me to the guest room, where his father was already seated in one corner. I sat across from him, with a low table between us. Kamal served us tea and a warm fresh-baked bread (naan). I was given permission to pray for the meeting and the food, so I thanked the Lord for the day and the food, and then blessed Kamal, his father, and the rest of the family in the name of Jesus Christ. Afterwards, I taught again about the patriarchs in the Bible, starting with Adam from Genesis 1. I had agreed to come to Kamal's house four times, so I paced the study on the "prophets of the Bible" with focus on the people of faith like Noah, Abraham and Sarah, Joseph, Moses, David, and eventually, Jesus.

After the study, Kamal brought in a wonderful meal of osh pilaf (delicious fried rice with chunks of lamb meat, carrots, garlic, and chick peas) and fresh garden salad. I prayed one last time, especially for God's blessing upon Kamal's father, and then left for the afternoon bus. Kamal walked two kilometers with me to the bus station, and explained to me that his father's health is failing, and would pass away soon. He wanted me to teach his father about the things of God so that somehow the extra knowledge about the ancient prophets (or patriarchs) would be counted by Allah as a "good deed." Muslims believe that Allah will bring out a scale on the judgment day, and weigh each person's good deeds on one side against his bad deeds (sins) on the other. If there are more good deeds than bad, that person may have a chance to enter paradise; however, the ultimate decision is up to Allah. There is no assurance of salvation in Islam. Even Muhammad, on his deathbed, did not know where he was going afterwards.

I made three more visits to Kamal's home, and finished our study on the lives of the prophets. The last study on the life of Jesus dovetailed well with the earlier study about the substitutional sacrifice of the ram in place of Isaac. Each time both Kamal and his father sat through the study. Once or twice his cousins joined us for several minutes. At the last study, I invited both Kamal and his father to surrender their lives to Jesus Christ, and put their faith in Him as their Lord and Savior. They were both hesitant to make that commitment.

A few months later, Kamal's father passed away. I don't know if he ever made a confession of faith in Jesus Christ, but at least he had heard the Good News about Jesus Christ in his own language. But Kamal began to come to the Bible study at Adam's house more regularly. Within a year, Kamal was baptized in the river along with few other believers.

I had made the trip to Kamal's home for the sake of his aging father, praying for the latter's salvation, but the Words of life, which had proceeded from the Bible in local language, had the most incredible and unexpected impact on the son.

John 3:8 - The wind blows where it wishes, and you hear its sound, but you do not know where it comes from or where it goes. So it is with everyone who is born of the Spirit.

As ambassadors of Jesus Christ, you and I are called to be faithful, humble, yet bold in testifying ("martyr," per Acts 1:8) of our Lord Jesus wherever the Spirit sends us. As we speak with those living in the kingdom of darkness, it is the Holy Spirit who plants seeds of Truth into their hearts. Some will reject the words of life; others will accept them and open their hearts to Jesus in an attitude of repentance and utter surrender.

As you step out of your home and into the lives of the broken and the lost, ask the Holy Spirit to fill you with His power and wisdom so that you may faithfully proclaim the Good News to whomever He leads you to. And afterwards, pray that the Holy Spirit will give eternal life to those whom He wills.

26 – Encountering God's Power

John 9:1-7, 35-38 - As he passed by, he saw a man blind from birth. And his disciples asked him, "Rabbi, who sinned, this man or his parents, that he was born blind?" Jesus answered, "It was not that this man sinned, or his parents, but that the works of God might be displayed in him. We must work the works of him who sent me while it is day; night is coming, when no one can work. As long as I am in the world, I am the light of the world." 6 Having said these things, he spit on the ground and made mud with the saliva. Then he anointed the man's eyes with the mud and said to him, "Go, wash in the pool of Siloam" (which means Sent). So he went and washed and came back seeing.

Jesus heard that they had cast him out, and having found him he said, "Do you believe in the Son of Man?" He answered, "And who is he, sir, that I may believe in him?" Jesus said to him, "You have seen him, and it is he who is speaking to you." He said, "Lord, I believe," and he worshiped him.

Mirzod was one of the Central Asians who came to Christ in a miraculous way. I met him while teaching computer classes at the local university. He was pursuing a PhD in philosophy, and was fluent in English. We hired him as our teacher for the Central Asian language, and asked him to teach us using the Bible. It was the first time that he even saw a Bible in his own language, and he read the entire New Testament in two months. Then began a struggle in his heart: Which is true, the Bible or the Quran? Who is the true prophet of God: Jesus or Muhammad? God answered his questioning heart in an amazing way.

One night he was awakened by someone coming into his room. At first he assumed that it was his father, coming home after his last prayer at the mosque. But the figure was absolutely black, and he felt the chill of death in the air. This figure came closer and started choking him. It was the spirit of death. Mirzod could not speak at all. So he cried out in his heart: "Help me, Allah!" Nothing happened. He also yelled, "Help me, Hudo!" (Hudo is the generic term for "God" in the local dialect.) Still nothing. And then he screamed, "Help me, Muhammad!" Again, nothing. Finally, he shouted in his heart, "Help me, Jesus Christ!" Just then, a bright beam of light appeared and struck the evil spirit, vaporizing it in an instant. Mirzod could breathe again, and he felt the peace of heaven enter into his heart. He then knew clearly who was the true Savior: Jesus Christ.

Even though he came to believe in Jesus as His Savior, Mirzod waited two years before he was baptized. This was because of his fear of his father, who was a leader amongst his clan. But after two years, Mirzod, his wife, and younger sister were baptized in the river. A month after their baptism, the parents of Mirzod came to our house. The father was upset with us. He demanded that his children be returned to him as Muslims. Their conversion to Christianity was very shameful to their family and to the clan. When we told him that we did not force his children, who are grown adults, to trust in Jesus, neither could we force them then to return to Islam. They had made the decision on their own. The father then threatened to turn us over to the local KGB office. What follows will be covered in another chapter.

For those living in Muslim societies, the Lord of the harvest is sovereignly sending them dreams and visions or rescuing them from demonic attacks (like Mirzod) to open their hearts wide to the gospel. Some Christians in the U.S. have asked me why this doesn't happen to them (Western Christians) in America. I believe that these miraculous encounters are more frequent and regular with the Muslims for two reasons.

First, the Muslims function within a worldview (commonly described by cultural anthropologists as the "fear and power" worldview) that acknowledges and believes in the existence of angels and demons, as well as communication with the spiritual realm through dreams and visions. They firmly believe that Muhammad truly had visions and visitations from an angel sent by Allah. When a Muslim has an unusual dream or a vision of a man in white holding out his arms and saying, "Come to me, all who are weary and heavy burdened, and I will give rest for your souls" (Matthew 11:28), he or she is ready to believe that the dream is of life-changing significance. In the West we subscribe to a worldview (called a "guilt and innocence" worldview) that promotes a more rational and scientific approach to explaining daily experiences. A majority of Christians in Western churches believe that God no longer communicates in supernatural ways (dreams, visions, prophecies, etc.).

Second, for a Muslim to turn away from his religion (and his community) and embrace Jesus Christ as His God and Savior is to face a possible death sentence. At the least he will be harassed by his own family and disowned by his parents. Why would a Muslim young man turn away from his family, his community, and the promises of a prosperous life for a few paragraphs printed in a gospel tract? When the Lord Jesus reveals Himself powerfully and miraculously to a Muslim, the latter is convinced that Jesus is really the Son of God who conquered sin, Satan, and death, and is more than able to protect him from any threat here on earth.

A closer look at John 9 will reveal that Jesus waited until the man who was just healed was thrown out of the synagogue before He revealed His identity as the Messiah and subsequently received worship. Jesus healed the man first of his physical blindness in a miraculous way before addressing his spiritual blindness. Mirzod had to be convinced that Jesus Christ, the One he was reading about in the New Testament, was truly the One who had all authority in heaven and on earth, even over the demons. When Jesus saved Mirzod from the evil spirit who came to take his life, the young Muslim man was ready to turn his back on his religion and follow his Savior, even if it meant persecution and death.

Would you pray that the Lord of the harvest would send dreams and visions of Jesus to your Muslim, Hindu, and Buddhist friends? Ask the Lord Jesus to show His power to them through miraculous healings and deliverances from evil spirits.

27 – Are You Satisfied?

Proverbs 11:3 – The integrity of the upright guides them, but the crookedness of the treacherous destroys them.

About two years after we settled down in the Iranian neighborhood of our city, we decided to open up an English library nearby. Many of our Muslim neighbors would come to our home and ask us to tutor their children (of all ages) in English. They recognized us as a channel of opportunity for their children's success. We decided that rather than offer private English lessons, we would open up an English library with a large classroom for group lessons. We would charge a minimal fee for each student.

I met with the deputy mayor, who happened to live just across the street from our home. His son was a professor at the local language institute, and the deputy mayor was very excited about the idea of starting an English library. I asked if the town would partner with us and provide an empty building for us to use as the library. He walked us over to a small building with two large rooms. The building was located in the center of the residential neighborhood, far away from the noise of larger streets. It was an ideal location for a library. One of the rooms could serve as the library with shelves of books and tables; the other room could be used for English lessons. Because the building had not been used for several years, however, it needed repairs and remodeling. We proposed that we would make all the necessary repairs (replace windows, doors, paint the walls, etc.) if the town would allow us to use the building for free.

The deputy mayor agreed and we both signed the contract in the summer of 2003. During our first furlough we collected and shipped nearly 3,000 books from the U.S. to our Central Asian country. In the early months of 2004 we finished all the repairs in the building. We purchased library and classroom furniture and furnished both rooms. We tasked a short-term mission team from Canada to start cataloguing the books. We also hired several university students to help us teach English classes and serve as librarians. Joy English Library officially opened that summer.

In the summer of 2004 we had to return to the U.S. for my back surgery (herniated disc), and we flew back to the field in October to continue with our ministry. The English lessons at Joy English Library had continued faithfully, but a threat loomed in the horizon. The deputy mayor was no longer in charge; the mayor had returned from his business travels abroad and resumed his authority. He was also an Iranian Muslim, but was often seen drinking alcohol, and his eyes and face showed signs of occasional drug use.

He asked to meet me in January of 2005. He explained to me that the contract that I had signed with the deputy mayor was null and void since he was not present. I told him that it had the legal seal of the town, but that did not matter to him. He demanded that we pay $100 each month or move out of the building. I showed him the list of students from the neighborhood who were benefitting from the library and English class programs, but that was of no concern to him. He only wanted some money to pad his pocket.

I talked with several local Christian and Muslim friends who had knowledge of the local legal system. I told them about the contract with the deputy mayor and asked them if I went to court with the contract, could we win the case against the corrupt mayor? They had heard about this particular mayor and that he would win legal cases through bribes offered to the court officials. They did not advise that I take the case to court.

We had spent several thousand dollars to ship thirty boxes of books, repair and remodel the building, and furnish it with necessary furniture. We also spent countless hours to prepare the library as well as pay salary to library staff. We prayed that God would change the heart of the mayor, but he did not budge.

I even visited the deputy mayor and asked for his advice. He was very apologetic and said that the mayor was acting very foolishly. He was known for being greedy. He told me that the current mayor's house, a very stately mansion with an outdoor marble pool, was built on free labor. He had hired a crew of craftsmen and artisans to help him build a "dream house" and then when they came to collect their pay, he told them that the house was actually built for his son (who was about seven at the time). He further explained that when his son became an adult (about twenty years later), the son himself would make the payment. The building crew complained bitterly, but they had no recourse since the mayor was the local authority.

When I heard this aspect of the mayor's corrupt and deceptive dealings with people, I realized that his heart would not change. One spring day in 2005, the library staff and I moved the books out of the building. The mayor didn't seem too happy that we were moving out of the building with all the furnishings. He had hoped that we would stay and agree to the ridiculous rental fee.

As I turned over the keys and walked away from the mayor, he asked in the local dialect, "Are you satisfied?" You see amongst the Muslims of our city, whenever there is a business contract or transaction, both parties have to say that they are content/satisfied in order to receive blessing from God. And then one of them may even offer up a closing prayer. He wanted to hear a verbal consent that I was satisfied.

I turned around and held up my two hands in a gesture of prayer. And then I prayed in the local dialect, "Lord, you see the hearts of men. You know what the mayor has done to us, to the town library, and to the children. You be the judge. I am not satisfied." And I walked away. The mayor began to shout and scream towards me, "You are not the only one who talks to God. I also talk to God."

A week later, the mayor was removed from his post. We don't know what exactly happened, but the long history of corruption of the mayor must have finally caught up to him. The city officials finally made their decision to remove him. Although his wife and children continued to live in their mansion, the deposed mayor was no longer at that house.

As for the Joy English Library, we decided to relocate it to another part of the city where we had better access to university students.

Over the next few months, several different businesses tried to use the empty library building. However, it seemed to us that God did not bless anyone else using that building. Until we left the country a year later with forced deportation, there was no long-term successor to our tenancy.

Perhaps you are a missionary serving the Lord in an impoverished community, and you may face similar challenges of threat from corrupt and greedy leaders. Those who were elected or appointed to take care of their citizens often take advantage of them for the sake of personal financial gain. Remember that you have been called by the Lord to bring His blessing to the nations (people groups).

God called Abram (later Abraham) to be a blessing to the nations (people groups). He made a promise to bless those who bless Abraham, and curse those who curse him (Genesis 12:1-3). In Christ, we have now become children of Abraham by faith, and we are both recipients of the Abrahamic blessing as well as those who are to help fulfill the Abrahamic commission.

Galatians 3:8-9,14 - And the Scripture, foreseeing that God would justify the Gentiles by faith, preached the gospel beforehand to Abraham, saying, "In you shall all the nations be blessed." So then, those who are of faith are blessed along with Abraham, the man of faith...so that in Christ Jesus the blessing of Abraham might come to the Gentiles, so that we might receive the promised Spirit through faith.

We have been commanded to be a light to the nations. *Acts 13:47 - For so the Lord has commanded us, saying, "I have made you a light for the Gentiles, that you may bring salvation to the ends of the earth."* God has sent you to bring His blessing to the nations. On the mission field, you will meet people who are genuinely seeking their Creator. However, you will also encounter people, especially government officials, whose hearts are corrupt and wicked, and whose purpose in life seems to be to oppose everything that is of God. At those times, you can pray in bold faith for the Lord to either change the heart of the corrupt leaders or remove them from their position. apostle Paul prayed against the wicked interference of Elymas the sorcerer at Cyprus (Acts 13:4-12), and the Lord struck the sorcerer with temporary blindness. Subsequently, the proconsul put his faith in Jesus. Ask the One who has all authority in heaven and on earth to do as He wills as you face opposition, sometimes even from wicked men.

28 – Blessings Follow Persecution

Matthew 5:10-12 - "Blessed are those who are persecuted for righteousness' sake, for theirs is the kingdom of heaven. "Blessed are you when others revile you and persecute you and utter all kinds of evil against you falsely on my account. Rejoice and be glad, for your reward is great in heaven, for so they persecuted the prophets who were before you.

1 Peter 4:14-16 - If you are insulted for the name of Christ, you are blessed, because the Spirit of glory and of God rests upon you. But let none of you suffer as a murderer or a thief or an evildoer or as a meddler. Yet if anyone suffers as a Christian, let him not be ashamed, but let him glorify God in that name.

The words of our Lord Jesus Christ above are meant for everyone who would put his/her faith in Him and follow Him. He gave these "beatitudes" knowing that hundreds of thousands (perhaps even millions) of men and women, boys and girls who choose to follow Him, will face persecution and even death. He said that those who are persecuted for the sake of His name are BLESSED. While on the field in Central Asia, the Lord encouraged our family to preach this message faithfully to the Muslim converts in our city. As a Korean-American from a comfortable and affluent community of suburban northern Virginia, I felt like I had no right to deliver this message. Yet, the words are His, not mine. The promises of blessing are His, not mine. And so we encouraged our believers to be bold in their faith and choose to see persecution as a blessing. And the blessing came. Here are a couple of testimonies.

Dawud was a Central Asian Muslim, and one of my students at the state university. He came to Christ after reading the four Gospels in one week. He was thirsty for the living water! The day he became a believer, he was filled with joy, and went home and told his parents. Of course they were upset with him, and his mother slapped and beat him on the head. Dawud did not fight back, but took the punishment. The next day his mother awoke to find both knees swollen. She could not walk and had to hobble and crawl around for several weeks. Dawud lived with his uncle's and aunt's family (common in Central Asia), and whoever persecuted Dawud in any way, something bad happened to him/her that day. Everyone in that compound soon realized that this Jesus of Dawud is greater than their Allah. (Dawud didn't tell me anything of this persecution at his home for two years…it was his mother's confession after she became a believer two years later.)

And then over the next few months the word got out in Dawud's neighborhood that there was a young Muslim who just became a Christian. One evening Dawud was going home on a mini-bus after our Bible study. The driver, seeing the Injil (New Testament) in Dawud's hand, told him to get out of the bus…even though Dawud had paid the full fare to his street. Dawud asked him why, and the driver said that he didn't want to give a ride to any local citizen who betrayed his people and became a "Russian Baptist." The other passengers also mocked and jeered at Dawud. And he was pushed off the bus. It was past 10 p.m., and he had to walk three kilometers to get home. At first he was angry at the driver and the other passengers, but then he remembered what Jesus had said in Matthew 5. And he started giving thanks and praising God. At that very moment, the Holy Spirit came upon him and filled his heart, and he received the gift of tongue, much like Cornelius in Acts 10. Dawud never knew what praying in tongues was about. (I grew up in a Presbyterian church, and although I believe that all the gifts of the Holy Spirit are alive today, I don't usually encourage my disciples to seek the gift of tongue, nor do I lay hands on them and pray for them to receive this gift.) A few weeks later, the Lord began giving him lyrics and tunes to praise music, and Dawud started writing worship songs in the local dialect. A couple of them are being sung in house churches throughout his country. One of those songs is titled "Don't be sad, but rejoice!" It's about rejoicing in times of persecution. He also received the gift of prophecy. What a blessing! (And Jesus promises that more blessings await him and other persecuted BMBs in heaven!)

A similar testimony comes from another sister in our city. After her baptism in the river, her parents tied her up to a chair and beat her. Her own mother began to strangle her, and the girl was slowly dying. If it were not for the father pushing away the mom, this new convert would have died as a martyr. However, it was at that moment of near death that the girl felt such a peaceful, warm, and joyful presence of God! She said that the glory of God filled the room (1 Peter 4:14). What an amazing blessing! [She came and stayed at our home one night, and then we had to find a "safer" place for her...because, as we had expected, her parents came to our home the next day.]

Sometimes, we struggle with the temptation of wanting to avoid persecution...to protect ourselves and our disciples. We think that persecution is not what God intends for us (nor our disciples), that it's unfortunate that someone is going through persecution, that living in comfort and security should be the norm for all Christians. But didn't the Lord tell us plainly on many occasions that the world will hate and persecute the believers because of Him? I am grateful for the freedom we have in the U.S. to worship Jesus openly. I am also thankful to be a U.S. citizen...the Central Asian authorities usually deport and do not physically harm American missionaries. (There were a few exceptions, including one horrible murder in the capital city.) But God taught me on the mission field not to let the feelings of guilt of enjoying such freedom/privilege preclude the faithful and necessary preaching of the Beatitudes (and other similar passages concerning

144

persecution) to the recent converts. It is God's promise that He will bless the persecuted. The promise is His, not ours...and I believe that we should encourage the BMBs to embrace this message; otherwise, they are missing out on God's amazing blessing. We can inadvertently stand in the way of God's mighty work in and through the lives of our disciples.

And when persecution does come to our disciples, we need to stand with them in prayer, and even house and feed them and help them find another job if they lose it because of Jesus. Pray for the Holy Spirit to lead and guide you and those entrusted to you through times of persecution. Sometimes, you will be able to walk through the crowds that intend to harm you (Luke 4:29-30); other times, you may have to endure the stoning (2 Corinthians 11:24-25).

And perhaps in the near future, persecution will come to the millions of Christians in America...so that we too may share in this blessing of heaven.

Recommended reading:
Killing Christians by Tom Dole

29 – Paul's Message for the Church Today

Galatians 2:11-14 - But when Cephas came to Antioch, I opposed him to his face, because he stood condemned. For before certain men came from James, he was eating with the Gentiles; but when they came he drew back and separated himself, fearing the circumcision party. And the rest of the Jews acted hypocritically along with him, so that even Barnabas was led astray by their hypocrisy. But when I saw that their conduct was not in step with the truth of the gospel, I said to Cephas before them all, "If you, though a Jew, live like a Gentile and not like a Jew, how can you force the Gentiles to live like Jews?"

Dawud, the young BMB (believer from Muslim background), continued to grow in his faith. While he was still enrolled in the university, he began to work part time at our computer center. He had a good command of four languages (Russian, English, and two local dialects), and also had talent in IT and programming. With each monthly pay, Dawud put aside ten percent for tithe, and then gave the rest to his mother to support the family. Besides attending men's weekly Bible studies and Sunday services, I met with Dawud on Saturday mornings for more focused discipleship. I taught him a few chords on the acoustic guitar, and within six months he was ready to lead worship with me on Sundays. After a few more months, he was learning new chords from the internet...he had surpassed his teacher by leaps and bounds.

Eventually, another convert, Mirzod, would join our Saturday morning meetings. From that point on, we began to work through SEAN International's "Life of Christ" series for pastoral training. We had been introduced to this excellent pastors' training material while at Columbia Biblical Seminary. As Dawud and Mirzod progressed through the six-book series, I also invited them to take turns preaching with me on Sundays and during early morning prayer times. Our house church met every other morning at 6:00 a.m. during the week for worship and extended time of prayer. Dawud and Mirzod grew in their hermeneutic and preaching skills through such opportunities. We began to go through selected Old Testament and New Testament books during the morning services.

One of those books was Galatians, and Dawud was assigned to preach from Galatians 2:11-14. After reading the above passage, Dawud preached to the ten of us who were in that room. He first gave a brief overview of what was happening in the church at Antioch. He explained how there was a great division between the Jewish Christians and Gentile Christians, mainly due to the influence of the culture around the church. And then Dawud gave an amazing insight into how the passage applies to the local house churches in Central Asia.

Central Asian Muslims believe that Christianity is the religion of the Russians, the very people who had conquered and occupied their lands for more than seventy years. There are scatterings of Russian Orthodox, Baptist and Pentecostal churches throughout the region. For a Central Asian Muslim to become a Christian signifies not only a change in religion, but also a change in ethnic identity. To be Kazakh, Tajik, Turkmen, Kyrgyz, Uzbek, or Uyghur is to be Muslim; once Dawud became a Christian, his people saw him as a "Russian." Naturally, when Dawud chose to follow Christ, his friends and family immediately accused him of becoming a "Russian." To disprove their accusations, Dawud would try all the more to stay connected to his culture, as long as such actions did not dishonor Jesus. He tried to avoid speaking to Russian friends on the street, even if some of them were brothers in the Lord. He didn't want to be seen by his Muslim friends and relatives that he had indeed become a Russian.

But on that Wednesday morning, as Dawud was preaching on a Galatians 2 passage, we saw and heard the transformative work of the Holy Spirit in his life. He confessed that he (and probably the other BMBs in the room) was guilty of behaving like Peter when it came to relating to Russian Christians in the public. In private gatherings or inside the walls of the local Russian-speaking churches, Dawud would embrace the brothers and fellowship with them. But on the street, he had been ignoring them; he was ashamed of them. After studying the Galatians passage, however, Dawud was convicted of this hypocrisy. And thus that morning, he challenged his fellow Central Asian Christians to openly acknowledge and embrace the Russian Christians in the public. (By this time, the Russian population in Central Asian countries had become a minority, and Russian Christians even fewer still.) Dawud himself decided that the next time he saw Sasha, a dear Russian brother in the Lord, he would walk up to him in front of his Muslim friends, and greet him in Russian! Dawud concluded his message by saying that Sasha was part of his eternal family; if his Central Asian friends did not come to faith in Christ, they would be forever separated from him (Dawud). Dawud needs to acknowledge and love his true family in Christ, and not be ashamed of (or ignore) them because of their ethnicity. He was affirming what Jesus had said in Luke 18:21 – *My mother and my brothers are those who hear the word of God and do it.*

As I sat listening to his short sermon, I praised God for the inspiration of the Holy Spirit; I could not have preached the same message. I was not able to fathom the heart and mind of a Central Asian BMB, wrestling with the issues of faith, identity, and multi-ethnic relationships. Only the Spirit of God can do that.

As an expatriate missionary, I began to understand what the Holy Spirit was saying to the Bride of Jesus Christ through a national (indigenous) believer. The Lord's desire is to see the Church become a house of prayer for all nations, a faint reflection of what will come to be realized

148

in heaven one day (Revelations 7:9). However, in Central Asia, both the national believers and the foreign missionaries were behaving as if such gatherings of diverse ethnic groups would be contrary to God's will, and even hazardous to the growth of the church. The national believers are encouraged to stay within their own "heart language" community and often discouraged from connecting or fellowshipping with those from Russian-speaking people groups for several reasons.

First, the concern is over the safety of the converts. Russian churches are registered as legal entities; churches using Central Asian languages are prohibited. Second, there was a foreign missionary-led impetus to keep the BMB in his community and not be cut off or ostracized (for the sake of evangelization). Third, and again mostly instigated by the foreign missionaries, the house churches comprised of former Muslims are encouraged to stay to themselves and not be connected with any of the established Russian-speaking churches to prevent negative influences on the nascent indigenous churches by the older and inflexible denominations.

Most of the foreign missionaries working with a given unreached people group desire to see the start of a church planting movement amongst that group. Some missionaries subscribe to a purist or idealistic notion that in order for the movement to succeed, they must isolate the nascent indigenous churches from the more established, traditional churches in geographical proximity. There may be some legitimate reasons for such thinking, but I believe that the missionaries are imposing their biases and fears upon the local churches, and inadvertently bringing division between the greater body of Christ on the field. I believe that the Lord Jesus desires all nations to worship Him in the unity of the Spirit in the U.S. as well as on the mission field.

If we truly believe that the Lord has determined the times and places where everyone should live (Acts 17:26,27), then isn't this also true of the indigenous churches that He is building across the world? Does He not want open, humble, and committed fellowship between the ethnic believers and churches in Almaty as well as in Atlanta? Are we not praying for the Lord's will to be done on earth as it is in heaven? If the Lord's desire is to see all nations worship Him in Revelations 7:9, then why do we think that promoting such worship here on earth is contrary to His will and detrimental to the advancement of His Kingdom?

Long-established denominational churches may have traditions and practices that may negatively influence indigenous churches in a country hostile to the gospel; however, there are also ways in which the traditional churches can be a source of tremendous encouragement and blessing to the nascent churches of another people group or tongue. Let me share just one example.

Mrs. Park was an elderly Korean woman was in her 70s. She grew up in a remote part of Korea where girls were kept from school; instead, they were trained to care for younger siblings and tend to kitchen duties. When she became a Christian as an adult, she had the desire to read the Bible for herself. Through literacy classes established by missionaries, she was able to read both the Korean hymnal and the Bible. However, because she lacked formal education, she had difficulty understanding what she read in the Bible. Furthermore, she confessed that she did not fully understand many of the Sunday sermons. And then she admitted that the only way that her faith grew with correct doctrine was through hymns. She was able to read, memorize and sing translated hymns like "Jesus Loves Me This I Know," "Amazing Grace," "Nothing But the Blood of Jesus," "What a Fellowship," etc. As she sang them over and over to the Lord while cooking in the kitchen or sweeping the courtyard, the Holy Spirit would use the confessions of saints of old from Europe and America to bless her soul...to remind her of the things that Jesus had taught His disciples (John 14:26). She grew in her love for

Jesus and gained insights into living as His disciple through the translated hymns!

Hymns are melodious and Christ-exalting testimonies of sinners redeemed by grace like Fanny Crosby, Isaac Watts, and John Newton. There are some missionaries who disdain translated worship songs and hymns and only promote usage of indigenous worship music in the house churches. I am sure that God can raise up local believers to write worship songs (e.g., Dawud); however, they cannot replace the volumes of testimonies of God's work of grace across cultural boundaries and seasons of time. I am thankful that the missionaries who came to Korea translated both the Bible and the hymns; God has used both to bless the people of Korea for many generations.

Over and over again, our disciples from Central Asia were able to join worship services in Russian and English (and even in Korean) as they visited or worked in different countries across the world. They rejoiced in knowing that many of the worship songs sung in their Central Asian house church gatherings are "universal"…the tunes were not foreign to them, even if the lyrics were in another language. On those occasions, they felt very acutely assured that they were part of the universal family of God…and often even more grateful that our God is God of all people groups and languages. Ask the Holy Spirit to give you wisdom on how to introduce teachings, rituals, or traditions of the universal Church that will edify and encourage your local believers.

As I left the early morning prayer gathering that day, I realized that Dawud was now ready to be a shepherd who could lead the house church. The manner in which the Holy Spirit, using the Word of God, interacted with and transformed Dawud's thinking and worldview was truly incredible. Dawud was growing more and more into the image of His Savior, becoming a shepherd after God's own heart (Jeremiah 3:14,15).

I offered to God a silent prayer of thanksgiving, and told Him that I was now ready to move to another place if that was part of His will. And so, a few weeks later, the Lord began to open the EXIT door...

30 – When You Are Arrested

Mark 13:9-13 - "But be on your guard. For they will deliver you over to councils, and you will be beaten in synagogues, and you will stand before governors and kings for my sake, to bear witness before them. And the gospel must first be proclaimed to all nations. And when they bring you to trial and deliver you over, do not be anxious beforehand what you are to say, but say whatever is given you in that hour, for it is not you who speak, but the Holy Spirit. And brother will deliver brother over to death, and the father his child, and children will rise against parents and have them put to death. And you will be hated by all for my name's sake. But the one who endures to the end will be saved.

Luke 21:12-15 – But before all this they will lay their hands on you and persecute you, delivering you up to the synagogues and prisons, and you will be brought before kings and governors for my name's sake. This will be your opportunity to bear witness. Settle it therefore in your minds not to meditate beforehand how to answer, for I will give you a mouth and wisdom, which none of your adversaries will be able to withstand or contradict.

A few weeks later, while I was having Bible study with four men, the police came into the building to arrest us. They took us to the nearby police station and began to interrogate each of the local believers, starting with Mirzod. When the police chief asked them who was their leader, who had told them about Jesus Christ, they all replied honestly, "Mr. Cha." And so the four men were released, and I had to go to the police station over the next few days for interrogation. Just in case I needed help with translation, I asked Dawud to accompany me. He graciously obliged.

The police chief who began to question me was a large man, about six feet tall, weighing 250 pounds. He was fascinated that I could speak the local dialect, so he began with the following question: "Aren't you supposed to be teaching computer classes at the university? What are you doing teaching our people another religion?" It was at this moment that God provided the words to say, just as He promised in Mark 13 passage above.

Instead of answering the police chief's question, I gave him a question. On several occasions, Jesus had also responded to a question with a question (Matthew 22:20; Luke 20:4). I told the police chief, "Look at your country. You have no jobs here, so many are leaving your country to look for work elsewhere. More than half of the men from our city have gone to other countries to look for work. Many left for Russia, America, Europe and Korea with illegal visa to find jobs."

When I mentioned "Korea," the chief chuckled and said, "That's true. My nephew is in Korea right now working at a factory. He sends me a couple hundred dollars a month."

This is when I asked him, "How long do you want your people to go to other countries illegally and work as slaves in those countries? Don't you want God to bless your country so that people from other countries will come to your country to look for work?" The police chief started to listen more seriously.

"Let me tell you something about your country. Your country is not poor; the land has abundance of gold, natural gas, and cotton. But all that wealth has not been bringing blessing to your people. You need to know that the blessings of God are not the same as money or wealth. Just because you have money, it doesn't mean that you have God's blessing. There are so many families here in our city who live in nice homes with several cars, but the kids are having problems with drugs and alcohol. That's not the blessing of God. When God's blessing comes, there is peace and joy in the family. Everyone is blessed, not just the father. Furthermore, the wealth of your country is resting in the hands of those who are at top—the

154

government officials. The general population is not seeing the blessing flowing down to them. School teacher's salary is $20 in our city. How can anyone live on such paltry income in the 21st Century? My professor's salary is $100 per month. And yet some of my colleagues at the university drive used Mercedes-Benz imported from Germany. How did they earn enough money to buy such luxury cars? It's because a few days before the exams, they sell the answer key of the exam to the students for several hundred dollars. As a matter of fact, I know that you can buy a university diploma for around $5,000. There is bribery and corruption in other sectors of the society. This is not God's blessing. I believe that God's blessing will come to your country when there are people worthy of His blessing. And that worthiness comes through His Truth.

"Let me tell you about my country, Korea. About a hundred years ago, Korea was a very poor and desolate nation. We worshiped all kinds of idols, and because of this, we were not receiving blessings from the living God. Then people from America, Canada, and United Kingdom came to Korea to bring God's blessing. They built schools, colleges, and hospitals. But most importantly, they taught us about the living God through the Bible. They taught us to turn away from worthless idols and believe in the one true God. They taught us to live honestly. And our people began to change. Koreans became people who knew how to share God's blessing with others. Now look at Korea; it is one of the leading nations in all of Asia. And people from your country are going there to find God's blessing.

"I came to your country to bring God's blessing. At the university I am not only teaching the students about computer programming, but also about how to become honest people so that in the future, they can become righteous leaders of this country. Again, I came to your country to bring God's blessing, not His curse. But if you don't like what I'm doing, you can kick me out of the country tomorrow."

The police chief stood up, pounded on the table with his fist, and said to other officers in the room (including a KGB agent in the corner), "No, I want you in my country. We need more people like you in my country. You can stay in this city as long as you want. However, because you have been arrested, you have to face the judge this Saturday. When he signs off on the arrest document, then your case will be closed, and you will be able to stay in our country. But when you see the judge, you must make two statements: 'I'm sorry' and 'I will not do it again.'"

I thought about the police chief's words for a few seconds and then asked him two questions. "In your country there are two kings: the president and God. Who is greater?"

"God," he answered.

"And if the two kings issue laws that are in conflict, whose law should I obey?" I asked.

"You should obey God's law," he stated.

"Well, my God tells me that I need to proclaim His truth and promises to the people this country. I can say to the judge that I'm sorry for causing all this trouble. However, I cannot say that I will not do it again, for this means that I will not be able to teach about God or His ways to your people. Then the blessing of God will never come," I said.

"If you cannot say those two things to the judge, then I cannot guarantee what will happen to you. You may be put into jail, fined a few thousand dollars, and then deported from our country," responded the police chief.

I was released to go home, but was told not to leave the city until after the court appearance. The Lord gave us a reprieve to fast and pray for the next round of questioning and perhaps even face the possibility of deportation.

2 Timothy 4:18 - The Lord will rescue me from every evil deed and bring me safely into his heavenly kingdom. To him be the glory forever and ever. Amen.

Regardless of what you are currently going through (or may experience in the days to come), remember that He is

156

able to rescue you from every evil attack. Put your trust in the Lord Jesus once more, and ask Him to carry you through the fire and the water (Isaiah 43:1-2).

31 – Cancel or Continue?

Daniel 6:10 - When Daniel knew that the document had been signed, he went to his house where he had windows in his upper chamber open toward Jerusalem. He got down on his knees three times a day and prayed and gave thanks before his God, as he had done previously.

The arrest had happened on Monday evening. Interrogation took place over the following couple of days, with the Holy Spirit providing words that convinced the police chief that we should stay in his country and continue the work of God's blessing to his people. On Thursday night, however, four police officers made a sudden, unannounced visit to our home. They banged loudly on our metal gate with their sticks, and I met them at the gate. They simply said that they were confirming the address that I had given them, and also reminded me of the court appearance on Saturday afternoon.

My wife and I lay awake for several hours after their abrupt visit, and took some time to pray and seek peace and strength from the Lord again. The next day, we had to make a very critical decision. As a church we had decided to make our semiannual prayer walk through the city on the following Saturday morning. This event had been written into the church calendar weeks before, and the question we faced as leaders of the church was simple: "Should we continue with the prayer walk as planned?"

By now it was obvious to us that the local authorities knew of our residence, and perhaps had informants or officers monitoring our phone conversations as well as our every move. If we stayed with the prayer walk, would we not be endangering the lives of our local believers? The most likely consequence for us, should the authorities have arrested us on Saturday, was deportation. However, for the local believers, they could face harsher penalties, including severe fine, physical beating, and prison sentence.

But then the Lord reminded us of the challenging message from the missionary to Pakistan at the retreat four years prior: "Will you teach fear of man to your disciples?" We felt that the Lord was taking us through the refining fire as a church. The Lord knew that we were going to have a prayer walk ministry through our city on Saturday, and so He allowed the arrest to happen a few days earlier. He wanted to see if we would cancel the prayer walk, or like Daniel, continue with the event?

Furthermore, it would be very difficult to communicate with every member of the house church about the change in plan because the final and definitive announcement had been made at the past Sunday service. Many church members did not own a phone, and we did not have the time nor the manpower to visit each village where they lived. Hence, we decided to continue with the prayer walk on Saturday morning.

By Friday evening, the regional leaders from our missionary agency joined us. They were a great source of blessing and strengthened our hearts with words of encouragement and prayers. The fact that they were willing to take the risk of being associated with us after the arrest spoke volumes of solidarity for the sake of the gospel. The next morning they would join us for the prayer walk.

Ironically, the place that we had decided to meet, a park in the center of the city, was less than a hundred meters from the police station where I was interrogated. About twenty of us, expatriate missionaries and local believers, came together in a circle. We sang a couple of worship songs in the local language, and then divided up into small groups of two to three, and dispersed throughout the city to pray for God's kingdom to advance powerfully. Whether the local authorities were observing us or not, we may never know, but the Lord watched over our church as we walked through the city. We believe that whatever cloud of fear of man that was lingering over our church was broken that morning through the time of the prayer walk.

Later that afternoon, I had to go to the municipal court to hear about the outcome of my arrest. Dawud (our church leader) and the two regional leaders from our missionary agency accompanied me. When we arrived at the courthouse, I was met by a young police officer. He had my arrest document in his hands and told me to wait a few minutes outside the courtroom. He would first introduce the case, and then call me in to see the judge. He reminded me of the warning from the police chief: "You must say two things: I'm sorry and I will not do it again." I replied that I could say that I'm sorry, but that I could not commit to not preaching the gospel again. The police officer scowled at me and then stepped into the courtroom. I stood outside, praying silently to the Lord. What would I say to the judge? The police chief was willing to help me, but he was also asking to meet him halfway and make the two necessary statements.

Less than five minutes after he went in, the police officer came out of the courtroom with a smile. He said that the judge signed off on the document to officially close the case. I asked him what had just happened? He said that the judge had asked who was the man waiting outside to see him. And the police officer responded that the man was a Korean from America who came to bring God's blessing to the country. The judge must have read a quick summary form the police chief as well, and decided to release me and clear me of all charges. Praise the Lord!

We had chosen not to cancel the prayer walk, and instead decided to honor the One who has all authority. In turn, Jesus honored us with His sovereign grace and allowed us to continue with our ministry in country.

[Note: God gave us another eight months to stay in the country and raise up the leaders of the church. In February 2006, Mirzod's parents reported us to the KGB in the capital city, and we were forced to leave in March. At our final service at Harvest Church, we anointed seven BMBs as leaders of the church. The church leaders, in turn, read

160

the first few verses of Acts 13, and then commissioned us as God's ambassadors to the people groups in the neighboring Central Asian country.]

Jesus clearly wants us to know that in His hands are the outcomes of every arrest, every trial, and every visa approval. We are the ambassadors of the King of kings, and we must fear and revere only Him and no one else.

As we close this chapter, I want to draw your attention to one of my heroes from the past. Hugh Latimer was a Protestant preacher in the 16th Century England. He was known for boldly proclaiming the truth of the gospel, regardless of the audience in the pews. One such occasion was to give a sermon before the King of England, Henry VIII. He was contemplating whether to change his sermon once he was informed that the king would be joining as a guest. Reportedly, Latimer began that day's sermon with the following words: "Latimer, Latimer, thou art going to speak before the high and mighty King, Henry VIII, who is able, if he think fit, to take thy life away. Be careful what thou sayest. But Latimer, Latimer, remember thou art also about to speak before the King of kings and Lord of lords. Take heed thou dost not displease Him."

Latimer was not arrested for the content of the message on that Sunday. He would continue to serve as the Bishop of Worcester for several years. Eventually, Latimer was imprisoned and burned at the stake by King Henry VIII's daughter, Mary, a staunch Roman Catholic.

Ask the Lord to fill you with the Holy Spirit, and give you the boldness to face any type of persecution or threat with an overflowing joy and confidence in Him! And then be ready to face the lions, just like Daniel of long ago.

32 – Jesus Restores Peter

John 21:15-16 - When they had finished breakfast, Jesus said to Simon Peter, "Simon, son of John, do you love me more than these?" He said to him, "Yes, Lord; you know that I love you." He said to him, "Feed my lambs." He said to him a second time, "Simon, son of John, do you love me?" He said to him, "Yes, Lord; you know that I love you." He said to him, "Tend my sheep."

While being questioned at the local police station, Mirzod was forced to sign an agreement that he will no longer attend nor preach at unregistered church gatherings. They threatened not only to keep him in prison, but also bring harm to his wife and infant son if he did not sign the agreement. Out of fear and concern for the welfare of his family, Mirzod signed the document.

Two weeks after the arrest, Mirzod did come to Sunday meetings, but he resigned from leadership and preaching duties. Over the next few weeks, he and his wife continued to worship with us, but we could see that he lacked passion and joy in his life. Perhaps he felt like Peter, who had denied Jesus three times after the Lord's arrest (Luke 22:54-62). My wife and I and other church members tried to encourage Mirzod, but the weight of his guilt and shame could only be lifted up from him by the Lord Himself.

And so as we continued our weekly fasting and prayer times on Wednesdays, we pleaded for the Lord Jesus to come to Mirzod as He came to Peter (John 21). One fall Sunday, we had a guest preacher from a distant city. Bakir was a former Muslim who was struggling with addiction to alcohol and immoral lifestyle. He was a gifted musician, and was often invited to play at weddings for a nominal fee and lots of vodka. He wanted to break free from alcoholism, but found no way out. And then, through the invitation of a Christian friend, he went to the Sunday service of a Russian Pentecostal Church in the capital city.

The Lord began to open Bakir's heart to the gospel of Jesus Christ during the sermon. At the end of the service, a group of believers gathered around him and began to pray in tongue. It was at this moment that the Holy Spirit came upon him with power, and he broke down and wept, repenting of his sins and turning his life over to Jesus. He also received the gift of tongue…and soon was called into the ministry of preaching the gospel to his own people.

He went back to his hometown, and began to share the gospel with his neighbors and friends. Some began to believe, but several of his neighbors began to beat him severely and called the police to arrest him for committing religious crimes. Bakir was thrown into the regional prison, badly bruised and bloody.

Once in prison, the inmates and even prison guards asked about his criminal past. He then began to share the reason for his beating and imprisonment, and many Muslims began to hear the gospel for the first time in their lives. After a month of imprisonment, Bakir was released; the local authorities had decided that a one-month sentence was adequate for the crime of religious (Christian) proselytism.

Over the next few months, inmates who were released from the same prison began to look for Bakir and came to faith in Christ. Some of the prison guards also came to faith and joined his house church. They also brought their friends and neighbors. Within two years, his house church network had over one hundred believers!

Bakir concluded his message with the following astounding statement: "Dear brothers and sisters. I know that a few weeks ago some of you were arrested by the local police. But rejoice that you were arrested. How else would the police and KGB hear the gospel? How else would other prisoners hear the gospel unless you are arrested? The Lord Jesus used my arrest to build His church in my city."

His bold confession infused new hope and courage into our church. Bakir was absolutely right. Who in his right mind would go up to the local police chief or KGB agent and share the gospel? And it would also be near impossible for a pastor to step into a Central Asian prison to preach the gospel. However, when a believer is arrested, then he is given the opportunity to preach freely of Jesus Christ to both the authorities and the inmates. Hallelujah!

Mirzod was especially encouraged by this message. About two weeks later, the Lord arranged for a second arrest. This time, my family and I were in a different city for a meeting with the leaders of an affiliate ministry, and Mirzod and two other men were having a Bible study. Suddenly, ten policemen rushed in and arrested the three Christians and took them to a different police station than the one where they were first arrested. Perhaps it was again Mirzod's father who tipped off the local authorities on the time and location of the gathering.

The police chief who questioned Mirzod knew of the latter's arrest a few months prior. He wanted to threaten Mirzod with severe and harsh punishment, but this time the young man was ready. His faith had been restored by the Holy Spirit through the recent testimony of Bakir. When the police chief asked him why an intelligent Muslim young man would leave his religion to follow after a man who claimed to be God, Mirzod was ready to defend his faith. He shared a lengthy explanation of the gospel and even gave the police chief a copy of the New Testament. When the authorities asked Mirzod who was the leader of the "illegal" religious group, he did not disclose my name, but instead said, "Holy Spirit." Mirzod confidently said that he receives guidance for life's decisions from the Spirit of the living God. And when the police chief tried again to have Mirzod sign the agreement not to attend unregistered house church meetings, the young man refused. He said, "You can beat me or put me in prison, but I will never stop going to church nor stop preaching the gospel." Seeing that

Mirzod, and the other two Christians, were resolute in their commitment to Jesus, they made verbal threats but eventually released them around midnight.

The following Sunday, Mirzod was worshiping the Lord with full joy and passion. And a few weeks later, he came up to me and said that he was ready to resume his role as a preacher in our house church. Jesus had indeed come to Mirzod as He had come to Peter. Praise the Good Shepherd for His faithfulness to His flock. He allowed Mirzod to be sifted as wheat (Luke 22:31-32) by Satan, but He also prayed for the young pastor to be restored. Indeed, Jesus Christ is the High Priest who intercedes on behalf of His flock. What a wonderful Savior!

Hebrews 7:22-25 – This makes Jesus the guarantor of a better covenant. The former priests were many in number, because they were prevented by death from continuing in office, but he holds his priesthood permanently, because he continues forever. Consequently, he is able to save to the uttermost those who draw near to God through him, since he always lives to make intercession for them.

As you disciple and raise up leaders for your church, pray for the Lord to guide them through victories as well as defeats. A faithful servant of God has to know how to rise up again after failures and disappointments. They need to know intimately the Shepherd who has promised them these words:

John 10:27-28 - My sheep hear my voice, and I know them, and they follow me. I give them eternal life, and they will never perish, and no one will snatch them out of my hand.

33 – Storming the Gates of Hades

Matthew 16:16-19 - Simon Peter replied, "You are the Christ, the Son of the living God." And Jesus answered him, "Blessed are you, Simon Bar-Jonah! For flesh and blood has not revealed this to you, but my Father who is in heaven. And I tell you, you are Peter, and on this rock I will build my church, and the gates of hell shall not prevail against it. I will give you the keys of the kingdom of heaven, and whatever you bind on earth shall be bound in heaven, and whatever you loose on earth shall be loosed in heaven."

When a Muslim dies, he or she has to be buried by sundown on the same day. Both men and women are invited to the house of the deceased, and are entreated to pray for the dead. This is called the janazah prayer...asking Allah to have mercy on the dead soul and forgive his or her sins. However, only men are allowed to join the actual burial ceremony.

In the spring of 2003, about three years after arriving in Central Asia, we had to conduct the funeral of an infant. This girl was born prematurely with a very severe case of spina bifida. Her neural tubes had not closed properly while in the mother's womb, and the spinal fluids were oozing out at the base of her neck, between her shoulder blades. The local doctors could not treat her, and although we tried desperately to have the child sponsored for treatment by a children's hospital or clinic in the U.S., we had no success. The entire church fasted and prayed for her healing, but the Lord's will was not in her miraculous healing. The child suffered greatly, and within a couple of months she passed away.

Her mother, Dilnoza, was one of our disciples. She had some mental limitations herself, and during childhood years her mother had taken Dilnoza to almost all the shamans and Muslim faith healers in town. The result of such exposure to demonic witchcraft was that Dilnoza had unclean spirits living in her. Through repentance and inner healing/deliverance prayer sessions, Dilnoza was eventually set free from the demons.

Dilnoza was never married, but she had relationships with several men over the years. A few years before we met her, she had already given birth to two children; the daughter (older child) died by accident on train tracks, and the son was living with Dilnoza. The boy would come to Bible study meetings with his mom whenever he could. Even after Dilnoza came to faith in Christ, she again became involved in an immoral relationship with a man, and was soon expecting a child. This was the child that perished within a few weeks after birth. Since there was no marriage commitment, the biological father did not want to be involved in the burial of the child. [Perhaps another reason was that he did not want to be publicly associated with someone like Dilnoza, whose life was similar to that of the Samaritan woman at the well in John 4.] Hence, it was up to our church to not only comfort the mother, but also help arrange for the burial.

After acquiring a proper death certificate from the local clinic, and all the required stamps from the local authorities, a handful of believers decided to come together at the town cemetery to bury the child. Normally the father, or another male relative, would bring the child to the undertakers for burial; but there was no male family representative. Those who were present were the mother, her three close Christian sisters (all former Muslims), my wife, and me. I was the only male at the funeral.

At first the two Muslim undertakers asked about the male head of the household's presence, but hearing the state of the mother and child, and being offered the required burial fee for the deceased, the two men readily agreed to proceed. They dug a small grave for the girl, and then waited nearby as we began perhaps the first and only Christian funeral service at the Muslim cemetery in the city. [According to Islamic tradition, Christians and other non-Muslims cannot be buried in a Muslim cemetery. The "Russian" cemetery, however, was too far away for us travel to for burial.]

We sang several songs of worship in the local dialect, and then I read Psalm 23 from the Bible. I gave a short message on the Lord being a faithful shepherd throughout our lives, for the young and the old. We can trust Him with the eternal state of the little girl who had suffered so much during her few weeks here on earth. And then each of the believers prayed.

We laid flowers on the little child and then left the two workers to finish the burial. The May sun shone on us brightly as we left the cemetery, but a few hours ago the entire city had been pummeled by heavy downpour along with lightning and thunder. As a matter of fact, the entire day was engulfed with turmoil and upheaval.

Faith and I had to come to the funeral separately. She had to homeschool our children, take our daughter to ballet school for an hour lesson, drop her back home, and then come to the cemetery. My responsibility was to pick up Dilnoza and her deceased daughter, along with several of her Christian sisters, who would join us. One of the sisters, Sarah, the local shaman who had come to faith in Christ less than a year ago, was accompanying Dilnoza and helping her prepare the infant for burial. As Sarah was resting over night in the room next to Dilnoza, she was exposed to dangerous amounts of natural gas from a leaky pipe. When I went to pick up the group of women, Sarah was already unconscious; her skin had turned pale grey and very cold to the touch. She had a very faint pulse. We realized that she had inhaled significant amounts of natural gas. We had to carry Sarah out of the house and put her in the minivan, and then drove to her relative's home. We placed her in the open terrace. As I prayed for the Lord to restore her to health, I could still feel that her skin was cold and grey, but there was faint breathing.

168

As I drove to the cemetery with Dilnoza, her deceased daughter, and her Christian friends, the thunderstorm increased in intensity. The sky turned completely dark for about five to ten minutes. As we neared the cemetery, however, the rain slowed down and the clouds dissipated. Eventually, we were able to walk to the gravesite in the sun. Faith met us at the cemetery; she had come with a taxi. She also experienced terrible storm conditions in the taxi while coming to the cemetery. There were a few times when the taxi driver had to stop abruptly to avoid accidents. But the Risen Lord had protected all of us. We had come to honor the King of kings who had conquered death at a place where people are buried who had lived all their lives in the kingdom of darkness, serving the prince of this world, and will forever suffer in hell.

We had come to offer worship unto Jesus at the gates of Hades, and the enemy was not pleased. Satan nearly succeeded in taking the life of a former shaman. He had tried to discourage us and even harm us while coming to the cemetery through the violent thunderstorm. And he was not finished.

After the funeral, Faith and I came home. Our daughter Karis was playing on the rope swing, with her body seated about three feet above the ground. She accidentally lost her grip and fell back wards, hitting the back of her head hard on the concrete below. She lost her consciousness for a few seconds, and then began to wail once she recovered her senses. We immediately put an ice pack on her wound to keep the swelling down. About an hour later she experienced nausea and vomited; the fall had been quite severe.

As my wife and I lay down to sleep that night, we gave thanks to God for watching over us throughout the day. Perhaps we did not fully understand the anger of the devil at what would be happening at the gateway into his kingdom. Had we known beforehand about the nature and intensity of spiritual warfare, we would have fasted and prayed several days leading up to the ceremony. But because there was a need for Dilnoza to bury her child quickly, and because we were her shepherds, we had decided to obey the Lord's leading to surround Dilnoza with worship and God's Word to bring comfort and peace to her. Unknowingly, we had stormed the gates of Hades, and we had experienced attacks from the enemy at multiple fronts. The day after the funeral, Sarah (the former shaman) came to our home with a bright smile. She had fully recovered from her near-death experience stemming from the natural gas inhalation. She said that someone dressed in white had come over her and prayed for her…and that's when she began to regain life and strength. I was surprised; I told her that I did pray for her, but I was wearing a black suit (which is customary for funeral services in the West). Apparently, the Lord sent an angel (or Jesus Himself came) to bring healing to the ill sister.

Joshua 1:3 - Every place that the sole of your foot will tread upon I have given to you, just as I promised to Moses.

Jesus Christ has all authority in heaven and on earth, including places where evil spirits are worshiped. When given the opportunity, we need to claim every hill, valley, and field for His kingdom…even if it means conducting a Christian funeral in Muslim cemeteries. Pray that the Lord will give you the opportunity today to proclaim Christ's victory over sin, Satan, and death in a new territory.

34 – Persevering in Evangelism

John 12:23-26 - And Jesus answered them, "The hour has come for the Son of Man to be glorified. Truly, truly, I say to you, unless a grain of wheat falls into the earth and dies, it remains alone; but if it dies, it bears much fruit. Whoever loves his life loses it, and whoever hates his life in this world will keep it for eternal life. If anyone serves me, he must follow me; and where I am, there will my servant be also. If anyone serves me, the Father will honor him.

While serving in Central Asia, I heard the following testimony of a BMB pastor. He shared about what happened at his church in the mid 1990's, a few months after he had come to faith in Christ.

The pastor of the local Russian Pentecostal church told his assistant, a local Muslim man who had converted from Islam, to go to an old section of their city (which is a conservative Muslim neighborhood) and preach the gospel to the Muslims living there. He obediently went to that neighborhood and knocked on the gate of the first house he encountered. An older man wearing the traditional Muslim prayer cap opened the door. The young believer began to tell him about Iso Masih ("Jesus Christ" in the local dialect). As soon as the man heard the name "Iso Masih," he got upset and asked the visitor if he was a Christian, to which the young man said, "Yes." The older man then said, "Shame on you. You have betrayed your people and your religion." He told the young man to leave his house and never come back. So the young evangelist left.

When the pastor heard what happened, he told the evangelist to go back to the same house and preach again. So the young evangelist went back and started to talk to the owner again about Jesus. This time, the older man started shouting and cursing at him, and threatened to beat him if he ever came back again. So the evangelist left and went back to tell his pastor what happened.

When the pastor heard what happened, he told the evangelist to go back to the same house one more time. The evangelist began to refuse, saying that the Muslim man will certainly beat him, and even kill him. However, the pastor did not change his mind; he prayed for the young evangelist and sent him out again. The young man obeyed and prayed along the way. The previous two times he had prayed for God to open the hearts of the people he would meet; this time, however, he prayed for God to protect him. He was fearful for his life.

When he arrived at the same house the third time, he saw a five-year-old girl playing with her toys at the front of the gate. So he knelt down next to her and began to tell her about God, about creation, and about the life and teachings of Jesus Christ, including all the miracles that Jesus performed. After a while, the owner of the house discovered what was happening just outside his gate, and came out with a large stick to beat up the evangelist. As he was about to strike the evangelist on the head, the girl shouted, "Papa, stop. Don't hit him. You must listen to what he says about Jesus, and from now on we're going to church every Sunday."

The father dropped the stick, fell to the ground, and began to weep as he embraced the little girl.

Would you like to know why? Because the girl had been deaf and mute since birth, and Jesus Christ had miraculously healed her. The evangelist had not known that the girl was deaf and mute. He was simply being obedient to the command...to preach the gospel to the lost. Even if it meant that he would be beaten and possibly killed. But as he faithfully preached the gospel to the little girl, Jesus showed up. And He healed the little girl! As an ambassador of Jesus Christ, the evangelist's job was to preach to the little girl; the work of Jesus Christ was to heal her. The entire Muslim family of seven came to faith in Christ that day.

172

Let us pray for the Lord to give us this kind of faith and obedience. We sing/preach/pray so freely and easily about Jesus Christ having all authority in heaven and on earth, and yet we tend to live in fear when there are rumors of threat (persecutions, deportations, pandemics like coronavirus, etc.). As Christ's ambassadors in hostile lands, we can easily struggle with the fear of becoming the kernel of wheat that falls to the ground and dies. But didn't Jesus say that such a sacrifice is needed to produce much fruit?

Pray that you would trust Jesus at His every word and obediently preach the gospel to the lost, even if it means facing persecution...so that His glory and power may be revealed. What testimony(s) of Jesus' power, love, and glory will you share with all of us when we gather in heaven?

35 – Spiritual Disciplines

Ephesians 6:10-12 - Finally, be strong in the Lord and in the strength of his might. Put on the whole armor of God, that you may be able to stand against the schemes of the devil. For we do not wrestle against flesh and blood, but against the rulers, against the authorities, against the cosmic powers over this present darkness, against the spiritual forces of evil in the heavenly places.

In the passage above, apostle Paul exhorts the believers to be disciplined and ready at all times to be engaged in the kingdom warfare against Satan and his minions. Towards that end, we are encouraged to be committed and steadfast in our spiritual disciplines. I list below the spiritual disciplines that I believe are crucial to the faith maturity of the individual believer as well as the corporate body of Christ.

Growing in Prayer Life - Early Morning Prayers: In our Central Asian city, we met as a church for early morning prayer three times a week (Tuesday, Thursday, and Saturday) from 6am to 7:30am. Each prayer meeting included one-half hour of praise, one-half hour of teaching from God's Word, and one-half hour of prayer. Prayer time would include intercession on behalf of the nation, the people groups, the city, and the lost individuals around us. The two young local leaders took turns with me in preaching at the morning prayer times. Dawud and Mirzod both grew in their confidence in preaching and teaching through morning prayer times. For the first few months they preached from Bible passages of their choice. After a while we took turns preaching from the same book of the Bible (e.g., Galatians, John, 1 Samuel, etc.). Their preaching improved greatly during those morning prayer times. The believers who came in the mornings were usually more passionate and committed, and received the messages well and with enthusiasm. Their intimacy with the Lord grew significantly through these prayer meetings, and many experienced the joy and miracle of God answering their specific prayer requests.

Weekly Fasting: As a church we decided to fast once a week (Wednesdays) for breakfast and lunch. Some fasted the entire twenty-four-hour period. This gave everyone an opportunity to pray for special needs within the church— salvation of loved ones, persecution from parents, sick children, need for job, etc. Several women decided to fast and pray for three days on their own for those times when there seemed to be intense persecution or suffering in their lives.

Through early morning prayer and fasting, the believers began to grow in their understanding of how spiritual battle is fought on their knees. We told them that "prayer is the battle, and ministry is the prize." Without fervent prayer on our knees, we may not be able to see God's kingdom advance powerfully like the early church in the Book of Acts.

Prayer Walks: Twice a year (spring and fall) we went throughout the city on a prayer walk. Transformations I video (by Sentinel Group) was available in Russian, and the believers have been challenged by it to see our city transformed by the power of the gospel. We also prayed that God would one day fill up the local soccer stadium with thousands of believers from the region, gathered to worship, and lift up the name of Jesus our Lord. One of the most significant prayer walks was during the time of our arrest (Chapter 31).

Prayer Vigils: In the fall of 2005, we held our first all night prayer gathering (vigil) at a member's house. The purpose of the meeting was to strengthen our intimacy with Christ through deeper prayer life. There were those who

175

came with some life pains and dire needs, and we had extended times of intercession for them. We also focused on praying for those family members who still did not come to faith. One of the great blessings of the first prayer vigil was that God spoke to Dawud that night and called him into a lifetime of ministering as a house church leader.

Scripture Reading: Whenever a Muslim came to Christ, we encouraged him/her to immediately read through the children's Bible in the language of their choice (Russian or local dialect). The children's Bible not only is written in simple indigenous language but also includes beautiful and helpful illustrations. By reading the children's Bible, the new convert gains a good understanding of the story of God's loving redemption of mankind, from Creation to Christ. Subsequently, we encouraged the new believers to have daily devotional readings, starting with the gospels. The men and women would also join respective weekly Bible studies, which are usually topical and cover selected passages of both the Old and New Testaments. The entire house church members were also encouraged to participate in bimonthly Bible exams. They were given two months to read and study one of the books of the Bible (James, Matthew, Esther, etc.) and then participate in a written exam at the end of that period. The three highest scores received prizes. This approach has helped both youth and adults to read (and reread) the Bible with attention to details, which they often recorded in a separate notebook. The notebook would later help them in times of personal spiritual need or when sharing their faith. We also encouraged our disciples to memorize Scripture (e.g., topical memory verses by Navigators) to help them with daily living situations as well as for sharing their faith.

Giving and Tithing: We challenged our disciples to come to church on Sunday with something to give back to the Lord. Those who had jobs were encouraged to give a tenth of their earnings. Those who were not employed were encouraged to bring even a loaf of bread (naan) to share with the church during lunch. Those who had the means were encouraged to give beyond tithe towards the needs of other church members who needed financial assistance. Everyone in the church needed to see that all our provisions came from the Lord, and that it is not solely the work of our hands that produce wealth for us (Deuteronomy 8:17-18). And God is glorified when we share with generously with those in need, especially within the body of Christ (Acts 4:32-36).

Evangelism and Outreach: As soon as a local Muslim came to Christ, it opened the opportunity for him/her to share their testimony with their family members and close friends. We encouraged our disciples to pray for God to open doors so that Acts 16:31 would become a reality in their home. As mentioned above, we fasted and prayed for unsaved family members on Wednesdays; we also trained our disciples to share the gospel using the Word of God and their personal testimonies. We also encouraged our disciples to invite their friends and family to weekly Bible study meetings as well as Sunday services. Many came to Christ through these gatherings.

Fellowship with Other Churches and Believers in the City: We encouraged our disciples to have open and supportive relationship with other house groups as well as with registered churches. There was one particular registered church, a Russian Pentecostal church with an Iranian pastor, with which our house church and other house churches in the city had favorable relationship. This registered church opened up its doors to a monthly gathering of house groups and other registered churches in the city for prayer and worship. Such gatherings allowed the believers to meet for mutual edification.

We discouraged believers from other house churches to come and join our group. We did this for three reasons. First, we wanted our house group to grow by evangelism, and not by transfer. Second, we didn't want "sheep stealing" to become a pattern in our relationship with other churches. Third, as long as the church leaders or pastors are doing their job and not teaching heresy, we wanted to encourage the local believers to stay with the house group where they came to faith. In the corporate world, it is often encouraged for a new entrant into the marketplace (e.g., a recent college graduate) to stay with the first company for two to three years. This gives enough time for the employer to train and equip the employee with skills and knowledge, which he will need for the rest of his career life. Similarly, we believe that a new believer needs significant input from his/her discipler during the first few years after coming to faith in Christ. Switching from one church to another during this critical time could hurt, more than help, the new convert's spiritual growth (unless there is clear evidence of abuse or heresy).

As the lost are coming to faith in Jesus Christ through you, what is God laying on your heart about their discipleship? Read carefully through the gospels, the Book of Acts, and the Epistles to rediscover the approach the early church leaders took to disciple the new believers. Whatever spiritual disciplines they taught and modeled, it would be wise for us to implement as well.

Recommended readings:
Celebration of Discipline by Richard Foster
Prayer: Finding the Heart's True Home by Richard Foster

36 – First Temptation of Christ

Matthew 4:1-4 - Then Jesus was led up by the Spirit into the wilderness to be tempted by the devil. And after fasting forty days and forty nights, he was hungry. And the tempter came and said to him, "If you are the Son of God, command these stones to become loaves of bread." But he answered, "It is written, 'Man shall not live by bread alone, but by every word that comes from the mouth of God.'"

During our first year at Columbia Biblical Seminary, we met a Korean missionary couple that had faithfully served over seven years in South East Asia. As they were entering their seventh year of ministry, their sending agency and church encouraged them to take a sabbatical year to rest and pursue further seminary training. They were free to choose any place in the world for their furlough (within the limits of a set budget), and the couple eagerly chose the U.S. The man would spend the year pursuing a master's degree at the seminary, and their two sons would attend the local high school. In anticipation of the upcoming visit to the U.S., the couple decided to save up enough funds to purchase a vehicle when they arrived in South Carolina. Several thousand dollars (in cash) were carefully packed into a small suitcase. As they were transitioning through Hawaii for layover, however, the suitcase was stolen.

This couple was part of our seminary small group at Columbia, and during our first gathering, they openly shared about this tragic loss. The man shared how the Lord used the theft to teach him and his wife a lesson. The money that the churches in Korea had sent sacrificially was for him to use for living expenses as well as for ministry. But he had saved up the money to purchase a vehicle in the U.S., and the Lord had taken that money away. He could not trust the Lord to provide a vehicle for him, so he had redirected the funds. He and his wife shared this testimony with a genuine, repentant heart. We were all convicted, and challenged once again to trust in the God who provides for His servants.

Ironically, when the missionary family arrived in Columbia, a local church was generous enough to bless them with a vehicle to use during their stay in the U.S. The Lord took away, only to give according to His sovereign will and wisdom.

I am so thankful that the missionary couple did not hesitate to share openly and humbly about their sin of doubt and unbelief towards God's provision. Their testimony stayed with me and my wife over the past twenty-five years, especially when we were serving the Lord in Central Asia.

We had chosen not to buy a home stateside for several reasons. First, we wanted to focus our finances on paying off student loans, car loans and any other debts that we had acquired over the years. Second, we wanted to send several hundred dollars to each of our widowed mothers in appreciation of their raising us faithfully. Third, renting an apartment or condominium would allow us the freedom to move quickly to another state or country for seminary and/or missions training. Last (and not the least), we didn't want our hearts to be tied to our home in the U.S.: should anything happen on the mission field, we may have been tempted to pack up and "return home." If we didn't purchase a home in the U.S., then our home would be wherever God's pillar of fire and the pillar of cloud would take us (Exodus 13). We would have to trust the Lord to faithfully provide a shelter everywhere we went.

During our ten years on the mission field, we noticed an interesting trend amongst expatriate missionaries. There were some missionaries who had the financial means to buy a house or an apartment (or several houses). We also purchased a house—it was a thirty-year-old mud-brick house built by a Crimean Tatar family. They were eager to sell their home and move back to Ukraine, so we were able to purchase the ten-room home for less than $10,000. A partnering church in Urbana, IL, generously provided us the necessary funds. Over the next year I spent many off-hours each week in fixing up the house to make it more "comfortable." The local Russian term for repairing and remodeling of a building is "remont." A local proverb rightly quips that remonting your home never ends in Central Asia; there is always something to improve or fix. Two big remont projects were to build indoor kitchen and bathroom to the existing structure. We also had to place two large metal tanks in the attic for storing hot and cold water. Our neighborhood suffered from poor water supply throughout the year, especially during the summer months, and the elevated storage tanks would help to provide some margin of water supply as well as adequate water pressure to run the plumbing system in the house. It would cost another $10,000 (labor and material) to accomplish the tasks just described. When we were forced to leave the country four years later, the market price for the "modernized" home was around $60,000. Rather than selling the home to the highest bidder, we decided to sell it to one of our house church leaders who was in need of a home. His brother had worked several years in Korea, and had enough money to purchase the home for $18,000, which was less than the amount we invested into the house. (We also left all the furniture and appliances in the house, distributing such items to various members of the house church.) Because the funds to purchase the home and complete the remont were all from the Lord (through supporters from the U.S. and Korea), we decided not to ask for the market price.

Some of the other missionaries in our country, however, sold their properties for three to ten times what they had invested. There were even a few missionaries who purchased multiple properties and hired local contractors to oversee several remonting projects simultaneously. Their reasoning was that they needed to be "good stewards" of the Lord's money, and be financially able to purchase a house when they return to their home country. Or they may have to put their kids through college. But Jesus did not send us to the mission field to "fix and flip" homes.

After fasting forty days in the desert, Jesus was painfully hungry. Satan was challenging the reality of Jesus' identity: "If (or since in some translation) you are the Son of God..." How is it possible for the Son of God to be hungry? After all, is He not the One who sent manna from heaven to nearly two million Israelites in the desert? But Jesus would choose to rely fully on the Father to provide food, clothing, and shelter per His sovereign will. He did not listen to the words of Satan; instead Jesus fixed His mind on the words of truth proclaimed in Deuteronomy 8:3.

Perhaps you are tempted to listen to the wisdom of the world to establish financial security for yourself and your children in our unpredictable economic climate. What Jesus promised two thousand years ago, He is still more than able to fulfill. Ask the Lord to renew your understanding of His words in Mark 10:28-30 - *Peter began to say to him, "See, we have left everything and followed you." Jesus said, "Truly, I say to you, there is no one who has left house or brothers or sisters or mother or father or children or lands, for my sake and for the gospel, who will not receive a hundredfold now in this time, houses and brothers and sisters and mothers and children and lands, with persecutions, and in the age to come eternal life."*

Have you left everything to follow Jesus? If so, He will provide for you hundredfold. Quite often it is because we have not left everything, that we struggle with what we do not have at the present moment. Perhaps the Lord is asking you even now to give up one or all of your earthly "treasures" to follow Him even closer. The rich young ruler lost the opportunity to become a disciple of Jesus. He passed up on the joys of having an amazing adventure with Jesus...healing the sick, casting out demons, and even raising the dead. Of course, this adventure would also include severe persecution and even martyrdom. But isn't that the kind of life we are called to live?

37 – When Missionaries Have More

1 John 3:17 - But if anyone has the world's goods and sees his brother in need, yet closes his heart against him, how does God's love abide in him?
1 Thessalonians 2:7-9 - But we were gentle among you, like a nursing mother taking care of her own children. So, being affectionately desirous of you, we were ready to share with you not only the gospel of God but also our own selves, because you had become very dear to us. For you remember, brothers, our labor and toil: we worked night and day, that we might not be a burden to any of you, while we proclaimed to you the gospel of God.

Our mission agency recommended that we set aside part of our monthly support towards attending the organization's annual regional conference in Thailand. This would usually take place in the January of each year. For many missionaries working in harsh environmental conditions or restrictive societies (like Muslim nations where foreign women are not allowed to dress in shorts in the public), Thailand is a welcome respite. Many missionaries would attend the conference for a week and then stay another week for personal vacation at a beach resort, enjoying abundance of tropical fruit and seafood as well as the cool, ocean waves. The cost for such first-world privileges, however, would range from $3,000 to $7,000 (including airfare, food and lodging, and entertainment) for a family of five serving in Central Asia.

The purpose for such a conference is to bring spiritual, emotional, mental, and physical refreshment to the missionary (and his family) so that he/she (they) can serve the Lord more effectively and persevere on the field. The conference would include wonderful programs for the missionary kids (MKs) of all ages as well as vibrant worship and excellent Bible teaching for the adults. Missionary families looked forward to these conferences and a weeklong vacation by the beach subsequent to the conference.

Even before we left for the mission field, we had already decided to attend our first conference after being in the target country for at least a year. So in the cold January of 2002, we flew off to Thailand for our first missions conference. Our kids enjoyed the entire Thailand experience immensely: roasted corn by the seashore, sweet pineapples and mangoes, grilled chicken satay, snorkeling in clear blue waters at Koh Samui, connecting with other MKs, the cartoon network, and sleeping in air-conditioned rooms. Faith and I quenched our thirst for Spirit-filled worship with hundreds of other missionaries and great Bible teaching from one of the professors at Dallas Theological Seminary. As we were flying back to frigid Central Asia, we understood why missionaries are drawn to these annual conferences.

The inner struggle began at that point. Even though we made our best attempt to live simply and at the lifestyle of the local believers, we knew that we were economically many notches above them; the fact that we had the luxury of flying out of the country to enjoy a retreat or vacation in the warm sands of Thailand testified to our hidden wealth. By this time we were also painfully aware of the desperate financial needs of our disciples. Some were widows or divorcees who had children to feed, clothe, and educate. Some lacked proper education and were barely literate; they faced challenges in acquiring well-paid posts at either the government or private sector.

In light of their needs, we decided to attend our mission agency's regional conference every three years. With the funds that we were able to save, we decided to help our disciples start businesses or provide scholarship for higher education. We also opened up an education center with a dozen computer stations and classroom furniture for teaching English classes. We hired three of my computer class students as teaching staff at the center upon their graduation from the university; one of them was our disciple. The staff's monthly salaries were disbursed from our support account.

We wanted to pursue apostle Paul's model of 1 Thessalonians 2:8...to share not only the gospel, but also our lives and whatever financial blessings we had. Our disciples had become like family to us, and the Lord gave us the heart and the desire to help meet their physical needs.

You may have people around you who are in need of financial help. Even today, there may be someone in your life who is in need of financial help. May the Lord give you wisdom and the means to tangibly express His love and kindness to the local church and the surrounding community.

I want to close this chapter with a testimony concerning ministry vehicles. During our time in the second Central Asian country, Faith and I each drove a car to carry on our ministry. They were both used Japanese vehicles; I drove a diesel van that could climb any mountain and Faith drove a small but reliable Mazda hatchback. As we were preparing to leave Central Asia, we needed to make decisions concerning the two vehicles. Most missionaries would sell their vehicles to reclaim the funds to purchase new/used vehicles upon their return to the U.S. (home country). As we were praying, we sensed that the Holy Spirit wanted us to give the two vehicles away (combined purchase cost was about $10,000). And so we gifted the diesel van to a fellow missionary family from Korea; during the past three years we had become close to their family, and saw genuine compassion and integrity in their ministry. There are all types of missionaries on the field; and from our perspective, their lives matched their words. They were in need of a reliable van, and we knew that it would be several years before they could raise enough funds to purchase a reliable vehicle. The Lord used us to meet their need. The smaller hatchback was gifted to a local couple that served as staff at a nearby university campus. Their lives, too, exhibited passionate love for Jesus and a great commitment to reach the lost souls. They had become like family to us, even though we were not on the same missionary team. They were also in need of a ministry vehicle. Upon our return to the U.S. in 2010, we were right away faced with the need for a family vehicle, preferably a van or a minivan. And within a week the Lord provided us with a British SUV and eventually a reliable Japanese minivan. Over the past ten years the Lord has faithfully provided our family with vehicles of various manufacturers...Acura, BMW, Ford, Honda, Hyundai, Jeep, Mazda, Mercury, Oldsmobile, Range Rover, Toyota, and Volkswagen. Of course they were all used vehicles, and some needed more attention than others. (We are grateful to our dear mechanic friend, Steve Kim, for taking good care of each one of them.) Just recently our friends Bud and Brenda gifted us with enough funds to purchase a reliable, used Toyota Highlander. It is serving us very well...no more breakdowns on the road and emergency calls to AAA.

Perhaps you are struggling to find reliable vehicles each time you return for home assignment. Would you consider giving away your vehicles, furniture, or appliances each time you move...if that is what the Lord is laying on your heart? As you give to the Lord and bless other expatriate missionaries or the local pastors/friends, the Lord will bless you, as He promised in Luke 6:38 – *"...give, and it will be given to you. Good measure, pressed down, shaken together, running over, will be put into your lap. For with the measure you use it will be measured back to you."*

38 – Second Temptation of Christ

Matthew 4:5-7 - Then the devil took him to the holy city and set him on the pinnacle of the temple and said to him, "If you are the Son of God, throw yourself down, for it is written, "'He will command his angels concerning you,' and "'On their hands they will bear you up, lest you strike your foot against a stone.'" Jesus said to him, "Again it is written, 'You shall not put the Lord your God to the test.'"

In the second temptation, Satan wants the Son of God to doubt in the ability of the heavenly Father to protect Him. Satan knew that Jesus was already aware of the amount of suffering He would have to face in the few years to come, and He wanted to work fear and doubt into the Savior's mind at the onset of His public ministry. Isaiah 53 is not a nursery rhyme but a very graphic death sentence. Perhaps the Lamb could be tempted to try the protective hand of God? Would the Father really send the angels to save the Son? Or since Jesus emptied Himself of all divine prerogatives when He came into our world (Philippians 2:7), was Satan tempting Him to reclaim His divine power just for a second to save Himself?

Again, Jesus responds with a very definitive and appropriate verse from the Book of Deuteronomy. He will not test the Father because He has no doubt about the Father's desire and ability to protect the Son. Jesus is completely secure in His relationship with the Father; the Son does not need to protect Himself.

Whenever you serve the Lord in a hostile setting (e.g., Syria or North Korea), you will often face the dilemma of how much "religious activity" to be engaged in. Overt engagement may result in arrest, imprisonment and/or deportation by the local authorities, or severe persecution from the local citizens. Little or no engagement for a prolonged period means the kingdom of God does not advance, and you begin to wonder why you are even in the country. Our Lord Jesus was never inactive. Of course there were days when He (and the disciples) went away by Himself for rest and renewal, but He consistently advanced God's kingdom boldly by preaching the gospel and setting people free from diseases and demons, even in the face of strong opposition (Mark 3:1-6).

What can often happen on a hostile mission field is that you and I will be tempted to listen to the voice of Satan, and go along with his suggestion. Obviously, Satan will not manifest himself to us visibly and speak to us, but his words will reach our hearts through even local believers as well missionary colleagues. I want to share from a segment of Korean Church history where the assembly of pastors and foreign missionaries failed in the second temptation of Christ, and decided to heed the voice of Satan rather than stand on the promises of God. It occurred during the Japanese occupation (1910-1945).

The gospel first came to Korea through Protestant missionaries around the 1860s. Rev. Robert Thomas, of Welsh descent, came on a U.S. merchant ship to Pyongyang, which was at that time the capital of Korea. He was executed along the shores of Taedong River by the Korean soldiers, but before he was martyred (Acts 1:8), he offered up copies of the Korean Bible to his executioner and other soldiers present. According to local historians, the executioner, the official in charge of the military dispatch, and some of their family members came to faith in Jesus Christ by reading God's Word. Truly, Rev. Thomas' sacrifice yielded fruit that he may not have expected (John 12:24). Eventually, more missionaries, especially from the U.S., came to serve the Lord in Korea. Hundreds gave up their lives, either at the hands of enemies of the gospel or by succumbing to diseases and harsh living conditions of Korea.

Gradually, the Lord blessed the work of the missionaries with churches sprouting not just in Pyongyang, but also through out the Korean peninsula. Then in 1907, the Lord poured out the Holy Spirit across all the churches of Korea. Tongues of fire rested on the believers just as in the Book of Acts, Chapter 2. [*The Korean Pentecost* by Blair and Hunt. Draper chronicles similar outpouring of the Holy Spirit in other parts of the world: Wales, Azusa Street, Norway, Chile, China, and Brazil—*The Almanac of the Christian World*, p.320.] I believe that the Lord generously poured out His Spirit upon the Korean Church in 1907 for two major reasons: first, to consecrate His Bride to be His faithful witness (martyr) to the ends of the earth (Acts 1:8), and second, to prepare them for the persecution to come under the hands of the Japanese Empire.

When the Japanese invaded Korea and officially took over the land in 1910, they brought with them Shintoism, their state religion. Shintoism is the worship of the sun goddess. Gradually, the Japanese officials imposed the law that all Koreans must worship their sun goddess.

Starting in 1938, the Japanese officials began to impose Shinto worship in the Korean churches. They placed kamidana, a miniature Shinto shrine, on the pulpit in the church sanctuaries and demanded the pastors to lead the congregation in bowing to their sun goddess before starting the church service. If the pastors did not comply, then they would be imprisoned and/or executed, and the church doors would be shut. The Japanese were trying to coerce the Korean Christians to turn their backs on the living God and worship the sun inside God's house, similar to what the Temple priests did in Ezekiel 8.

Ezekiel 8:16-18 - And he brought me into the inner court of the house of the LORD. And behold, at the entrance of the temple of the LORD, between the porch and the altar, were about twenty-five men, with their backs to the temple of the LORD, and their faces toward the east, worshiping the sun toward the east. Then he said to me, "Have you seen this, O son of man? Is it too light a thing for the house of Judah to commit the abominations that they commit here, that they should fill the land with violence and provoke me still further to anger? Behold, they put the branch to their nose. Therefore I will act in wrath. My eye will not spare, nor will I have pity. And though they cry in my ears with a loud voice, I will not hear them."

It was while he was living as an exile in Babylon that Ezekiel had the above vision from the Lord. This man was a priest-prophet, and the Lord "transported" him to Jerusalem to show His people how offended He was by their grotesque idolatry. They turned their backs on the living God, the Creator of the universe, to worship the creation (sun). Over time, the Israelites have become like the gods that they have come to worship, committing all kinds of abominations.

Psalm 115:8 - Those who make them become like them; so do all who trust in them.

If they had continued to faithfully worship Yahweh, the living God, they would have become like Him...merciful, compassionate, just, kind, and holy (Micah 6:8). But the descendants of Abraham, Isaac, and Jacob have now become like the pagans around them...their lives filling up with violence, greed, and immorality as their hearts were offered up to the pagan idols and the associated demonic spirits. And after centuries of rejecting repeated warnings from the Lord (Deuteronomy 28:15-68; 2 Chronicles 7:19-22), the children of Israel are exiled to distant lands.

Less than a hundred years since its birth, the Church of Korea was facing its greatest challenge with the issue of forced Shinto worship. Should the Korean believers choose the path of peace and security, and embrace Shinto worship, or should they refuse to commit idolatry, even if it meant persecution?

One of the pastors who refused to compromise with Shinto worship was Rev. Kichul Chu, who was overseeing the flock at the largest church in Pyongyang at that time. The Japanese officials were especially concerned about Rev. Chu's response to their demand, since he was seen as the key figure in the Korean Church movement. As Rev.

Chu was being installed as the pastor of the new, five-story church building in Pyongyang, he preached boldly the following lines in his sermon:

Shinto shrine worship is a violation of the First Commandment and is a crime against the holy name of the Lord; it is an act of betrayal against our Lord God. [More than Conquerors by Chu, p. 31.]

For this act of defiance, the Japanese soon arrested and imprisoned him. Over the next six years, Rev. Chu would have to endure series of arrests, imprisonment, interrogation and torture, brief release to convalesce at home, and then rearrest for not capitulating. They had decided against quick execution because they believed that if Rev. Chu capitulated and agreed to Shinto worship, then the majority of the Korean pastors would follow his footsteps and compromise. However, by God's grace, Rev. Church never gave in to their demands and would end up dying under the cruel hands of the Japanese officials.

Besides Rev. Chu, there were other church leaders (elders, deacons as well as pastors) who were either arrested and tortured or killed. As these attacks were unfolding before the eyes of other Korean pastors yet to face the visits by the Japanese officials, a steady movement towards Shinto worship compromise began to grow. These Korean pastors began to say to themselves: "If we are all arrested, who will shepherd the churches? And if all church doors are closed, how can the gospel advance in our country?"

Hence, in September of 1938, a total of 193 delegates from 27 presbyteries, including ordained pastors, elders, and about two-dozen missionaries, met together in Pyongyang to sign a pro-Shinto worship resolution:

"We ministers understand that Shinto shrine worship has nothing to do with religious matters, nor is it against Christian doctrine. We are also aware that Shinto shrine worship is a patriotic and nationalistic ceremony. Thus as citizens of imperial Japan, we vow to show our loyalty

through voluntary participation in the practice..." [*More Than Conquerors* by Chu, p.37]

Truly, this foolish resolution was exactly what the Lord meant in Proverbs 29:25 - *The fear of man lays a snare, but whoever trusts in the Lord is safe.* The resolution was the second temptation of Christ, repackaged for the cowering leaders of the Korean Church. After signing the resolution, twenty-seven ministers, representing twenty-seven presbyteries, went voluntarily to Pyongyang Shinto Shrine and bowed towards the sun goddess on behalf of the entire assembly of churches. For the next seven years, from 1938 to 1945, in every church with its doors open, the ministers were leading the congregation to worship the sun goddess before starting their Christian service.

On the early morning of this resolution, the wife of Rev. Chu was praying alone at the church. Her husband was being tortured in the local prison, but her heart was more burdened by what the assembly would decide to do later that day. As she was laboring in prayer, she received a profound vision from the Lord: a young student came into the sanctuary and told her to read Hosea, Chapter Nine. She began to read the opening verses of that chapter and understood what the Lord was about to do.

Hosea 9:1-3 - Rejoice not, O Israel! Exult not like the peoples; for you have played the whore, forsaking your God. You have loved a prostitute's wages on all threshing floors. Threshing floor and wine vat shall not feed them, and the new wine shall fail them. They shall not remain in the land of the Lord, but Ephraim shall return to Egypt, and they shall eat unclean food in Assyria.

Mrs. Chu understood from reading this passage that the assembly would compromise with Shinto worship later that day, and that consequently the Spirit of God would leave the Korean Church. The Lord's glory and presence left Jerusalem when His people worshiped the sun (Ezekiel 8:16; 10:18). Eventually, He would send His chosen people away to foreign lands as exiles (Ezekiel 12:10). The same

193

fate would happen to the people of Korea; only in this instance the nation would be divided in two.

At the conclusion of WWII, Korea would briefly enjoy a period of freedom. Within a few years, however, the leaders of communist China and Soviet Union installed Ilsung Kim as ruler over northern region of Korea, and the West supported Syngman Rhee as ruler over southern region of Korea. Then in June of 1950, the Korean War erupted, and after three years of grueling fighting, the nation signed a ceasefire agreement with the north being governed by communist regime (Kim dynasty) and the south governed by a more open and democratic government. The people living in North Korea began to suffer from unspeakable conditions of famine, police brutality, and impoverishment. Pyongyang, which was once called the Jerusalem of the East because of the powerful presence and work of the Holy Spirit, had become the seat of communist power. And when Ilsung Kim came into power, he proclaimed himself to be "God the Father," his wife to be "God the Spirit," and his son Jongil Kim to be "God the Son." Ironically the name "Ilsung" means "the sun is established" and "Jongil" means "the righteous sun." Because the Church of Korea voluntarily worshiped the sun goddess during the Japanese occupation, the Lord has exiled the northern half of the country to worship the "sun" despots under coercion. Even to this day, the people of North Korea are forced to worship the statues of the two deceased leaders as deity.

How does this tragic story of Shinto worship compromise of the Korean Church speak to the missionaries of today? Do you trust God to protect you in all circumstances and settings? What would you do when there is rumor of terrorist activities targeting expatriate missionaries? Would you trust in the Lord who led you to the place of ministry? Would He not protect you, as He did with Elisha when this prophet of God was surrounded by the Aramean army (2 Kings 6)? Or would He not tell you to escape from the hands of a violent ruler like King Herod, just as He did with Joseph and Mary (Matthew 2)? We need to learn how to hear the voice of God so that we do not make decisions based on man's wisdom (often influenced by the voice of Satan).

Expatriate missionaries, especially from the Western (First World) countries where the societies have placed personal safety and security as a high premium, struggle in mission fields where the threat of terrorism or other forms of physical danger (like coronavirus) are present. We can easily make personal security an idol in our lives. As Christ's ambassadors, we must learn to overcome every occurrence of the second temptation, which will only increase in frequency and magnitude as the time of the Lord's second coming draws near.

It has been seventy years since the nation of Korea has been divided...may the Lord be merciful and relent, and allow the period of "exile" to end. I want to close this chapter with an excerpt from one of Rev. Chu's earlier sermons (entitled "The Authority of the Prophet") before his arrest:

Prophet Jeremiah cried out for the repentance of his people with many tears, foreseeing the destruction of his nation. Instead of shedding such tears of sorrow, why do our ministers today only aim to flatter the Japanese by praising their prosperity, becoming accomplices to their wickedness in these dark and evil times? John the Baptist boldly rebuked King Herod for committing adultery with his brother's wife. He was prepared to die when he confronted this king who had the power to kill or to save him; he chose to speak the truth as a prophet of God even if it meant certain death and it was after he did so that his authority as a prophet was established. Why don't any of the ministers gathered here today urge action? Are you ignorant, or are you simply feigning ignorance? Why are you mute, merely trembling with fear?

195

Recommended readings:
More Than Conquerors by Chu
The Korean Pentecost by Blair and Hunt

39 – Third Temptation of Christ

Matthew 4:8-10 - Again, the devil took him to a very high mountain and showed him all the kingdoms of the world and their glory. And he said to him, "All these I will give you, if you will fall down and worship me." Then Jesus said to him, "Be gone, Satan! For it is written, "'You shall worship the Lord your God and him only shall you serve.'"

Matthew 22:37-39 - And he said to him, "You shall love the Lord your God with all your heart and with all your soul and with all your mind. This is the great and first commandment. And a second is like it: You shall love your neighbor as yourself.

Matthew 28:18-20 - And Jesus came and said to them, "All authority in heaven and on earth has been given to me. Go therefore and make disciples of all nations, baptizing them in the name of the Father and of the Son and of the Holy Spirit, teaching them to observe all that I have commanded you. And behold, I am with you always, to the end of the age."

The Great Commission flows out of the Greatest Commandment. It is because of our love for God that we choose to obey Him in taking the gospel to the ends of the earth. And the second commandment (to love our neighbor as ourselves) is most wonderfully fulfilled when the lost hear the Good News through us and attain eternal life through Jesus Christ. However, we must remember that the Great Commission ends with the return of Jesus Christ our Lord; the Greatest Commandment (to love the Lord) stretches into eternity. We will forever pour out our adoration and worship unto our God. Hence, it is imperative that as we fulfill the Great Commission, we do not break the Greatest Commandment.

During our ten years of ministry in Central Asia, we challenged our Muslim friends who were ready to come to faith in Jesus Christ, to repent (confess and turn away from) their sins and past ways, traditions, and allegiances and believe the Good News (see Mark 1 and Acts 2 verses below).

Mark 1:14-15 - Now after John was arrested, Jesus came into Galilee, proclaiming the gospel of God, and saying, "The time is fulfilled, and the kingdom of God is at hand; repent and believe in the gospel."

Acts 2:38-39 - And Peter said to them, "Repent and be baptized every one of you in the name of Jesus Christ for the forgiveness of your sins, and you will receive the gift of the Holy Spirit. For the promise is for you and for your children and for all who are far off, everyone whom the Lord our God calls to himself."

We challenged them to reject the Quran as a holy book from God, to reject Muhammad as a prophet of God (he is a false prophet, an anti-Christ according to 1 John 2:22-23), and to stop the daily prayers towards Mecca since it is idolatry. When Muslims bow towards the Ka'ba, they are bowing to a created object, as well as to the spirit of Satan that stands behind it.

When we first arrived on the mission field in the fall of 2000, we were introduced to diverse Muslim outreach methods. There were articles and workshops on "The Camel Method" and the Insider Movement. At the beginning of our ministry we were not as upfront and bold about our thoughts and convictions concerning Muhammad and Islam. We did not want to offend the "seekers" from Muslim backgrounds and we wanted to see quick and easy conversion. We were drawn to this new strategy that promised mass number of conversions...movements of Muslim people groups turning to Christ. We allowed our Muslim friends to put their faith in Jesus without challenging them to turn away from Islam. However, two things emerged from this compromising/soft approach: 1) the converts who came to believe in Jesus without renouncing Islam altogether were weak in their faith and tended to hold onto both faiths (Christianity and Islam) and often equivocated in their identity before others, and 2) Jesus was not being honored solely, per His proclamation (John 14:6; Isaiah 42:8). We later decided to have our Muslim friends turn completely away from Islam before coming to faith in Jesus Christ as their Lord and Savior. We had fewer numbers (of conversion), but these new group of converts were not afraid to identify themselves as Christians ("Masihi" in Central Asia). They lived out 1 Peter 4:16 regularly - *Yet if anyone suffers as a Christian, let him not be ashamed, but let him glorify God in that name.*

We also decided to baptize our believers in the open mountain river rather than in the privacy of a bathtub or indoor pool. At the time most Central Asian governments allowed freedom of religion; hence outdoor, public baptism was not illegal.

A few years into our church plant, several of our disciples (all BMBs) came and told us: "Thank you so much for being up front about your views on Islam, especially concerning Muhammad and the Quran. Some of our friends who came to Christ through other missionaries in our city say that they feel very deceived." The missionaries had encouraged their Muslim friends to study the Quran and the Bible together to see similar truths and words of wisdom. Many months after the Muslims had come to Christ, the missionaries told them that the Quran is not to be trusted because it is not from God. Consequently, the BMBs felt deceived by the missionaries. Why weren't they (the nationals) told from the very beginning the missionaries' true views on the Quran and Muhammad?

Our disciples told us that they had struggled with the idea of rejecting the Quran when they first met us. But when they finally made the decision and "burned the bridge" and gave full allegiance only to Christ and the Bible, they knew that there was no turning back. They knew where we stood on Islam, and they felt that we honored them (no deception) and Jesus Christ!

There are foreign missionaries who are not only teaching that it is acceptable for the BMBs to continue to practice Muslim rituals, including prayers at the mosque, but there are some missionaries who are also joining their Muslim friends at the mosque to pray with them. These missionaries believe that they are taking a deeper step towards becoming incarnational and promoting strong bonding with the local community. Hence, when they pray and bow at the mosque, "in the name of Jesus," they are becoming like the local people group in order to gain access to their hearts months or years later.

However, I believe that they are failing at the third temptation that Jesus faced. Satan was promising Jesus all the glory, riches, and fame of the kingdoms of the world if the latter bowed down and worshiped him. Perhaps embedded in this offer was the promise too of all the people groups of the world. If Jesus would only have worshiped Satan, then the Son of God would not have gone through the humiliation and the pain of the Cross; He could have accomplished His mission the easy way and gone back to the Father in heaven. However, this was not the path that Jesus chose. He would rather face the cross and redeem the peoples of the world per Father's will, than to compromise the Greatest Commandment and fall prostrate before a created being.

However, this is what some missionaries (and even pastors in the U.S.) are doing. To win a few converts, they are ready to adopt whatever methodology or strategy that will help them accomplish that goal. To them, the end justifies the means.

As ambassadors of Jesus Christ, may we love and honor our Muslim friends (by being open and honest) and more importantly, love and honor our Lord and Savior Jesus Christ! How are you being tempted to compromise your faith for the sake of winning a few converts?

As Christ's shepherd over your local church, would you watch your disciple (BMB) continue to beat his wife, even a year after coming to faith? Would you confront him (using Scripture) to stop such violence, or would you simply look the other way and pray that the Holy Spirit would bring him to a biblical understanding of how a husband should treat his wife?

Let us now consider another scenario. What would you do if your disciple continues in his readings of the Quran and occasionally prays at the mosque with his father and brothers? Would you instruct him to stop committing idolatry, or would you pray that the Holy Spirit would guide the convert to his own convictions on this matter?

If you intervene in the first and not the second, you have just placed the Second Commandment (to love his wife as himself) above the Greatest Commandment (to love God with all our heart, soul, and mind). Our God is a jealous God (Exodus 34:14), and He alone deserves complete and sole allegiance from us and our disciples.

40 – How Will You Build?

1 Corinthians 3:9-15 - ...for we are God's fellow workers. You are God's field, God's building. According to the grace of God given to me, like a skilled master builder I laid a foundation, and someone else is building upon it. Let each one take care how he builds upon it. For no one can lay a foundation other than that which is laid, which is Jesus Christ. Now if anyone builds on the foundation with gold, silver, precious stones, wood, hay, straw— each one's work will become manifest, for the Day will disclose it, because it will be revealed by fire, and the fire will test what sort of work each one has done. If the work that anyone has built on the foundation survives, he will receive a reward. If anyone's work is burned up, he will suffer loss, though he himself will be saved, but only as through fire.

Shukrat was a Central Asian Muslim who grew up in a small village that was known in the region for raising up fundamental Muslims, some of who became violent jihadists. He was over six feet tall, weighed over 220 pounds, and perhaps because he grew up working on the farm and milking cows, his hands were huge and strong. He had a penchant for drinking and starting fights, especially at wedding parties. Furthermore, he would often take money from the wallets of the men he would beat up. That was his means for supplementing his meager income from farming his land.

One day, as he was walking back home from the bazaar, a Russian Baptist grandmother (babushka) accosted him and berated him in Russian. She told him that his notoriety as a wicked, drunken man had frequented her ears too often, and she was sent by God to warn him of his precarious state; if he did not repent of his sinful lifestyle, he would end up in hell. She then thrust a copy of the Russian New Testament into his hands and walked away. Shukrat was incredulous. No one dared to talk to him that way; he never lost a fight, and all the men in his town feared him. But what could Shukrat do? It would not be culturally right for him to beat up an old Russian woman. So he shouted a few curse words in Russian at the woman and then stormed back home in anger. He did not discard the Russian Bible, however. He kept it in his coat pocket.

That same night, Shukrat found it difficult to fall asleep, and decided to read the New Testament that the woman had given him. As he read chapter after chapter, the Holy Spirit began to open his heart to the reality of Jesus' divinity. A few hours later, he was led to repent of his sins and put his faith in Jesus Christ as his Lord and Savior. Shukrat had an unusually restful sleep that night.

The next morning Shukrat woke up to find his mind clear and his heart tender towards his wife and children. He recalled the past day's events in his mind, and thought that perhaps the late night conversion to the Christian faith was just a random emotional act. So he decided to gulp down a glass of vodka and forget about the entire experience with the Russian woman. Then a very surprising thing happened; he vomited the alcohol. He was shocked...he had never thrown up vodka before. It was what he relished for the past fifteen years, ever since he was a teenager. Suddenly, he realized that he no longer had the desire to drink alcohol again. Furthermore, the Lord took away his desire to smoke (he would smoke two packs of cigarette each day) and also purified his lustful heart. Seeing this drastic transformation in Shukrat, his wife came to faith in Christ. And so did his younger brother and his wife, and his cousin and his wife.

The wife of his younger brother, was the daughter of the town imam (priest). Upon her conversion to Christian faith, the father was furious with Shukrat and after one Friday afternoon prayer, instigated two thousand men to join him in attacking Shukrat. They congregated at a clearing a few hundred feet in front of Shukrat's house, armed with ax, sticks and shovels. They were intent on killing the three men who had just turned away from Islam to follow Christ. They called out the names of the three Christians, who stepped through the metal gate and closed it tightly behind them. Shukrat was sure that he would never see his wife and daughter again. They walked to the middle of the crowd; the Muslim men opened up a passageway for the three men, and then quickly closed up behind them. There would be no escape. The men shouted: "Allahu-akbar" (Allah is great) and shook their weapons and tools above their heads.

When Shukrat reached the middle of the clearing, he was prompted by the Holy Spirit to lift up his right arm and point his finger towards heaven. At that very moment a divine wind came down from heaven, gently falling upon the three believers, but as it spread outwards, the force of the wind knocked over five to six layers of men who were immediately surrounding Shukrat. Then the entire crowd felt the presence of the living God (1 Peter 4:14). The fear of the LORD was upon them, and the crowd of two thousand angry Muslim men became deathly quiet. The terror from God was upon them, just as in Genesis 35:5 - *And as they journeyed, a terror from God fell upon the cities that were around them, so that they did not pursue the sons of Jacob.*

Psalm 34:7 – The angel of the LORD encamps around those who fear Him, and delivers them.

They had never felt such a thick and powerful presence of the holy God. No one dared to say a word, or even breathe, in fear of their lives. Shukrat recognized that this must be the presence of the holy God, and spoke to the crowd as he lifted up his Bible: "Fellow brothers. You know who I am and what kind of lifestyle I led. I used to get drunk, smoke, commit adultery, and fight with many of you. And going to the prayers at the mosque did not change any bit of that sinful lifestyle. But one day with Jesus Christ, who is described in this Holy Book, my life was completely changed. God has set me free from my bondage to all kinds of sin. What the Quran could not do, Jesus Christ did in an instant. Brothers, you can do whatever you want with me today, but I will never turn away from the One who has saved me from sin and death."

The crowd kept silent. The imam who had organized this rioting crowd was furious and shouted to the men: "How come none of you is responding to what this Christian just said? Speak up!"

But everyone kept their mouth shut; no one dared to incur the wrath of God in any way. Just then the local police car pulled up and drove right to the middle of the crowd. The policemen stepped out and arrested the three men before any violent rioting could take place.

As they were spending the next few days in jail, the news of their arrest reached the ears of Christian congressmen in the U.S. A petition was drafted by the congressmen to urge the government officials to ensure that the jailed Uzbek Christians would be protected from the hostile Muslim community; otherwise, the annual aid from the U.S. could be reduced or terminated. Eventually, the mayor of the town convinced the Muslim community to let the three Christians live.

Although the Lord had saved Shukrat from the hands of his enemies, because of his bold stand for Christ and his clear and public identification with Him, his neighbors began to cut off all ties with him and his family. Even his uncle, who lived just next door, stopped greeting him. A few townspeople did come to visit him, but late at night or very early in the morning.

A few years later, Shukrat was invited to a ministry training conference for local pastors in the capital city. By this time he had already taken several semesters of Bible classes at the Assembly of God seminary in the same city. The speaker at this conference was from Canada, and delivered a message that was shockingly new. He advised that the Muslims who come to faith in Christ should strive to remain in their community. They didn't have to declare themselves to be Christians; instead, they could explain to their friends and family that they were now Muslims who follow Jesus. This would prevent the unfortunate mishap of being persecuted and ostracized from the community. The missionary encouraged the BMBs (Muslim background believers) to act like they were still Muslims so that they could maintain the relationships and keep the doors open to share the gospel, resulting in greater number of conversion.

Shukrat's heart began to stir up with anger; he did not like what he had just heard from this foreign, Western missionary. The latter was telling the local BMBs that they should act like cowards and hide their identity as Christians. Shukrat especially felt like this teaching was a slap in his face because it was saying that his stand for Christ in front of two thousand men was a mistake. He walked out of the conference with great disappointment. If the speaker had not been a foreign missionary, he would have stood up and openly challenged the man; but out of respect for the fact that he was a guest to his country, he kept quiet.

When I met him for the first time (a few years after this conference), Shukrat still had some lingering questions concerning the conference teaching. He asked me what I thought. I told him that what he did in front of the crowd was absolutely right, biblical, and Christ-honoring. I told him to never hide his identity as a Christian, and God would carry him through every evil attack and opposition (2 Timothy 4:18).

It was at this time that our second son, Josiah, had a dream in which he saw Shukrat preaching at a second floor building, but the foundations began to crumble. And the Lord spoke the reference 2 Corinthians 3:10 into Josiah's mind. He awoke to tell me of his vivid dream, and immediately, I knew that the Lord wanted me to strengthen and affirm Shukrat's resolve to stand boldly for Jesus.

The next time I met him, I reassured him that what he did was admirable and that Jesus was truly honored in front

206

of his townspeople. During the one year that we were in his town, we partnered with him in ministry at several villages, and about forty Muslims came to faith in Christ.

2 Timothy 3:12 – Indeed, all who desire to live a godly life in Christ will be persecuted.

Have you been persecuted by your community? If so, rejoice that God's Word is being fulfilled in your life. If not, perhaps you are not living out the testimony as Christ's true disciple.

Are your disciples being persecuted for turning their backs on their traditional faith or spiritual allegiance, and putting their faith in Jesus Christ? Remind them that they are walking through what the early Church had experienced, just as Jesus declared in John 15:18-25. But remind them also that the Lord will never leave them nor forsake them (Isaiah 43:1-2; Hebrews 13:5).

Recommended readings/viewing:
Insider Movements by Jeff Morton
Hast Thou No Scar? by Amy Carmichael (poem)
Half Devil Half Child by Bill Nikides (video)

41 – Who Do You Say I Am?

Matthew 16:13-17 - Now when Jesus came into the district of Caesarea Philippi, he asked his disciples, "Who do people say that the Son of Man is?" And they said, "Some say John the Baptist, others say Elijah, and others Jeremiah or one of the prophets." He said to them, "But who do you say that I am?" Simon Peter replied, "You are the Christ, the Son of the living God." And Jesus answered him, "Blessed are you, Simon Bar-Jonah! For flesh and blood has not revealed this to you, but my Father who is in heaven."

The Lord Jesus Christ would not only commend Peter with the words recorded in verse 17, He would also proclaim that Peter's confession and his life would become instrumental in the building of the Church in the days and years to come.

In an earlier chapter we read about how the Holy Spirit inspired Dawud (the local BMB pastor) to point out the need to keep the diverse ethnic groups of believers in a state of dynamic unity. Language and culture can often cause divisions. Another pervasive and divisive issue concerns the confession of Peter above (Matthew 16).

Muhammad taught in the Quran that the Christians believe in three Gods: God the Father, Mary the Mother and, through their sexual union, Jesus the Son (Q5:116). Of course he was in grave error, because this is not what the Christians (both Catholic and Protestant) believe. Most likely Muhammad was misled by one or more heretical sects that had flourished in the Mediterranean region before his time. This misunderstanding, however, has been passed down from one generation of Muslims to another. A typical Muslim will vehemently reject the name or title of Jesus as being the Son of God, simply because that title invokes the thought that God had sexual relationship with a human. All Bible-believing Christians will decidedly reject such notion as well; to suggest that our God had sexual relationship with a woman is indeed blasphemous. However, that is not what is meant by the term "Son of God." We cannot reject the familial titles of God within the Trinity because of some misguided Quranic teaching. The triune nature of God is an eternal reality established by God Himself; we can neither reject nor modify that truth.

There are many Western and non-Western Bible translators who have taken the liberty and initiative to remove the familial titles from the Bible in order not to offend the Muslim readers. Furthermore, there are foreign missionaries (many from the West) who are purposely following this approach and excluding the title of Jesus being the Son of God in their conversations with both Muslims and converts (disciples). This is a grave error and sin because it goes against the warning in Revelations 22:18-19. The translators and missionaries are liberally removing and/or replacing titles and identities of God the Father and God the Son.

Matthew 3:17 in a Muslim-Compliant Translation would read: *A voice came from heaven saying, This is The Beloved and We are very pleased with him!*

In the ESV Bible, the verse reads: *and behold, a voice from heaven said, "This is my beloved Son, with whom I am well pleased."*

What was an inspired revelation to Peter by the Father is no longer a bold, triumphant proclamation (Matthew 16:13-17). It has now become a shameful and painful text that needs to be edited for today's politically correct and man-fearing Christians.

Does the Bible not say that only he who confesses that Jesus is the Son of God would not only find eternal life, but also abide in Him?

1 John 5:11-12 – And this is the testimony, that God gave us eternal life, and this life is in his Son. Whoever has the Son has life; whoever does not have the Son of God does not have life.

1 John 4:15 - Whoever confesses that Jesus is the Son of God, God abides in him, and he in God.

The Bible states that he who denies the Father and the Son is an antichrist; Muhammad was such a figure 1,400 years ago, and now some in the Church are honoring his erroneous teaching and allowing it to perpetuate even into the gatherings of believers.

1 John 2:22-23 - Who is the liar but he who denies that Jesus is the Christ? This is the antichrist, he who denies the Father and the Son. No one who denies the Son has the Father. Whoever confesses the Son has the Father also.

Even if some Muslims come to faith in Christ without the explicit confession of Him as the Son of God, how will the Church worship together? What if a BMB from a house church that rejects (or omits purposely) the title of Jesus as the Son, emigrates to a foreign country, and eventually comes to worship at a Ukrainian, Latino, Korean, or American church? When the Bible is read from the pulpit, or, a hymn or gospel song is projected on the screen, and the BMB comes across the title of Jesus as the Son of God, will he continue with the worship or react so aversely that he has to leave the service? Or even worse, what if he attacks and condemns the congregation as being blasphemous?

Is the Body of Christ divided? Will one group of congregation exalt and celebrate Jesus as the Son of God while another refuse to acknowledge the title and even condemn it with equal passion? The foreign missionaries amongst Muslim people groups must think carefully and deeply into the future and see the outcome of our approach. More importantly, everything we do and say must bring glory to the Father, Son, and the Holy Spirit. This includes the celebration of the new believer's baptism:

Matthew 28:19 - Go therefore and make disciples of all nations, baptizing them in the name of the Father and of the Son and of the Holy Spirit...

210

42 – Pork or Pornography?

Mark 7:14-23 – And he called the people to him again and said to them, "Hear me, all of you, and understand: There is nothing outside a person that by going into him can defile him, but the things that come out of a person are what defile him." And when he had entered the house and left the people, his disciples asked him about the parable. And he said to them, "Then are you also without understanding? Do you not see that whatever goes into a person from outside cannot defile him, since it enters not his heart but his stomach, and is expelled?" (Thus he declared all foods clean.) And he said, "What comes out of a person is what defiles him. For from within, out of the heart of man, come evil thoughts, sexual immorality, theft, murder, adultery, coveting, wickedness, deceit, sensuality, envy, slander, pride, foolishness. All these evil things come from within, and they defile a person."

Matthew 5:27-28 - "You have heard that it was said, 'You shall not commit adultery.' But I say to you that everyone who looks at a woman with lustful intent has already committed adultery with her in his heart.

One day I stepped into a computer store in our small Central Asian town to purchase blank CDs. I was promptly greeted by two young Muslim men. One was the store owner and the other was his Quranic teacher. When I gave them the usual "assalomu-allaikum" they responded in kind and then asked me if I was a Muslim. I told them "no," and said that I was a "Masihi"—a Christian in Central Asian language. They said something like, "Well, that's too bad. You would be so blessed if you were a Muslim." My immediate response in my head was…you are talking to the wrong guy. So then I asked them a simple question.

Me: "Do you sell pork here?"

MM (Muslim merchant): "Of course not! Pork is haram (unclean). I neither sell nor eat pork."

Me: "But you are selling something worse than pork in your store."

MM: ??? "What's that?"

Me: "Those bad horror movies and pornographic DVDs in your store. If a man is not allowed to eat pork, and he inadvertently does eat some pork, the meat will go out of his system after a few days. And he can ask God to forgive him. But if the man watches a pornographic movie, it will stay in his mind for the rest of his life, tempting him to sin against God. You are selling many bad movies in your store, and even ten-year-old boys are coming in to buy those movies. You are defiling the hearts and minds of the next generation of your people by selling these movies. If I were you, I would get rid of such DVDs. They are worse than pork."

MM: (silence)

A few years ago I asked the same question to a young Pakistani Muslim man living in northern Virginia. He thought about it, and responded that pornography was worse than pork. I asked him "why"…and he could not explain clearly, but he just thought that it was worse than eating pork. (He had been attending evangelistic Bible study at a local church for the past two years.) I told him that I agreed with his answer, and gave him the same explanation as above.

And then he said the following: "I know that Muhammad taught that if you even look at a woman lustfully, you have committed adultery in your heart."

Me: "Oh really? I've read through the Quran, but I don't remember ever reading Muhammad saying those words."

PM (Pakistani Muslim): "Or maybe it's in the hadith. I'm sure Muhammad said that."

Me: "If you ever find the reference in the Quran or the hadith, please tell me. I'd be very interested to find out. But I do know that Jesus said what you just quoted in His Sermon on the Mount. You see, Jesus is our Creator. He made you and me. And because He is our Creator, He knows what is in the heart of a man. He knows that external things (like eating pork) are insignificant compared to what goes in (like pornography) and comes out of our hearts (lust and immorality)."

The Pakistani young man nodded and walked away, deep in thought.

Our desire and aim in conversation with any nonbeliever should be to elevate our Lord Jesus above any man, any religious founder...like Muhammad. Let us remember heroes like King David in his youth; he could not just stand back and watch Goliath defy the God of Israel. God rewarded the young man's passion to lift up the name of Yahweh with an unbelievable defeat of the giant with a stone (1 Samuel 17). Prophet Elijah also wanted to lift up the name and glory of Yahweh above all gods and idols, including Baal. And the Lord honored his desire with a resounding defeat of the prophets of Baal (1 Kings 18). Are you so close in your walk with the risen Lord that you will do anything to lift up the name of Jesus over and above any other name?

43 – Kingdom Detours

Acts 8:26-31 - Now an angel of the Lord said to Philip, "Rise and go toward the south to the road that goes down from Jerusalem to Gaza." This is a desert place. And he rose and went. And there was an Ethiopian, a eunuch, a court official of Candace, queen of the Ethiopians, who was in charge of all her treasure. He had come to Jerusalem to worship and was returning, seated in his chariot, and he was reading the prophet Isaiah. And the Spirit said to Philip, "Go over and join this chariot." So Philip ran to him and heard him reading Isaiah the prophet and asked, "Do you understand what you are reading?" And he said, "How can I, unless someone guides me?" And he invited Philip to come up and sit with him.

Acts 16:6-10 - And they went through the region of Phrygia and Galatia, having been forbidden by the Holy Spirit to speak the word in Asia. And when they had come up to Mysia, they attempted to go into Bithynia, but the Spirit of Jesus did not allow them. So, passing by Mysia, they went down to Troas. And a vision appeared to Paul in the night: a man of Macedonia was standing there, urging him and saying, "Come over to Macedonia and help us." And when Paul had seen the vision, immediately we sought to go on into Macedonia, concluding that God had called us to preach the gospel to them.

It was the spring of 2003, and we had planned to baptize another dozen or so Muslims who had come to faith in Jesus Christ over the winter months. There were young and old, men and women, who were excited about publicly proclaiming through baptism in the near-freezing mountain river that they were now followers of Jesus Christ. They were ready to confess that Jesus Christ is the Son of God (1 John 4:15), and rejoice in the truth that God lives in them. Everyone showed up at the designated bus stop for the final trip to the mountainous region where a river was patiently waiting, being warmed by the late May sun of Central Asia. Everyone was there but Dawud; because of some miscommunication (probably a mispronounced Persian word on my part) he was waiting for our group at the other end of the city. The next day, I met Dawud at the university, realized what had happened, and we decided to set another date to baptize him and possibly another recent convert.

We would be returning to the States for our first furlough, and because of time constraints, we decided that the best venue for the baptism would be at the outdoor pool of a neighbor's house. At about this time, we received an email from Erick Schenkel, the director of the organization that sponsored our visa in the host country. [We are very grateful for the Christ-honoring leadership of Erick. He encouraged us to be bold for the gospel. While most of the organizations placed restrictions on religious activities of the missionaries in order to avoid deportation, Erick and his organization encouraged us to share the gospel boldly. He reminded us that we were in the country for the purpose of sharing Christ, and not for the purpose of preserving our visa.] He asked if we could welcome and receive a short-term missions team of fourteen members from the U.S. The majority of the team were college students from Tennessee...blond and red-haired American youths with a passion for Jesus and love for the lost, and some with thick southern accent. This particular fourteen-member short-term mission team was scheduled to serve the King of kings in China that summer, but due to the SARS (severe acute respiratory syndrome) outbreak in China, they were prohibited from entering that country.

And because the short-term team had already committed their time and resources to prepare for a summer of evangelism, particularly to the college students, the umbrella ministry that was directing their program decided to reroute them to our city in Central Asia. However, because of this unexpected eleventh hour detour, the team members were not happy; rather, some of them were discouraged and disheartened. They had invested valuable time learning Chinese and praying for the Chinese college students, but they were now in a place where chopsticks and the "ni-hao-ma" greeting were no longer useful. As Faith and I prayed for this team, we sensed that the Sovereign Lord was the One who brought them to our city for a special purpose. He was the One who was responsible for their welfare, and eventually, the outcome of their visit. The short-term team needed to submit to God's sovereignty.

And so as we met them at a guesthouse and said a few words of warm greeting in Persian dialect, I told them that it was the Lord of the harvest who brought them here to our city because He had prepared a special assignment for them. I shared about the growing number of believers from Muslim backgrounds who were joining our house church. And as a testimony to that, we invited them to the baptism of Dawud and another man (also a former Muslim) at a nearby house with a pool. And then we surprised the team to a delicious meal of rice pilaf and beef, chicken and lamb kabob.

A few days later Dawud and another man were baptized in the pool. After the baptism, the men in the short-term team joined me in praying for the two converts. As the men prayed, the women were praising and worshiping Jesus in the background in the local language with some of our sisters from our house church. It was a precious and sacred moment.

A week later our family flew back to the U.S. to start our six-month home assignment. The short-term team stayed in our city for the next two months, reaching out to the university students on several campuses. More than a dozen Muslim young men and women came to Christ through their outreach efforts, and in the fall a team of long-term missionaries came to the city to start a permanent ministry base at the campuses.

216

It was just like the apostle Paul being diverted away from Bithynia towards Macedonia by the Holy Spirit. When Paul obeyed and followed the Lord's leading, he was used by God to bring many to salvation and plant house churches in that region, including in the city of Philippi. God diverted the short-term team that was meant to go to China to our Muslim city because there were souls ripe for harvest.

That was not the only time Paul was diverted from his planned course. In Acts 28 we discover that Paul's journey to Rome was diverted to Malta because of a shipwreck. Once on the island, the Lord used Paul to bring heal the sick, including the father of the chief official. Although it was not explicitly written in the Bible, I believe Paul had numerous opportunities to share about Jesus Christ, by whose authority he was able to heal the sick.

Galatians 4:13 - You know it was because of a bodily ailment that I preached the gospel to you at first.

Also, Paul began his ministry in Galatia because of an illness. Perhaps he had originally planned to travel through that region, but an unexpected illness required him to stop and rest. The Lord used this opportunity of Paul's convalescence to launch a network of churches in the region.

Thursday afternoons I am usually at the county jail to lead Bible study with the male inmates. During an eight-month period in 2017, there were a dozen lockdowns. Unexpected events like a medical emergency, inmate conflict, or equipment failure can trigger a lockdown. No outside volunteers are allowed into the facility, and all scheduled programs, including Bible studies, are canceled. During two of those lockdowns, a fellow volunteer and I decided to stay in the lobby to catch up and pray for one another. As we were sharing our prayer requests, both times we met a young male inmate who was just released. Both times we were able to share the gospel, and they came to faith in Christ. Another time, an elderly woman was in the lobby to pick up her granddaughter who was being released. As I gave a tract for her granddaughter, I asked the woman if she had assurance of salvation. She responded with a "No," and the Lord gave me the opportunity to lead her to faith in Christ. If the lockdowns had not happened, I would not have met the three lost sheep who needed to meet their Savior.

The Lord wants us to surrender the detours He places in our lives unto Him so that He can accomplish His purposes. Kingdom detours (like coronavirus pandemic) can often result in a lost sheep finding his or her eternal home. Perhaps the Lord has placed several detours in your life…from the moment you came to faith in Christ until now. Perhaps where you are now is not what was on your mind when you first joined your mission agency. Ask the Lord of the harvest to guide your steps to those places where the lost sheep are ready to hear the voice of Jesus, the Good Shepherd (John 10:16).

44 – Why Did Jesus and Muhammad Come?

John 8:31-36 - So Jesus said to the Jews who had believed him, "If you abide in my word, you are truly my disciples, and you will know the truth, and the truth will set you free." They answered him, "We are offspring of Abraham and have never been enslaved to anyone. How is it that you say, 'You will become free'?" Jesus answered them, "Truly, truly, I say to you, everyone who practices sin is a slave to sin. The slave does not remain in the house forever; the son remains forever. So if the Son sets you free, you will be free indeed."

The Lord has called us to shine His light everywhere we go, even at the new mosque in your neighborhood. Faith and I have been teaching Crescent Project's "BRIDGES" classes (Muslim outreach training seminar) at various churches in our area. After one class, a group of us decided to go on a "prayer walk" at the site of the new mosque in Leesburg. A Muslim group had purchased a plot of land near the airport, and in the coming years they will start building a place for prayer. We asked the Lord to give us the souls of the Muslims who would be gathering at this new mosque (Joshua 1:3). During the prayer walk, a fellow pastor and I decided to go up to the old house on the property and introduce ourselves…in the spirit of Jonathan (1 Samuel 14:6). That afternoon we met Musa, a devout Muslim from Afghanistan who immigrated to America in the 1990s. Several weeks later I paid him a visit with a bag of clementine, persimmons, pomegranates, a Bible, and a copy of the *Life of Jesus* DVD. Musa and I sat down and talked for nearly two hours. As usual, he and I went back and forth in conversation, feverishly trying to convert each other. Near the end of our time, the Holy Spirit guided me to ask a simple question to Musa; God wanted us to focus on the purpose of both Jesus and Muhammad's coming.

Me: "Why do you think Muhammad was born? What was he struggling against throughout his life? Anytime there is a new movement, there will invariably be opposition to that movement. I know that he had mortal enemies whom he slayed with the sword...Jews, Christians and pagans...but did he struggle against anyone else?"

Musa: "Yes. Muhammad also struggled against shaiton. You call him Satan. Everyone has his own struggle against shaiton. We call this the greater jihad."

Me: "Did Muhammad win?"

Musa: "Yes, I believe that he won."

Me: "But how could he have won? He is dead and buried. His tomb is in Medina. He did not win, but lost, because he remains dead. Let me tell you what Jesus came to struggle against. Jesus came to us 2000 years ago not to fight against any mortal enemy. At the time of His coming, the Jews were suffering under the oppressive rule of the Roman Empire. But He did not overthrow the Roman government. With one breath He could have slayed every Roman soldier in Israel, just like the angel of God that put to death 185,000 Assyrian soldiers during Hezekiah's time (Isaiah 37). But He did not come to fight against men. He came to fight against something that we could not. Can I show you what His enemies were? Can you read from these few verses in the Bible? First from John 8:31-36."

Musa: " '...truly, truly, I say to you, everyone who practices sin is a slave to sin...' What does it mean that everyone who sins is a slave to sin?"

Me: "The Bible tells us that when we sin, we are slaves to sin. You and I don't want to sin, but something keeps us in bondage so that we do things that we don't want to do. We want to live a pleasing life to God, but we end up sinning against Him. Jesus came to set us free from such slavery. He accomplished this on the cross. If you read the Bible, it will explain how Jesus did this. Now can you read from Hebrews 2:14-15?"

Musa: "Since therefore the children share in flesh and blood, he himself likewise partook of the same things, that through death he might destroy the one who has the power of death, that is, the devil, and deliver all those who through fear of death were subject to lifelong slavery."

Me: "The Bible also tells us that Jesus came to set us free from Satan and slavery to fear of death. And Jesus won...because He rose again from the dead on the third day. His tomb in Jerusalem is empty. Jesus came to fight against and conquer an enemy that has defeated every man since the time of Adam."

Musa was intrigued by this concept that Jesus came to fight not against flesh and blood, not against the Roman or any other empire, but against powers that we cannot see. I gave him a copy of the Bible as a gift, and encouraged him to read from the Book of John.

As ambassadors of Jesus Christ, we must continually pursue what Paul confessed in Philippians 3:10 - *that I may know him and the power of his resurrection, and may share his sufferings, becoming like him in his death.*

It is only through our personal relationship, encounter, and intimacy with the Risen Christ that we can lift Him up above all else in our conversation with the lost world. If the supremacy of Christ is firmly fixed in our hearts, then we will not tolerate anyone or anything claiming to be His equal, or even greater. We will do our best to exalt His name to the highest place. Do you love your Lord? Are you jealous for His glory? Or are you ashamed to mention the name of Jesus in the midst of those who are hostile towards our Lord? Repent, and ask the Lord to come to you and strengthen your love for Him, and He will come to you as He came to Peter in John 21.

45 – Our Last Communion Together

Luke 22:14-18 - And when the hour came, he reclined at table, and the apostles with him. And he said to them, "I have earnestly desired to eat this Passover with you before I suffer. For I tell you I will not eat it until it is fulfilled in the kingdom of God." And he took a cup, and when he had given thanks he said, "Take this, and divide it among yourselves. For I tell you that from now on I will not drink of the fruit of the vine until the kingdom of God comes."

The first time I met Boris was in the fall of 2009, in the village of Living Water. He was ethnically Russian, but grew up and worked mostly in this Central Asian republic. He had studied at Moscow University and was a respected journalist during Soviet times. He had been single all his life; he had chosen career over romance or family. A year before we met, he had decided to retire from newspaper journalism and settle down in Living Water. He had heard about church meetings at the community center that I visited once a month to teach the Bible. A group of expatriate missionaries and local church leaders took turns teaching Bible every weekend at the Living Water community center. The first time he had heard about the church meetings, he made a visit to the community center. The director of the center, a former Muslim and now a devout Christian, was suspicious of the old Russian man, and denied that there were church meetings at the center. A few years later, he again heard rumors about the church meetings, and so he came and knocked on the community center on the night that I was teaching on the passage from John 6:35 where Jesus proclaims that He is the Bread of Life.

Boris took a seat amongst a dozen other people in the room, most of whom were already believers. My message was simple…Jesus is the only bread that will satisfy the hunger of our souls. As Boris listened, he felt like the Bible study was all about his life. He had been chasing after the bread that spoils...bread that never satisfies the longings of his heart. He needed the eternal, life-giving bread. That evening Boris surrendered His life to Jesus.

Over the next few weeks, Boris' faith grew in great strides. Because God had blessed him with a sharp mind and elite education, Boris was able to read through the Bible, commentaries and theological books very rapidly. He also had musical talent, and within a month he was leading worship with me with his guitar. But what was most amazing about Boris' faith was his humble and servant attitude, much like his Savior. There was a Russian woman about fifteen years younger than he who was part of the church at Living Water. Her name was Sonya. She was illiterate and was never married; yet, she had an eight-year-old son from a past relationship. She and her son were living in the shed of a town drunkard; they hardly owned a few change of clothes. She had come to faith in Christ few years prior, but there was no joy in her face when we first met her. She knew that she had ill reputation in the village, and brought that mask of shame with her into the church.

Boris began to take interest in Sonya. He understood very quickly that the Lord had shown him unconditional love and mercy, and now he was to share his blessing with others. He took time to check into Sonya's background, and even though she was not the kind of woman he would have courted thirty years ago, his new life in Christ opened his heart towards this "Samaritan woman at the well." Over the next few months, Boris and Sonya continued to deepen in their relationship, and the two eventually decided to get married. Our family was invited to the wedding ceremony; it was a glorious and blessed celebration of a couple much like Ruth and Boaz of the Old Testament. Ever since Boris poured out his love and affection on Sonya, her countenance began to change. She had more joy and confidence in her face. She and her son also began to dress better, and with improved diet, the Lord renewed their health. Boris also began to help the son with his school work, and his grades improved from D's and F's to A's and B's. The Lord had blessed Boris with new life, and in turn Boris decided to share this blessing with a woman and her son who had been scorned and rejected by the people of the village.

A few weeks before we left Central Asia, Boris called me with a special request. He asked me if I would baptize him, since he came to Christ through me. He knew that our family was leaving the country soon, and we had announced that on our last Sunday worship at Living Water, we would celebrate the Lord's Supper. He wanted to be baptized so that he can partake in the Lord's Supper with me and other believers at the house church.

There was need for caution, however; the local majority people group had overthrown the corrupt president a few weeks prior, and there was a strong sentiment of nationalism. In the weeks subsequent to the revolution, minority people groups were violently attacked and even killed. Since I was Korean and he was Russian, we did not know what the local people would do if they witnessed baptism in a lake. However, we decided that God who had brought Boris to Christ would be more than able to protect him. On a bright, sunny Friday at a nearby lake, Boris was baptized in the name of the Father, and the Son, and the Holy Spirit…it was a joyful and peaceful celebration.

The following Sunday we had our last worship with the believers of Living Water church. Boris and Sonya were with us. As we celebrated the Lord's Supper, I could see tears of joy in Boris. I had led many communions before, but this particular celebration in Living Water was perhaps one of the most meaningful and glorious.

As you disciple the local believers, there will be opportunities for you to live out your faith boldly with them. How is the Lord inviting you to do that today?

46 – God's Provision for Our Children

Isaiah 54:13 - All your children shall be taught by the LORD, and great shall be the peace of your children.

During our four years at Columbia Biblical Seminary, the Lord opened the door for my wife to start homeschooling our children. We knew that the Lord could send us to remote parts of the Muslim world where there would not be any access to international (or missionary kids) school. And after hearing numerous negative testimonies of boarding schools for missionary children, we decided that we would keep our children with us, at least until college. Hence the only option for our family would be homeschooling if there were no missionary kids (MK) schools nearby.

Although my wife graduated cum laude from Massachusetts College of Pharmacy with a bachelor's degree in pharmacy and worked as a pharmacist for ten years, she still felt inadequate to teach her own children. She would be responsible for their academic and holistic training that would greatly impact their lives. But after much prayer, and encouraged by the testimonies and prayers of homeschooling moms in our seminary community, Faith began taking small steps into the realm of homeschooling. She observed other moms, especially missionaries on furlough, teaching their children at home using a variety of curriculum.

And so Faith began to homeschool our two sons from their kindergarten years. Initially, they enrolled in the neighborhood elementary school, but my wife would supplement their education in the afternoon using Christian-based curriculum. By the time we left the seminary and came back to northern Virginia for fund raising and preparation for the mission field, Faith was fully engaged in homeschooling our three children: Joniel (age seven) in second grade, Josiah (age six) in first grade, and Karis (age three) in pre-kindergarten.

As our family was making the final preparation steps for departure to the field in the summer of 2000, some of our friends and church leaders showed their growing concern for our children's education. We were residents of Fairfax County, Virginia, and at that time, the public school system of this county was rated top in the nation. Some church members suggested that we leave our kids in the U.S. with them so that our children can receive proper education like other children. Others suggested that we either send our children to one of the boarding schools in nearby countries, or move only to a city where there is a well-established international (MK) school. Otherwise, they argued, our children may not be able to study at a well-known college (like University of Virginia)...they may only qualify to study at a community college. We responded by saying that the Lord has called our entire family, including the children, as Christ's ambassadors to the Muslim world to the city or town that He would designate, and that we would trust Him to raise up our children through homeschooling. One elderly deaconess said quietly with compassion, "Those poor kids. What sins have they committed that they must leave a blessed country like America and go to a hostile land and miss out on good education? I will pray for your children faithfully."

For those of you who are not Korean, you must understand that quality education is very important to us. We want our children to excel in schools...that's why people call us "A-sians" and not "B-sians" or "C-sians." Getting straight "A's" on report cards are expected from our children...so that they can study at Ivy League schools and become successful engineers, doctors, and lawyers.

During our ten years in Central Asia, there were several moments when Faith was struggling as a homeschool teacher. She felt inadequate in some of the subjects, and at the end of almost every school year, she would confess that she cannot continue. Words of doubt from some of the church members would echo in her mind, and she was fearful that perhaps they were right. What if our children are barely able to study at a community college when they finish 12th grade?

My role, as the principal of our homeschool, was to encourage my star teacher (my only teacher) and take her out on a lunch or dinner date every week to show my appreciation for her labor of love. The Lord also provided short-term missionaries who came to help with our homeschooling endeavors.

It was during this period that the Lord gave my wife the promise of Isaiah 54:13 concerning our three kids. He told her that He would watch over their education…and that He would take care of their future.

Faith continued to homeschool all three children until our oldest finished 9th grade. The Lord also provided opportunities for our children to study at the local (Russian-speaking) schools. Eventually, they would become fluent in Russian. By the time Joniel began 8th grade, I had to take on the role of teaching advanced math and sciences, and both Faith and I felt the tension of not having enough time for ministry to the Muslims and BMBs around us. Hence, after much prayer and thought, we decided to relocate to a city where there was an MK (international) school. The final three years of education for our children was at this MK school. Our children were blessed to have dedicated volunteer teachers from all over the world. The MK school also provided opportunities to engage in extracurricular activities like organized sports (soccer and basketball) and school drama.

In the fall of 2009, Joniel began applying to the universities in the U.S. By God's grace, he was accepted to several top universities in Virginia, including the University of Virginia (UVA). Both my wife and I were praising the Lord with tears in our eyes…truly He was watching over our children with favor. As the deadline for choosing a university drew near, we were faced with the challenge of paying for his tuition. Obviously, our monthly missionary support level was not enough to meet the $45,000 annual fee. Joniel applied for financial aid with UVA, and a staff from the administrative office emailed me within a week. She inquired about the discrepancy in addresses supplied to the university; our mailing address showed northern Virginia, but our residential address reflected a city in Central Asia. I explained that the mailing address (for correspondence purposes) was that of my younger brother (who held the power-of-attorney privilege on behalf of our family), but we actually lived and worked overseas for ten years. In her follow up email, she asked what we had been doing in Central Asia for all those years? I explained that my wife and I had lived and worked in Virginia for many years before going to Central Asia as missionaries. I also explained that in every Central Asian city where we lived, I taught engineering classes as a guest professor at the local university.

Two weeks later, we received an amazing email from UVA. They decided to consider our son, Joniel, as in-state resident (which reduced tuition by half), and furthermore, the school would provide full coverage for his college expenses. While the four of us were clapping and shouting with joy, my wife, the homeschool teacher, was crying with thanksgiving. Truly, the Lord was faithful, and redeemed her many years of labor and perseverance as a homeschool teacher.

The following year, our second son, Josiah, was also accepted to the University of Virginia, and again, with full financial coverage. Three years later, our daughter Karis was accepted to Princeton University, and again with full financial coverage.

Homeschooling is not for everyone. Some missionaries will have to enroll their children in nearby MK schools or even in a boarding school. They will have to hear from the Lord on what to do with their own children. But in every process of decision-making, may the primary determining factor be the pursuit of God's Kingdom and His righteousness, and not the children's education.

I have seen some missionaries from non-U.S. countries come to Central Asia not only to serve the Lord on the field but also to enroll their children in English-speaking schools, including the MK school where our children attended. For these missionaries, their children are being given a privilege or luxury that would be unattainable in their home country. Quality education at a MK school can easily be a bridge to studying at colleges in the US. When persecution mounts and the authorities become hostile towards the gospel, with increasing cases of deportation of missionaries, some of these missionaries will desist from all religious activity. They do not want to jeopardize their visa status and the future of their children's education. If they are deported, then they must face the possibility of returning to their home country where the children will not be able to survive in the highly competitive public school environment. Hence many missionaries decide to stay "hidden" until the environment is safe for ministry; however, such seasons may never come again in any given Muslim country. Sadly, they are putting their children's education and future above the advancement of God's Kingdom. Have you entrusted your children's education and future into the Lord's hands?

47 – The Blessing of Bethel Haven

Matthew 6:31-33 - Therefore do not be anxious, saying, 'What shall we eat?' or 'What shall we drink?' or 'What shall we wear?' For the Gentiles seek after all these things, and your heavenly Father knows that you need them all. But seek first the kingdom of God and his righteousness, and all these things will be added to you.

As we were getting married in 1991, I told Faith that we would not be buying a home in America. We had looked at some new townhomes for sale, but we decided that it would be better to pay off our student and car loans and other outstanding debts before heading off to the mission field. We also decided to support our widowed mothers each month from our salary, in honor of their labor of love in raising us in a foreign land. We knew that once we became fulltime missionaries, it would be challenging to support them financially, so we decided to bless them as much as we could while we had the financial ability.

I also believed that if we bought a home, we would soon fill it up with nice furniture. If we were renting, then we didn't mind furnishing it with secondhand items from the local thrift store. But once we own a home, we would be tempted to furnish it with more "permanent" and presentable furniture, which could easily cost up to thousands of dollars. Also, renting would allow us the flexibility of quickly moving to another state or country. Finally, if we owned a home in the U.S., our hearts would be tied to America. Should anything happen on the mission field, we would be tempted to turn back and go to our "real home." If we didn't own a home in the U.S., we would consider the place where Jesus took us to be our home here on earth.

I promised my wife that if we ever bought our own home, it would be on the mission field. As I had shared in an earlier chapter, we had the opportunity to purchase and own a nice mud-brick home on the field for about $10,000. We had to sell it rather abruptly when we were deported from our host country; for the rest of our time in Central Asia we lived in rented homes.

In 2008 we let our mission agency and home church leaders know that we would be coming back to the U.S. in 2010 to put our first son into college. We planned on staying for a year, during which time our second son (a high school senior) would apply to college. After that furlough year we would return to the field with our daughter.

In the spring of 2010 we heard from our church leaders that there was not a guest missionary house for our family. We would have to manage the rental costs ourselves. We were paying $500 per month for our three-bedroom in Central Asian home. In the northern Virginia area, we would have to pay four times that amount for a three-bedroom apartment. (Thankfully, our support team at our sending church managed to find enough funds in our account to help us cover for the one-year rent for a small townhome near the church.)

When I first heard the news that we had no guesthouse waiting for us in the U.S., I was discouraged. We had put in a request for a church-owned guest home for missionaries like us when we returned for the long (one-year) furlough, but that did not happen. I shared the news with my wife, and she also was disappointed. But that evening, after dinner was over and the table was cleared, we opened our Bibles for family devotion. We read from Matthew 6:25-34, especially focusing on verse 33: *But seek first the kingdom of God and his righteousness, and all these things will be added to you.*

And I said to my family, "This promise is from Jesus, not from our home church or mission agency. We left everything in America to follow Jesus to the mission field, and now we are going back to America to put Joniel into college. But the church tells us that we have no home for us. Since Jesus made the promise to provide for our needs, if He were to give us a home, what would you like in a home?" And I directed the question to the youngest first.

Karis (age thirteen) said that she wanted a swimming pool. Josiah (age sixteen) asked for a large yard where dogs can run around. Joniel (age seventeen) asked for lots of trees; Central Asia lacks lush, green forests. Faith asked for hardwood floors, and I asked for a brick home. We had lived four years in a trailer home while at seminary in South Carolina, and I remember the whole structure shaking whenever a violent thunderstorm passed through. We wrote down the requests on a whiteboard, held hands together, and prayed to Jesus. And we forgot about this prayer request until a couple of years later...

We moved back to the NoVA (northern Virginia) in the summer of 2010, stayed a few days at a hotel near the church, and graciously the Lord led us to a three-bedroom townhome for $2,000 per month. With the generosity of our home church, we were able to stay in the townhome for the first year. After that, we were on our own, and we knew that our monthly missionary support level was not enough to cover for the rental. By God's grace my parents had left us a sum of money as inheritance, but that fund was quickly drying up as we stayed another year at the same townhome.

[In another chapter I explain how the Lord led us to stay in America and reach out to the immigrants and refugees who are coming to this nation. I also left Pioneers and joined Crescent Project, since the latter was focused on equipping and mobilizing the churches of America to engage with the Muslims in their neighborhood.]

In the fall of 2011 we were desperately looking for a three-bedroom apartment or home with less than $1,000 monthly rental fee, and we could not find any in the NoVA region. Fairly soon we would have to move to another state or become homeless.

It was about this time that my old colleague from the engineering firm that I had previously worked at gave me a call. His name is Bob, a dear, white brother in the Lord, about ten years older, and a gifted engineer. He and his wife met us for dinner a day before we flew out to Asia to lead a retreat for a group of missionaries engaged with North Koreans. After the meal, Bob asked us how he and his wife could help us in our ministry. We had known them for over twenty years, and they had been faithful prayer and financial partners during that time.

We told them that the ministry to the Muslims and churches were going well, but the great need was for a home that we could rent for less than $1,000 a month. Bob and his wife exchanged a warm glance, and then looked at us with a smile. He told us that over the years, the Lord had blessed him and his wife to build a new home in southern part of Virginia. They were living in their new home, but the first home, which they had built with their own hands about thirty years ago, was empty. [He is the original "Bob-the-Builder."] Bob asked if we would like to live in his old home? He said that we would not have to pay any rent; just pay the utilities, home insurance and the property tax…which adds up to about $1,000. And then he said we could stay in his home as long as we want. We can live in this house until Jesus comes back!

A few weeks later, Faith and I made the drive out to Leesburg, to the house that Bob and his wife built. And guess what? It is a beautiful two-story brick house with four bedrooms. Except for the lobby, kitchen and bathrooms, all the rooms have hardwood flooring. The house sits on ten acres of land with lots of trees (evergreens, oaks, and other kinds that I have yet to identify), and two acres of open field (lawn) and even has a swimming pool. [Before leaving for the mission field, we had visited Bob's home before, but there was no swimming pool at the time. It was an addition to the property years after the house was built.] A year after we moved into the house, our neighbor blessed us with a puppy as a gift.

We named the house "Bethel Haven." In Hebrew, Bethel means the house of God. Truly, this was the house that God gave us. The Lord Jesus met our every request that we had written on the whiteboard in our Central Asian home a few months before we left the field. I want to state clearly that it was not our faith or prayer that made this house possible, but the faithfulness of our Lord Jesus Christ to His promises. He is trustworthy; His promises are true. Quite often, however, we missionaries choose to trust our own logic, ability and strength…and so we will fix and flip homes on the field instead of trusting the Lord to provide wherever we go.

During our ten years in Central Asia, there were several times when my wife would ask me if we did the right thing in not buying a home in the U.S. before we left for the mission field. We were meeting many missionaries who owned houses or condominiums back in their home country, and they seemed to have peace that comes from that knowledge. Others were feverishly fixing and flipping homes to be able to purchase a home upon their return to their home country. Faith thought that perhaps we had made a mistake not to buy a home in the US. At those moments, which were sometimes two or three o'clock in the morning, I would tell her: "I believe that because we left everything to follow Jesus to the mission field, He will give us a home when we go back to the US. There will be one person who comes to us and says, 'I have two homes. Would you like to live in the second home?'"

And that's exactly how the Lord provided for our family. Bob came to us and offered his second home. I know that there were many members of my home church who owned several real estate properties when we returned from the field; but the Lord did not provide us a home through them. Rather, God chose a man who, in his intimate relationship with the Lord, heard from the Holy Spirit and blessed others as he was led. The Holy Spirit has given him the gift of giving, and he and his wife exercised

234

that gift in accordance with the leading of the Holy Spirit. Is this not the way that the body of Christ should function?

Perhaps you are the missionary on the field, not knowing what will happen twenty years from now when you return to your home country. You may not have a house that you purchased before you left the field, nor a large sum of money to make such purchase possible. Will you trust the Lord to provide for you, per His promise in Matthew 6:33?

And if you are that person with two (or more) homes, would you prayerfully consider blessing a returning missionary family with your extra home so that the Lord's promise can be fulfilled through you (Acts 4:32-37)?

48 – Honoring the Lord

Isaiah 58:13-14 - "If you turn back your foot from the Sabbath, from doing your pleasure on my holy day, and call the Sabbath a delight and the holy day of the Lord honorable; if you honor it, not going your own ways, or seeking your own pleasure, or talking idly; then you shall take delight in the Lord, and I will make you ride on the heights of the earth; I will feed you with the heritage of Jacob your father, for the mouth of the Lord has spoken."
Malachi 3:8 - Will man rob God? Yet you are robbing me. But you say, 'How have we robbed you?' In your tithes and contributions.

A few months after we moved into Bethel Haven, my wife and I were driving home after church service on a rainy Sunday. Both our sons were studying at UVA, and one of them needed a dresser for his room. As we turned into a neighborhood road, we noticed signs for yard sale, and we stopped at the house to look for a bargain dresser. Although we did not find a dresser, we did purchase two ornamental plaster pillars for our plants in our dining room. We were able to buy them at half price (saved $40 total), and we proudly brought them into our home. [A Korean proverb: If you unsheathe your sword, at least sharpen a pencil before you put the sword away.] Half an hour later, lightning struck a tree that stood next to our garage...the flash of light and the resounding thunder shook our home. The tree had fallen away from home, and we thanked God for His protection. The next morning, I went out to open the garage door, and the automatic door opener had been damaged by the electrical surge. Just then, the Lord placed this thought in my heart: "The $40 you saved from the yard sale is nothing compared to what it will cost to fix the garage door. Do not do as you please on My Day." It would have cost at least $200 to fix the garage door; I decided not to fix it so that every time I open and close the door

236

manually, I am reminded of this lesson from the Lord. The Lord wants me to honor Him on the His Day. He does not want me to do as I please on His Day.

Just because we are "missionaries," we do not have the privilege to skip out on Sunday worship at church (whether at the local house church or with your team of missionary friends) and have devotion by ourselves on the plane, listening to a sermon by John Piper, Tim Keller, or Gary Hamrick, and consider that to be worship. This was a big issue with the missionaries on the field. We often noticed missionaries' cavalier attitude towards the Lord's day, and missionary families would travel or even go skiing on Sundays* (see anecdote below). As spiritual leaders (whether overseas or here), what we do sets a precedent for our disciples and peers...our children, our network of Christian friends, and even BMBs.

I offer the following four reasons for honoring the Lord's Day and worshiping with the body of believers near you.

First, we need to maintain our intimacy with God in our personal walk of faith...and that includes honoring the Lord's Day. God commanded His people to work six days and then rest and worship Him on the seventh (Fourth Commandment in Exodus 20). Jesus regularly went to the local synagogue to join the local congregation in their worship of the Father (Luke 4:16)...and it was His custom. The Old Testament tradition was to set aside one out of seven days. The New Testament way is to meet daily as a body of believers (Acts 2:46). Either way, the encouragement is to meet for corporate worship and fellowship at least once a week. This is to be practiced not out of legalism, but because we love Jesus (John 14:21), and we know that God is honored when we worship Him corporately (Hebrews 10:24,25; Acts 2). We have been called out of the kingdom of darkness to declare the praises of our Savior to one another and to those still living in darkness (1 Peter 2:9,10).

Second, if we are going to lead and disciple others, especially Muslim converts, then we should model a life of faith (with integrity) that does honor the Lord by joining in worship with the local body of Christ. If we believe in the importance and necessity of the local church and our commitment to its existence, purpose, and role, then we should live out what we teach and believe. This may mean making sacrifices of time and convenience in order to honor God and the local church. As missionaries, we should not plan on traveling to resorts for pleasure or staying home to watch sports games on Sundays.

Third, as we honor the Lord and put Him first in all things (Matthew 6:33), I believe that the Lord will bless our ministry and family endeavors. This is the principle that I (and my wife) have been following since heading off to seminary in 1995. As we tried our best to seek God's Kingdom and His righteousness first in our ministry setting (and we are guilty of falling short here and there), He has blessed us with fruit in our ministry as well as provision for our family in amazing ways.

Fourth, on the mission field, some of the missionaries would reference Romans 14:5 and argue that worshiping specifically on Sunday is not binding...every day is to be treated with honor. And yet, the reality is that in most countries (except for some Muslim nations), Sunday is the only day off for the entire family (i.e., no school or work). And so the kids can join their parents and come to the house church and worship only on Sundays. This was true of our experience in Central Asia (post-Soviet countries). Furthermore, would that missionary then choose to meet consistently for worship on another day? Or would he join worship at a local church at his convenience? And what if he starts a house church, and his own disciples opt to come irregularly to weekly worship because of their commitments to extended family gatherings, town events, weddings, and even children's sports games...how would he feel? I am so thankful that the missionaries who came to

Korea (many from the U.S.) taught fervently to honor the Lord on Sunday, and modeled such convictions themselves. The legacy of their faith is seen through the Church of Korea even today (over 26,000 full time missionaries from South Korea according to a report in 2016). My own father (conservative Presbyterian pastor) did not allow us to go to the theaters or even dine at restaurants on Sundays, definitely no long distance traveling on Sundays unless it was an emergency. Perhaps that's why God honored him with much fruit over the forty years of his ministry in North Korea, South Korea, and the U.S. And I must confess that I am no way near the spiritual maturity of my father.

This chapter is an exhortation to love the Lord our God with all our heart, soul, and mind (Matthew 22:37), including through corporate worship on Sundays with our family and friends. How are you honoring the Lord on His Day? Is it a day of worship and rest, or a day to catch up on errands, football games, bargain shopping, or doing other activities per your pleasure?

In the winter of 2009 our family decided to join three other missionary families on a weekend skiing trip. (We were all serving in the same Central Asian city at the time.) The plan was that we would arrive at the resort on Friday and leave on Sunday afternoon. When we looked at the schedule, there was no time for corporate worship on Sunday morning. The three families had planned on skiing on Sunday morning (to get the most time on the slopes)...as was their custom. We talked to the parents, and eventually, we compromised by having a short worship on Saturday evening. (We were all tired and sore after a day of skiing and snow boarding. Some of the kids were nodding off as we worshiped corporately at 9 p.m. on Saturday night. We gave God our "leftovers".) And then we all went to bed, looking forward to another day of fun on the slopes. That night an extremely cold front descended from the north and temperatures fell to −30' Celsius. All four families drove diesel-engine vans, and none of them started the next morning. (A firm reminder from God that He was still sovereign.) Our vehicles didn't start until Sunday afternoon...too late to go to the slopes. We didn't have another worship service that morning, but it turned out to be a very restful time catching up on sleep, taking leisurely strolls in the snow-covered fields, and having fellowship with one another. Some took time to sing worship songs together and pray for each other in smaller groups. We drove home that afternoon feeling well rested.

49 – Birth of i43 Ministry

Isaiah 43:6-7,21 - I will say to the north, Give up, and to the south, Do not withhold;

bring my sons from afar and my daughters from the end of the earth, everyone who is called by my name, whom I created for my glory, whom I formed and made... the people whom I formed for myself that they might declare my praise.

Isaiah 56:6-7 - "And the foreigners who join themselves to the LORD, to minister to him, to love the name of the LORD, and to be his servants, everyone who keeps the Sabbath and does not profane it, and holds fast my covenant— these I will bring to my holy mountain, and make them joyful in my house of prayer; their burnt offerings and their sacrifices will be accepted on my altar; for my house shall be called a house of prayer for all peoples."

Acts 17: 26-27 - And he made from one man every nation of mankind to live on all the face of the earth, having determined allotted periods and the boundaries of their dwelling place, that they should seek God, and perhaps feel their way toward him and find him. Yet he is actually not far from each one of us...

When we returned to the U.S. in the summer of 2010, our plan was to stay one year to help our first son adjust to college life and our second son to apply for college. However, within the first few months, the Lord redirected our focus away from Central Asia to the US. As I was helping with the weekly ministries at my home church in Herndon, VA, I began to hear rumors about a mosque in our neighborhood. I had not seen any minarets or anything that resembled a mosque, so one day I decided to walk around the streets adjacent to our church. Eventually, I was led to a small house about a hundred meters down the street from our church.

When I knocked on the door, a young bearded man greeted me with a smile. I introduced myself as one of the pastors from the huge Korean church down the street. And his surprising reply: "Nice to meet you. My name is Tolib. I am the priest of this mosque, and I am a missionary to your country." When I heard the phrase "missionary to your country," I was both shocked and a bit flustered. (The Muslims are now sending missionaries to my home country!) But it was as if the Lord wanted to open my eyes to the reality of global migration and the spread of Islam in the West. While the Church of America was sending missionaries to Muslim countries, they were sending missionaries to the U.S.

Tolib was the imam (priest) of the local Ahmadiyya Muslim Community in Herndon. He was born in Pakistan but grew up in Germany. [Ahmadiyya Muslims are considered cults by the orthodox Muslims, and are heavily persecuted in Pakistan. Hence the diaspora of the Ahmadiyya community to Europe and North America.] Tolib had been serving as a cleric for about a year, but the house mosque was in existence for several years. And somehow our Korean church, with about 2,500 members in the Korean congregation and over 600 in the English congregation, was not aware of their presence nor engaged in outreach to their Muslim neighbors with the gospel of Jesus Christ.

During our first meeting, which easily ran two hours, Tolib and I strove to convert each other. I began to realize that he had read portions of the Bible, and he understood that I had read through the Quran (in English) in my studies of his religion. Neither of us converted, of course, but we decided to exchange phone numbers and meet again soon.

The next week we met at a nearby Starbucks (always a good place to connect with Muslims). Before stepping into the café, I prayed to God to somehow reveal Himself to Tolib, and also give me the right words to say to him. What could I say to this Pakistani imam so that he could begin to understand that Jesus Christ is God, not just a prophet?

As we sat down together with coffee in our hands, the Holy Spirit planted a question in my mind. So I asked Tolib: "You are the priest of a house mosque, and I am a pastor at a Korean church. What do you think is the greatest threat to your religion in America?"

He looked a bit puzzled and smiled and didn't say a word beyond a quiet "I don't know." So I decided to answer for him. "It's not the FBI nor the CIA. It's not the Christians nor the Jews, nor even the Republican Party. Let me show you what is the greatest threat to Islam here in America. And the answer is found here in the Injil in Matthew 6:24."

And I opened up the Bible to Matthew and asked him to read the verse:

No one can serve two masters, for either he will hate the one and love the other, or he will be devoted to the one and despise the other. You cannot serve God and money.

Tolib still looked more puzzled after reading the verse, so I explained to him the words of Jesus. "When Jesus spoke these words of warning, He was speaking to His followers, His disciples. He could have pointed at Hinduism, Confucianism, Buddhism, or any other 'ism' that existed at the time, but He did not see them as the real threat to His Kingdom. He knew that money would be the greatest threat to His followers in loving and serving God. Look at the Church of America. We are so busy following the American Dream that we can give God only one to two hours on a Sunday. The rest of the time we are busy working to make payments on unnecessary purchases that we've made in pursuit of the American Dream. This is crippling the Church of America. I believe that Jesus is our Creator. He is God. And because He made us, He knows what we will struggle with, and appropriately warned us against the idolatry of money."

When I said these words, Tolib nodded and was honest enough to admit that his house mosque has registered membership of 800, but on a given Friday only 200 show up for prayer. As soon as his members buy a luxury car of a nice home, he does not see them any more…maybe they show up during Ramadan. And then Tolib asked me if he could preach on this topic at his mosque on Friday?

I smiled and told him, "Of course! As long as you give credit to the one who spoke those words." He said that he would, and even took a copy of the Bible as a gift from me. I knew that Muhammad uttered no words equivalent to what Jesus said in Matthew 6:24. Muhammad told his followers that if you are a good Muslim, Allah will bless you with the riches of the world. Jesus says just the opposite, warning His followers against the riches of the world that can easily make them go astray.

Tolib asked if we could meet again in the future. We met about five more times, including a time of marriage counseling over lunch with both our wives present. He and his wife had been married less than a year, and they appreciated our words of advice and counsel from nearly twenty years of marriage. His wife especially loved the passages from Ephesians 5, 1 Corinthians 13, and Proverbs 18:22 concerning how the husbands are to view and treat their wives.

Eventually, Tolib was reassigned to Europe, and we had to end our regular Bible study meetings on the teachings of Jesus. He did not come to faith in Jesus before he left, but I prayed that the Lord would soon open his heart to the gospel so that he and his household would be saved.

It was during these few months of interaction with Tolib that the Lord prompted me to seek His face concerning our next season of ministry. Faith and I began to attend early morning prayer service at a nearby Korean church. We also began to fast and pray once a week, and the Lord led me to the passage of Isaiah 43. He revealed to me that He was bringing the nations to the US, especially Muslims like

Tolib and his Muslim community, so that they could have the opportunity to hear the good news (Acts 17:26,27). If they remained in their home country of Pakistan, Syria or China, these lost people may never hear about Jesus. The Lord led us to stay in the U.S. and minister to the refugees and immigrants from all over the world. Subsequently, we launched a non-profit ministry called "i43" to fulfill the Great Commission, both here in the U.S. and overseas.

As the Lord is stirring up the nations, sending some unreached people groups to come in contact with you, would you join Him in seeking after the lost sheep? Perhaps there are refugees whom you are encountering even on the mission field. Ask the Holy Spirit to open the door for you to reach out to such "aliens," even as you and I are also aliens here on earth (1 Peter 2:11; Hebrews 11:13-16).

50 – Elijahs and Obadiahs

1 Kings 18:1-4 - After many days the word of the LORD came to Elijah, in the third year, saying, "Go, show yourself to Ahab, and I will send rain upon the earth." So Elijah went to show himself to Ahab. Now the famine was severe in Samaria. And Ahab called Obadiah, who was over the household. (Now Obadiah feared the LORD greatly, and when Jezebel cut off the prophets of the LORD, Obadiah took a hundred prophets and hid them by fifties in a cave and fed them with bread and water.)

Romans 14:4 - Who are you to pass judgment on the servant of another? It is before his own master - that he stands or falls. And he will be upheld, for the Lord is able to make him stand.

During our ministry years in one of the capital cities of Central Asia, I heard a very insightful sermon from the pastor of the International Church. He and his wife were from Scotland, and both had served faithfully on the field for many years. The sermon text was from 1 Kings 18, and he began to describe the important ministry of both Elijah and Obadiah. Prophet Elijah was the one who had a very spectacular ministry, chosen and empowered by God's Spirit to challenge and defeat the prophets of Baal. God even sent a private limousine in the form of a fiery chariot to whisk him away to glory. Obadiah, however, was not as well known. His name is mentioned in only a few verses, not over several chapters like Elijah. However, the Lord acknowledges him as a devout believer and one who feared God. And as a faithful servant of the Lord serving in the palace of Ahab, the King of Israel, Obadiah risked his life and position to hide a hundred prophets of the Lord. We can only imagine the challenge and struggle of Obadiah in the court of a very wicked and idolatrous king.

The Scottish pastor then addressed a very common problem that he has been observing on the mission field.

He grouped the expatriate missionaries into two categories: the Elijahs and the Obadiahs. The Elijahs are typically bold (even in public ministry), have strong convictions, and willing to take risks in ministry for the sake of the gospel. The Obadiahs are typically quiet about their faith in the public and their level of ministry engagement is geared towards longevity on the mission field...for the sake of the gospel. Both groups are on the mission field for the sake of the gospel; however, because their approaches differ, there often arise tension, criticism, and conflict between the two.

Generally, the Elijahs would label the Obadiahs as being fearful, slow in action, and even compromising. In response, the Obadiahs would criticize the Elijahs as being unwise and too aggressive, and a threat to the security of other missionaries on the field. The pastor reminded all the missionaries attending the service that morning to appreciate each other's ministry and to cease placing harsh judgments on one another.

My wife and I place ourselves in the Elijah category, and the Lord challenged us to appreciate and be thankful for the ministries of the Obadiahs around us. As long as the gospel is being preached without compromise, we should be rejoicing in what God is doing.

Philippians 1:18 - What then? Only that in every way, whether in pretense or in truth, Christ is proclaimed, and in that I rejoice.

Paul embodied the heart of a genuine bondservant of God who was committed to the gospel being preached to advance God's Kingdom. He knew that God is the only One who can truly evaluate and commend or reprimand each evangelist or missionary.

As you engage with the lost people around you, I encourage you to be bold like Elijah, but be willing to fellowship, embrace, and celebrate the Obadiahs in your network. The Lord's house is large enough to put all kinds of vessels to use (2 Timothy 2:20), and regardless of whether we are of the Elijah type or Obadiah type, the

Lord's desire is for every vessel to be consecrated unto Him. On the mission field, we have observed both the Elijah type and Obadiah type of missionaries struggle with sexual immorality and discredit the name of our Lord. Both types of missionaries need encouragement, accountability, prayer, and support. Would you commit to praying for and encouraging missionaries who are different from you (as long as they are not compromising the gospel)?

I want to close this chapter with my encounter with the Lord after the interview of a Presbyterian minister in Columbia, SC, many years ago. In the fall of my second year at Columbia Biblical seminary, I had to interview the pastor of a liberal Presbyterian church in town. The pastor was in his 70s, and had served the Lord faithfully for more than forty years, including about ten years in Korea. He had led evangelism campaigns in my birth country with Billy Graham, and had brought hundreds, if not thousands to Christ. The purpose of the interview was to describe the pastor's view of Scripture, and within half an hour I discovered that he did not hold to inerrancy of God's Word. He believed that some parts of the Old Testament (Genesis Chapters 1-3, the Book of Job, and the Book of Jonah) were to be read as fables/parables and not in literal sense.

At the conclusion of our two-hour interview, the pastor asked me, "Did I pass?" I responded with, "Excuse me?"

Then he challenged me, "Didn't you come to evaluate my ministry and my views about the Bible?" I felt my face flush with embarrassment, and I blurted out that I came to fulfill a class assignment, and was not evaluating him or his ministry at all.

However, in my heart I had already labeled him as a "liberal" pastor...simply because of his view of Scripture. As I came out of the church and took in the crisp autumn air, the Lord spoke to my heart: "Who are you to judge My servant?" And then the Lord reminded me of the hundreds, or even thousands, of people who had been saved through the faithful ministry of this pastor. I may never bring one-tenth of the lost into God's kingdom as this "liberal" pastor had done; by whose authority was I to judge this servant of God with spiritual pride? And thus as I sat down in the car, I lifted up a prayer of repentance and asked for God's forgiveness. I told God that He was right...I was in no place to judge His servants. Only He can commend and rebuke His servants justly.

I am not advocating for liberal views concerning Scripture nor adopting compromising methodologies that lean toward heresy, but I am encouraging you to be more understanding and accepting of what God is doing in the harvest field through diverse types of workers. By the way, did you know that C.S. Lewis also subscribed to the view that some sections of the Bible are mythological? And we in the evangelical circle have placed him high on the pedestal as a gifted Christian scholar and apologist. [See *Decide for Yourself: How History Views the Bible* by Norman Geisler, p.102.]

51 – Burying Your Children in a Foreign Land

Isaiah 8:18 - Behold, I and the children whom the Lord has given me are signs and portents in Israel from the Lord of hosts, who dwells on Mount Zion.

The Lord first challenged me with the idea of releasing my children to Him for the sake of the gospel while my wife was pregnant with our first child. We did not know the gender of the child, but I sensed that the firstborn would be a son. I also knew his name would be Joniel. This name was spoken to me in a dream, where a voice said that name twice. Perhaps the name is a combination of "Joseph" and "Daniel," or a possible Hebrew name meaning "peace of God" (from "Jonah," meaning dove, and "El," meaning God.)

One day as I was praying for the child in the womb, I had a sudden thought of what may possibly happen to my son when we were eventually sent to a Muslim nation as missionaries. What if a group of fanatic Muslims captured our family and dragged my son in front of me and threatened to behead him for our crime of spreading the gospel? I would plead the leader to take my life instead, and spare my son. After all, it was I who made the decision to bring my family to the Muslim nation to share the gospel; my son was not involved in making that decision.

One thread of thought after another began to weave a tapestry of father's sacrificial love for his child, and I began to swell up with a sense of pride and amazement. I was not yet the father of a child to be born into this world (he was still in his mother's womb), and yet I had the capacity to love my unborn child with such self-sacrificial love. Although I knew that such love is from the Creator, and a reflection of the Father's love for us, I began to take pride in this newly discovered paternal love within me. It was at this very moment that the Father spoke very clearly to my prideful heart: "Do you think that I loved my Son any less that I watched Him die on the cross for the sins of the world?"

This penetrating question from the Father triggered the following thought. If it were possible, the Father would have taken the place of His Son on the cross, for the Father loves the Son very much. He proclaimed this unmistakably at the time of the Son's baptism (Matthew 3:17) and then before the crucifixion (Matthew 17:5). The Father could have sent every angel in heaven to prevent the arrest, beating, and crucifixion of His Son, but then His plan to redeem the world would not have been fulfilled. And so it was necessary for the Father to watch His Son be tortured and die cruelly on the cross....so that sinners like you and I could be saved.

I knelt before the Father that very moment and confessed my sin of pride, and asked Him to forgive me. There is no father on earth that could ever love his son or daughter more than the Father in heaven who loved (loves) His Son. If the time comes for me to surrender my wife, my child, my life for the sake of the gospel, then may the Father give me His perfect love to accomplish it.

In the summer of 2014 my wife and I were in Seoul, Korea, to present seminars on world missions. The day before we were to return to the U.S., I had a free afternoon. I decided to take the subway to visit Yanghwajin...a cemetery where nearly 400 foreigners are buried. Amongst them are over a hundred missionaries, both adults and children. I had heard about this sacred plot of land, and as it was the middle of a hot day, there were few other visitors. I walked quietly and prayerfully between the memorials of many missionaries. And then I came to the memorial of Ruby Kendrick with the inscription: "If I had a thousand lives, Korea should have them all." I began to weep...it cost numerous lives to bring the gospel to the people of Korea, including me. How could I ever pay the debt owed to these servants of God?

251

After a few hours of online research, I discovered the following letter from Ruby Kendrick to her parents, written from Korea in 1908.

Dear Mom and Dad,

This land, Chosun, is truly a beautiful land. They all resemble God. I see their good heart and zeal for the gospel, and I believe that in a few years it will be a land overflowing with the love of Christ. I saw children walking over ten miles on barefoot to hear the gospel, and the love of God in them encourages me.

But the persecution is getting stronger. Two days ago, three or four of those who had just accepted Christ less than a week were dragged away and martyred. Missionaries Thomas and James were also martyred. There were orders from the mission board to return, but most of the missionaries are in hiding, and worshiping with those with whom they have shared the gospel. It seems that they are all planning to be martyred. Tonight, I have a strong desire to return home.

I remember how you, Mom, resisted to the last moment of my leaving the port because of the stories of hostility towards the foreigners and opposition to the gospel.

Mom, Dad, perhaps this may be my last letter. The seeds that were sown in the backyard before I came out here must be filling our neighborhood with flowers. There is another Seed bearing many flowers in the land of Chosun, and they will be seeds to other nations.

I will bury my heart in this land. I realized that this passion for Chosun that I have is not mine but God's passion towards Chosun.

Mom, Dad, I love you.

Ruby Kendrick

Ruby was originally from Plano, TX. (May God bless the Texans...to raise up more servants like Ruby!) She had come to Korea by ship as a single woman. She served a year in Korea and then died of appendicitis at the age of twenty-five.

252

One deep-rooted prayer that came out of spending that quiet afternoon at Yanghwajin was that the Father in heaven would allow all five of us to be buried overseas, preferably in different lands. It would be my joy and honor to be buried in the very land that my wife and I would serve until He takes us home. And similarly, my desire is that our children, too, will be buried in the land and amongst the people loved by God. Perhaps the people in those lands may initially be hostile to the gospel, but may the labor of our children bless the nation, just as Ruby Kendrick blessed the people of Korea.

I believe that if we, as Christian parents, only focus on bringing up "godly" children, then they will become our idols. As parents, we are to pursue God-given calling in our lives first and foremost, and then the Lord will help us in raising up our children to bring Him glory. Too often the parents neglect the Great Commission opportunities at their workplace or in their neighborhood, and focus only on raising their kids to be healthy, prosperous, and "godly." The offspring have now become their idols. I believe that the Lord wants each parent to faithfully live out Matthew 6:33 in his or her own life context. As a father reaches out to a Muslim or homosexual person in his office, and shares about the challenges and victories with his family (especially with his children), the children will learn to tackle their own challenges with prayer and Christ-like attitude. As a mother shows compassion and love to a Syrian Muslim refugee woman and her war-crippled toddler, her children will learn to be compassionate towards children who are different from them.

My wife and I have adapted this maxim we heard at a pastors' gathering in Leesburg: "May our ceiling become the floor of the next generation!" We want our children (and grandchildren) to go beyond where we went…to break through to the hearts of the LGBTQ community with the love of Jesus Christ, to boldly take the gospel into the isolated land of North Korea, and to stop the killing of millions of babies (abortions) across the world.

Your children and grandchildren do not belong to you. They belong to the One who created them...the One who died and rose again for them (2 Corinthians 5:15). Would you release your children and grandchildren to the Lord Jesus Christ so that He may send them to the ends of the earth for His Kingdom sake?

Recommended song:
Keith Green - "Pledge My Head To Heaven"

52 – Into the River of Life

Ezekiel 47:1-6 - Then he brought me back to the door of the temple, and behold, water was issuing from below the threshold of the temple toward the east (for the temple faced east). The water was flowing down from below the south end of the threshold of the temple, south of the altar. Then he brought me out by way of the north gate and led me around on the outside to the outer gate that faces toward the east; and behold, the water was trickling out on the south side. Going on eastward with a measuring line in his hand, the man measured a thousand cubits, and then led me through the water, and it was ankle-deep. Again he measured a thousand, and led me through the water, and it was knee-deep. Again he measured a thousand, and led me through the water, and it was waist-deep. Again he measured a thousand, and it was a river that I could not pass through, for the water had risen. It was deep enough to swim in, a river that could not be passed through. And he said to me, "Son of man, have you seen this?" Then he led me back to the bank of the river.

In Ezekiel's vision above, we can make two important observations: 1) the deeper a man walks into the river of life, the less control he has over his own movement, and 2) wherever the water flows, there is life.

I believe that this is an apt metaphor of what it means to follow Jesus Christ wherever He leads us. (I first heard this metaphor from a young Korean-American missionary to Africa, John Park, at one of his short-term missions workshops in Seoul, Korea. I want to give him the proper credit.) The closer we follow Christ, the less control we have over our own lives. Jesus determines where we go, how we are to live there, how much we would own, etc. However, wherever we go according to His will and leading, we will see the King of kings bring abundant life (John 10:10b). He will do this in very places where the prince of this world has brought only death and destruction (John 10:10a).

Following Jesus does not lead us to a permanent place of rest next to a tranquil, still lake, or pond nestled in the remotes of a vast forest. That's the aspiration of many of us who are immersed in American (First World) Christianity. We want the Good Shepherd to lead us to green pastures and keep us there, where life is comfortable and without worry. All the while there are people in other parts of the world who are suffering, and dying without having heard the gospel. The other problem with wanting to live permanently near a tranquil pond is that we end up drifting towards a section of the pond where garbage gathers; and slowly, our lives become contaminated by whatever pollutants that surround us.

Hebrews 2:1 - Therefore we must pay much closer attention to what we have heard, lest we drift away from it.

This is what happened with Lot and his family. Lot had chosen a land that seemed to promise prosperity and security for his wife, two daughters, and even future progeny. He was probably aware of the intense wickedness of the people of his town, Sodom, but he decided to stay as a resident; he lived about twenty-five years in Sodom after separating from Abram (Genesis 13). When his daughters became old enough to marry, he had intended to find husbands amongst the men of Sodom. And when the two angels arrived in Sodom to rescue Lot and his family from impending destruction, the two potential bridegrooms refused to leave their city.

Although the Lord took Lot and his daughters to a place of safety, removing them from the destruction of Sodom, we learn sadly that Sodom remained in the hearts of the two daughters. They would force themselves upon their inebriated father to bring forth sons who would carry on the family name, and perhaps even the immoral legacy of Sodom.

256

Jesus commands the Christians today to be living in the world but not to be part of it (John 17:14-16). If we follow Him closely, abiding in Him daily, then we can live in the truth and blessing of this command. How do we know if the rubbish of this world is beginning to pollute our souls? We can take a look at how we spend our time, treasures, and talents. Do we miss Sunday services at home church because of our children's sports games? Do we spend Sunday afternoons and evenings indulging in hours of football or basketball games on the screen? Do we accept or approve of abortion, same-sex marriage, or the practice of couples living together prior to marriage to test the relationship? Or do we indulge in pornographic images or videos on our iPhones, excusing ourselves by saying that *everyone else is doing it?*

We have been drinking the polluted still water of American culture, and our lives are beginning to reflect the patterns of this world. The Lord Jesus always takes us through the fresh waters; He is the source of life, and He is like the river of life in Ezekiel 47. As we follow Him, our lives will brush up against the drug addicts, idolaters, rapists, homosexuals, and murderers; but because Jesus is leading us through these relationships, we can trust Him to keep our hearts pure and fixed on Him.

Ezekiel 47:3-5 verses show us the man progressively walking deeper into the river. To walk ankle-deep, knee-deep, waist-deep, and finally completely immersed in the river of life is to show degrees of surrender in every arena of a Christian's life as he or she follows Jesus' leading. For instance, in the area of spending time in God's Word: ankle-deep—having daily quiet time with the Lord; knee-deep—joining a weekly Bible study, memorizing Bible verses or passages; waste-deep—reading the Bible through the year; immersed—taking seminary classes or pursuing a seminary degree.

In the area of financial giving: ankle-deep—tithing; knee-deep—percentage beyond tithe given to the church or missions; waist-deep—sacrificing next year's vacation trip to the Bahamas to help build an orphanage in Haiti; immersed—selling your investment property to support a refugee ministry or giving your second home to a missionary family that just came back from the field.

In the area of serving in ministry (local/overseas): ankle-deep—teaching Sunday school classes, volunteering at church VBS or local soup kitchen; knee-deep—leading weekly Bible study at church or county jail, volunteering as ESL teacher, or going on a short-term mission trip; waist-deep—serving as bi-vocational lay minister or long-term mission to another people group; immersed—committing to serve in another country for the remainder of one's life, willing to be buried there for the sake of the gospel.

Where are you in your pursuit of Jesus? Are you still enjoying the ankle-deep relationship with Jesus? Of course you will enter into eternity with Him because He is faithful to His word, but you will miss out on the adventure of following Him closely and seeing amazing works of God happening in and through you. There are some Christians who will faithfully attend Sunday worship and even Sunday school classes for fifty or more years; but because they don't take the opportunity to venture out on short-term mission or build relationships with Muslim refugees across the street, they will never experience the knee-deep pull of the rushing current. They may never experience the joy of leading Buddhists to Christ and baptizing them in the river. They may never have the opportunity of witnessing a Hindu family burning up their house idols and praising Jesus for their new found freedom and life!

Ezekiel 47:7-9 - As I went back, I saw on the bank of the river very many trees on the one side and on the other. And he said to me, "This water flows toward the eastern region and goes down into the Arabah, and enters the sea; when the water flows into the sea, the water will become fresh. And wherever the river goes, every living creature that swarms will live, and there will be very many fish. For this water goes there, that the waters of the sea may become fresh; so everything will live where the river goes.

Recommended reading:
Radical by David Platt
Don't Waste Your Life by John Piper

Epilogue: Is He Worth the Risk?

2 Timothy 1:7- 9 - for God gave us a spirit not of fear but of power and love and self-control. Therefore do not be ashamed of the testimony about our Lord, nor of me his prisoner, but share in suffering for the gospel by the power of God, who saved us and called us to a holy calling, not because of our works but because of his own purpose and grace, which he gave us in Christ Jesus before the ages began.

In chapter 20 (*Jars of Clay*), I had shared about my encounter with Dawud, a Muslim university student who had asked for a copy of an English Bible. I want to revisit that encounter and share some thoughts appropriate for the current situation we are facing in 2020 (coronavirus pandemic). When Dawud requested a Bible, I had told him that if I found one I would bring it the following week. On the way home, I was both excited and a bit anxious. The anxiety stemmed from the fact that a fellow missionary from South Korea had been deported just a few months prior for religious activities on campus. He had come to the field three years prior to us, and by the time we had arrived, he already had a dozen Muslim students who had come to faith in Christ. The missionary and his wife were actively discipling these new converts. He had established a computer center at the university, and had graciously allowed me to join him in teaching engineering classes at his center. About fifth year into his ministry on the field, one of his disciples turned him over to the secret police (KGB); subsequently, he and his family had to leave the country within three days. We opened up our home for a farewell meal and a time of prayer for his family. Many tears were shed that evening.

So, when Dawud asked for a copy of the Bible, I immediately thought about the possibility that he could be a KGB affiliate. He could gather enough evidence (Bibles and other religious resources obtained through me) and then turn them over to the local KGB office for a sizable sum of money. For the next few days, Faith and I prayed (even fasted a day) and asked the Lord for wisdom and guidance. We did not hear any "prophetic" words from the Lord, but the Holy Spirit gave us peace in our hearts (Philippians 4:6,7) that Dawud's request seemed to be in earnest. Hence, we decided to give him a copy of the Bible, knowing that there were risks involved. If Dawud were a KGB "plant", then we could be arrested and deported. The two years of investing into learning the language and culture, as well as the funds spent to move overseas and settle down in Central Asia, could all end up being a wash if we were kicked out of the country. *But we decided that Dawud was worth the risk.*

By God's grace, Dawud became a follower of Christ and was called of God to be a house church leader. (You can read the rest of the story in chapters 20 and 28.) He has led many to the Lord, including Muslims living in adjacent countries. If we had decided not to give Dawud a Bible (out of fear of being arrested and deported), then we would have missed out on the incredible blessing of seeing a Muslim student being transformed into a faithful follower of Christ and used of God powerfully in Central Asia.

As all of us continue to struggle with how to live out our faith during this extended time of quarantine and lockdowns due to the coronavirus, I believe that apostle Paul has a message for us from 2 Timothy...the very last letter that he wrote before his martyrdom. Paul penned this letter from a prison in Rome around A.D. 67, when Christians around the Mediterranean world were being persecuted heavily by the Roman authorities. If Paul were dying in a hospital room with coronavirus today, I believe that his message would not change. He would give us the same charge that he gave to Timothy two thousand years ago.

There are three points from his letter that I want to highlight. First, we must be committed to preaching the gospel regardless of the situation (2 Timothy 1:13; 4:2). We must be willing to endure any hardship, including persecution, and even a pandemic, as we advance God's Kingdom (2 Timothy 1:8; 3:10-12; 4:5). In 2 Corinthians 11, Paul recounts how he had been exposed to death over and over again (v.23) for the sake of the gospel. According to Bible scholars, Paul traveled 10,000 miles on foot to preach the gospel! That's an incredible commitment. If Paul were our contemporary, he would not limit himself to ZOOM teaching only; he would certainly travel to those places where in-person ministry would either be preferred or more effective.

Second, we must trust that the Lord will acknowledge and reward those who labor for His Kingdom (2 Timothy 4:8). We are all ESSENTIAL workers in God's harvest field (world), according to 2 Corinthians 5:17-20. There are healthcare professionals around the world who are past 60 and are continuing to provide services to their patients. Somehow, this pandemic has opened the door for fear and the voice of the world to come into the Church and instruct us that those of us who are non-ESSENTIAL (per government definition) should remain at home and not risk getting or giving the coronavirus. Online evangelism is possible and does result in fruit of conversion, but there are still many people who prefer or need in-person visit for dialogue, prayer, and even sharing of meals.

Third, we must trust fully in the Lord Jesus Christ to be able to deliver us from every evil attack (2 Timothy 4:18). Apostle Paul firmly believed this, and thus he faithfully went wherever the Holy Spirit led him to go and preach. In Acts 28, there's an incident where Paul comes on shore to an island from a shipwreck, and is unexpectedly bitten by a poisonous snake. However, nothing happens to him; he does not die, because it was not his time to be with the Lord. During this season, you and I may catch the coronavirus, but if it is not our time yet to be with the Lord, then He will heal us of this disease and restore us. If it is our time to be with Him, then He will take us home, whether through this virus, an auto accident, or some other means. We are "immortal" until we have everything that God has for us to do. Many of us are tempted to believe that this world is our "home," when in fact our permanent home is in heaven with Jesus (John 14:1-3; Hebrews 11:13-16). Like Paul, we should be eager to leave this world to be with the One we love (Philippians 1:23).

Your co-worker, neighbor, classmate, or even a random shopper at Walmart may be the person that needs to hear the Good News through you in person (and not via ZOOM only). Would you take the risk (of catching coronavirus) to meet with that person? Is he or she worth the risk, like Dawud?

A recent newscast featured an interview with a public school art teacher. She seemed to be in her 50s and was very popular with her students. Her county had decided to open the schools for "in-person" lessons, and she decided to stop teaching. Her words: "I love my students, but I don't love them enough to die for them."

How about us? Do we love the Lord enough to lay down our lives for the lost, the very ones He died for? If you were the only person on earth, would Jesus still come down from heaven to die for your sins? I believe that He would. He cares for even one lost sheep (Luke 15:4). And if my Savior is willing to give Himself up for me, how could I not take the risk (of catching coronavirus) to offer eternal life to someone that the Lord is bringing across my path?

May the Lord Jesus be glorified in and through our lives, and may His kingdom advance powerfully during this season of coronavirus pandemic.

Made in the USA
Monee, IL
20 November 2020